# JAPANESE MYTHOLOGY

**World Mythology in Theory and Everyday Life**

Series Editors: Tok Thompson and Robert W. Guyker, Jr.

This series presents an innovative and accessible overview of the world's mythological traditions. The inaugural volume provides a theoretical introduction to the study of myth, while the individual case studies from throughout time and around the world help guide the reader through the wondrous complexity and diversity of myths, and their widespread influences in human cultures, societies, and everyday lives.

The Truth of Myth: World Mythology in Theory and Everyday Life
Tok Thompson and Gregory Schrempp

Old Norse Mythology
John Lindow

Classical Mythology: From Creation to First Human
Carolina López-Ruiz

Mythology of the San Bushmen of Southern Africa
Mathias Guenther

Japanese Mythology: A Guide
Matthieu Felt

# JAPANESE MYTHOLOGY
## A Guide

Matthieu Felt

OXFORD
UNIVERSITY PRESS

# OXFORD
## UNIVERSITY PRESS

Oxford University Press is a department of the University of Oxford.
It furthers the University's objective of excellence in research, scholarship,
and education by publishing worldwide. Oxford is a registered trade mark of
Oxford University Press in the UK and in certain other countries.

Published in the United States of America by Oxford University Press
198 Madison Avenue, New York, NY 10016, United States of America.

Library of Congress Cataloging-in-Publication Data
Names: Felt, Matthieu author
Title: Japanese mythology : a guide / Matthieu Felt.
Description: New York : Oxford University Press, [2026] |
Series: World myth theo and everyday life series | Includes bibliographical
references.
Identifiers: LCCN 2025042947 | ISBN 9780197686034 hardback |
ISBN 9780197686041 paperback | ISBN 9780197686058 epub
Subjects: LCSH: Mythology, Japanese | Japan—Social life and customs
Classification: LCC BL2202.3 .F45 2026
LC record available at https://lccn.loc.gov/2025042947

Printed by Integrated Books International, United States of America

The manufacturer's authorized representative in the EU for product safety is
Oxford University Press España S.A. of Parque Empresarial San Fernando de Henares,
Avenida de Castilla, 2 – 28830 Madrid (www.oup.es/en or product.safety@oup.com).
OUP España S.A. also acts as importer into Spain of products made by the manufacturer.

# CONTENTS

# ACKNOWLEDGMENTS

This book would not have been written without the encouragement of Tok Thompson and Gregory Schrempp, whose invaluable feedback shaped its direction and contents, and Stefan Vranka, who originally suggested the project. I must also thank the anonymous reviewers for their feedback on both the proposal and the manuscript, whose questions, doubts, and corrections were of great help in considering how this project might come together.

There is no shortage of mythologists and myth enthusiasts who have given me suggestions or advice on what might go in this book, including Arthur Defrance, Joshua Frydman, Bonnie McClure, David Lurie, and Marjorie Burge. My wife, Tess Younker, has been immensely patient listening to my unending discussion of hypothetical contents and generously looked over the final version of the manuscript.

The fortunate invitation to a conference on mythology in Fall 2023 by Klaus Antoni, Julia Dolkovski, and Louise Neubronner was timely and eye-opening in how I considered putting the final volume together. I also want to thank Sarah Schmid for advice on presenting contemporary mythology and Raji Steineck for kindly answering my questions about his mythological research and suggesting the best ways to present it.

Finally, I owe a huge debt of thanks to Sarah G. Douglas for her editing, proofreading, and many valuable suggestions. Her voice of restraint and honest appraisal of the content were critical for making this book accessible to readers.

# LIST OF MAPS, FIGURES, AND TABLES

# Introduction

Japanese myths are a rich and complex collection of creation lore, supernatural tales, and legendary stories. Like Greek, Egyptian, and Norse myths, Japanese myths are full of human-like deities who love, murder, and betray each other. The human descendants of the Japanese gods are counted as some of Japan's greatest heroes. Their stories are filled with supernatural feats and tragic outcomes. Japanese myths also stretch across multiple worlds. The most important of these are the High Heavenly Plain, which is the abode of the heavenly gods; Yomi, known as the land of the dead; the Central Reed Plain Land, filled with earthly deities; and Tokoyo, a mysterious land of immortals.

Japanese myths have been studied for the past thousand years and, perhaps unlike Greek or Norse myth, were closely tied to the belief systems and ritual practices of everyday people until very recently. As late as 1945, the official line on Japanese myths was that they were true, especially concerning the divine status of the Japanese emperor. Even though the emperor renounced his divinity after defeat in World War II, Japanese myths are still a part of everyday life in Japan through their imaginative and fanciful adaptations. Japanese people also continue to visit shrines to the Japanese gods, especially on occasions like New Year's Day.

This book is a straightforward introductory guide to these deities, heroes, and worlds as they appear in the oldest recorded sources. This book also provides a basic introduction to the study of Japanese myths in Japan and around the world.

The core figures in Japanese myths are called kami. Kami are Japanese deities, and the term can be both singular and plural. Kami refer to an extremely wide variety of people and things. The eighteenth-century scholar Motoori Norinaga (1730–1801) wrote that kami could refer to heavenly deities such as the sun goddess or moon god, earthly and regional deities who live among us, human beings (especially the descendants of heavenly or earthly kami), animals (including foxes and tanuki), landscape features such as waterfalls or rock formations, or plants (especially trees). Because kami are abundant in the world around us, human beings need to treat the kami with respect or else their life will be made difficult. Kami are worshipped at shrines. There are about eighty thousand shrines in Japan where about twenty thousand Shinto priests work to appease the kami and serve their communities.

There are two major barriers to the study of Japanese myth. First, the wide variety of people or things that can be identified as kami, along with the sheer number of kami, can make narratives very complicated. The names of these kami are sometimes very long, which makes them difficult to remember. Most of the important kami also have more than one name. Sometimes this is because the kami develop and grow, taking on new roles, but more often it is because there are multiple written sources for Japanese myths and these names are recorded differently. This leads into the second major barrier for studying Japanese myths, which is that the mythical narratives in written sources do not match each other. Some major narrative events, such as the death of the creator goddess Izanami when giving birth to the fire kami, do not happen in some versions of the story. Since these narrative accounts cannot be easily reconciled, it is important in Japanese myth to keep track of versions and sources, and this can be difficult for readers and students.

In light of the complexities presented by kami and written sources for Japanese myth, this book provides abridged retellings of the most important Japanese myths. These retellings are based on the contents of ancient Japanese texts, but rather than providing an exhaustive rundown of every version and detail of a myth, I provide only the most important versions and information. These retellings are not direct translations but are very close to the original texts. I indicate the textual sources for the different parts of each retelling. Readers wishing to engage directly with the source material can follow up with the translations of primary sources listed in the References at the end of this book.

I take several measures to simplify kami. First, most kami will be referred to using only one name. For example, the sun goddess has the names Ō-hiru-me-no-muchi and Ama-terasu, but in this book, she will be referred to as Ama-terasu exclusively. Since the names can be quite long, in some cases, hyphens separate the name into its constituent words. For example, Ama-terasu is "Heaven Shining." Since the names of kami are usually related to their character or powers, and because they may also be part of the story, translations of these names are provided. For a few kami who appear frequently, the hyphenation may be dropped after the first instance their name appears. For example, Izana-mi will be called Izanami, and Ama-terasu will be Amaterasu. In modern Japanese, some kami are referred to with shortened names. For example, the kami Masa-katsu-a-katsu-kachi-haya-hi-ame-no-oshi-ho-mimi is usually just called "Oshi-ho-mimi." I use these shortened names after the first time these kami appear in the narrative. Finally, Japanese emperors are referred to using their so-called Chinese-style name, although the reader is cautioned that these monikers are anachronistic. For example, Emperor Kamu-yamato-iware-biko-hiko-ho-ho-demi is referred to as Emperor Jinmu, though "Jinmu" was not coined until after the earliest sources of Japanese myths were written.

This introduction provides the basic information needed to understand this book. This includes a summary of the main texts that record Japanese myths, an explanation of how the terms myth and mythology are used, and an introduction of modern methods and theories for studying myths. In the first four chapters of the book, each retelling of Japanese myths is followed by a selection of modern scholarship about what these myths mean, and these selections demonstrate a variety of methodological approaches. I provide a summary of the book chapters at the end of the introduction.

## *Kojiki, Nihon shoki,* and Other Mythical Accounts

The two main written sources for Japanese myths, and the two primary sources for the retellings in this book, are *Kojiki*, or *An Account of Ancient Matters*, and *Nihon shoki*, or *The Chronicles of Japan*. In this book, *Kojiki* is referred to as *Ancient Matters* and *Nihon shoki* as *Chronicles*. Both texts were completed in the early eighth century: 712 for *Ancient Matters* and 720 for *Chronicles*. The two texts can be read either as distinct mythical narratives or as a combined resource for Japanese myths. The former strategy is primarily used in literature studies, which stresses the unique details of the respective texts and demonstrates how the myths in each text constitute different worldviews. The latter strategy is primarily used in religion and mythology, when the primary object of interest is not the textual representation of myths, but rather their historic characteristics and connections with religious ritual.

According to its preface, *Ancient Matters* was completed in 712 by the court scholar Ō no Yasumaro (n.d.). Yasumaro's clan, the Ō, was associated with scholarship and higher learning. There are few details about the life of Yasumaro. His existence itself was debated until 1979, when a farmer plowing a field in Nara happened to discover Yasumaro's tombstone. The preface to *Ancient Matters* claims that Emperor Tenmu (n.d.–686, r. 673–686) asked the scholar Hieda no Are (n.d.) to compose a record of the imperial lineage. Tenmu's request was prompted by the state of disarray of the existing genealogical records, presumably because there were multiple powerful clans each holding different materials. Those materials were also probably recorded in a variety of writing styles, dialects, or even languages.

According to the preface of *Ancient Matters*, Hieda no Are was charged by Tenmu with collecting the various records from clans at court and learning how to read or recite them. However, Are died before completing the task that Tenmu had given him. Yasumaro then took the record that Are had created and wrote it down, creating the text we now know as *Ancient Matters*. The importance of clan narratives and lineage in the eighth century, and the fact that there is no corroborating record of the events that Yasumaro writes about in his preface, mean that we should consider the claims in the preface with some skepticism. It was certainly to Yasumaro's benefit to associate his work with Tenmu, who was long dead in 712 when *Ancient Matters* was written.

The myths in *Ancient Matters* and *Chronicles* describe the social organization of the clans that comprised the eighth-century court. When these texts were written, the head of each clan worshipped a patron deity. For example, the Fujiwara clan's patron deity was Ame-no-koyane, and the main shrine was the Kasuga Shrine in present-day Nara City. For the imperial clan, the patron deity was Amaterasu, the sun goddess. Clans whose patron deities played important roles in myths were assured prominent positions in the imperial court. For example, in one episode from Japanese myth, the sun goddess Amaterasu hides herself away in a heavenly rock cave. The patron deities of the Nakatomi and the Inbe clans performed rituals to draw her out of the cave. At court, the Nakatomi and the Inbe clans were charged with ritual, a role with a guaranteed court rank and a title of nobility for the clan itself. The titles of nobility granted different perks to clans. In one famous historical example, the patron of the Inbe clan submitted a petition to the emperor asking that his rank be raised on account of his mythical ancestor's prominent role in the creation of the Japanese state. That request was granted the following year.

Other materials besides the preface of *Ancient Matters* also point to the importance of genealogy in early Japan. The prefaces to the 815 *Shinsen shōjiroku* and the notes for the 812 reading of *Chronicles* at court also describe genealogical records in disarray and a court order for a scholar to correct them. *Shoku Nihongi*, the court history for the eighth century, records cases of petitions for changes in court rank or clan title based on lineage. Perhaps most confusingly, clans associated with immigrant lineages from the Korean Peninsula could claim that they were descended from kami who had migrated to the Korean Peninsula in ancient times. As such, they should be granted special privileges at court.

The oldest manuscript edition of *Ancient Matters* is from Shinpuku Temple. The manuscript dates from around the fourteenth century. There is a competing manuscript lineage, known as the Ise lineage, which is associated with the Urabe clan. The oldest manuscript in that lineage is from a slightly later date, around the sixteenth century. Both the paucity of *Account* manuscript lineages and the long gap between when *Account* was written in 712 and the date of the oldest manuscripts suggest that for the first millennium of its existence, *Account* was not widely read. This suggestion is further corroborated by the lack of records saying that *Ancient Matters* was read at court or studied by court scholars. At present, there are only three later texts that appear to have been drawn from or written with a strong cognizance of *Ancient Matters*, all from the ninth century.

The narrative of *Ancient Matters* is strongly informed by the concept of *musuhi*, which refers to a kind of generative force that produces living things. In modern Japanese the word *musu* is used to describe the growing of moss, because it seems to spontaneously appear on surfaces. The first kami that appear in *Ancient Matters* are associated with this generative force. Of particular importance are Taka-mi-musuhi or "High August Generative Force" and Kamu-musuhi or "Divine Generative Force." This generative force is responsible for the first kami appearing in the universe like reeds emerging from the waters. The kami who appear take residence in a location known as the High Heavenly Plain or Taka-ama-ga-hara.

In the narrative of *Ancient Matters*, the High Heavenly Plain is never actually created. It exists already when the narrative begins. As such, *Ancient Matters* only explains the creation of the Japanese archipelago. It does not explain the creation of the heavens, the earth, or the world. The heavenly kami order two of their own, Izanagi and Izanami, to create the Japanese archipelago.

The mythical creation narrative of *Ancient Matters* claims that Izanami died while giving birth to the fire god, and because of this, the creation of the world was never completed. When her husband goes to the Land of Yomi to confront her, he tells her, "Our work is not complete." However, he is unsuccessful at bringing his wife back from Yomi. Therefore, the Japanese archipelago, called the "Central Reed Plain Land," is never completed. Later, when Izanagi leaves Yomi, he performs a ritual ablution to remove the impurity of Yomi from his body. When he does, he creates three magnificent children: the sun goddess Amaterasu, the moon god Tsuku-yomi ("moon counting"), and a third god, Susa-no-o ("raging man"). He gives each of these kami a charge. Amaterasu is charged with rule of heaven. Tsuku-yomi is charged with the rule of the night. Susa-no-o is charged with the rule of the sea. The Central Reed Plain Land is left incomplete and without an assigned ruler.

In *Ancient Matters*, the completion of creation and the assignment of an appropriate ruler to the Central Reed Plain Land centers of the kami of Izumo, present-day Shimane Prefecture. Ō-kuni-nushi, the main deity worshipped at the Izumo Grand Shrine, completes the creation of the Central Reed Plain Land. Ō-kuni-nushi is a descendant of Susa-no-o, and the Kumano Shrine in Izumo is dedicated to Susa-no-o. After a series of travails, explained in detail in *Ancient Matters*, Ō-kuni-nushi completes creation and assumes the governance of the Central Reed Plain Land. Later, Amaterasu sends representatives from the High Heavenly Plain to force Ō-kuni-nushi to surrender the Central Reed Plain Land to her grandson, Ninigi.

From the perspective of the heavenly kami, the Central Reed Plain Land never had an assigned ruler, and Ō-kuni-nushi had simply seized it for himself in the interim.

The deep involvement of Ō-kuni-nushi in the plot of *Ancient Matters* suggests a concerted effort by the compiler Yasumaro to incorporate Ō-kuni-nushi and the myths associated with the Izumo region into the mythical narrative connected to Amaterasu and the leader of the imperial clan, who were based in Yamato, present-day Nara Prefecture. This has led some scholars to suggest that the Izumo and Yamato regions perhaps represented different polities in antiquity. After Izumo was conquered by Yamato, its mythical traditions were absorbed or fused with Yamato myths. At the most extreme position, scholars have even suggested that the kami Susano-o was invented to graft these two mythical traditions together.

After the mythical founding of the Japanese state by the first emperor, Jinmu, *Ancient Matters* moves through the reigns of historical emperors until around Kenzō, presently counted as the twenty-third emperor of Japan. After Kenzō, *Ancient Matters* provides only minimum details, including the emperor's name and place of burial, for ten more emperors. The last of these is Suiko, who ruled in the early seventh century. It seems that the primary objective of *Ancient Matters*, in terms of the history of the emperors, was to clarify the historical connection between emperors within recent memory of its compilation like Suiko, with those from the distant past like Kenzō and Jinmu. Given that most of the early emperors are legendary or mythical and that there were multiple major polities on the Japanese archipelago before the ultimate emergence of the Yamato state, one possibility is that the mythical and legendary emperors were based on rulers of the different polities from across the archipelago. Then, Yasumaro or someone slightly before his time put them together into a single lineage.

The circumstances for the creation of *Chronicles* were quite different. *Chronicles* was compiled in 720 by Prince Toneri, the son of Emperor Tenmu. The text does not have a preface explaining how it came to be. The annals for Tenmu's reign in *Chronicles* record that the court was interested in compiling a state history at that time. There are also claims in the annals for the reign of Suiko that Prince Shōtoku and Soga no Umako compiled a history of Japan and a record of its emperors, but the contents of these early reigns in *Chronicles* are apocryphal. One clear motivation for Toneri was to link his father's reign to those of the previous emperors. Tenmu led a coup in 671. Therefore, Tenmu could be characterized as a usurper instead of a legitimate emperor. Toneri's story in *Chronicles* resolves this issue by linking Tenmu to earlier rulers.

It is difficult to assess the reception of *Chronicles* in the eighth century, when it was first composed. The eighth-century poetry collection *Man'yōshū*, meaning "Myriad Poems Collection," cites *Chronicles*; however, these references do not match the version of *Chronicles* that we have at present. One likely reason for this is that *Chronicles* was adapted from a very early stage into a digest or some kind of genealogical chart of the emperors with years or era dates so that it could be easily referenced when doing historical research or writing. The compilers of the 797 history *Shoku Nihongi*, whose title literally means *Continued Chronicles of Japan*, clearly had *Chronicles* in mind when they titled their study. Few other sources from this period exist.

The oldest manuscript of *Chronicles* is the Tanaka manuscript, probably from the ninth century. There are about ten different manuscript lineages for *Chronicles*. Many of them, like the Tanaka, date back to the Heian Period of Japanese history (794–1185 CE).

Unlike *Ancient Matters*, *Chronicles* was extensively studied and read from the early ninth century onwards. In the ninth and tenth centuries, six public lectures on *Chronicles* were held at court, and at parties following these lectures, courtiers composed poetry about the gods, emperors, and court officials in the text. These materials are the oldest pieces of a large body of notes and commentary on *Chronicles* that continued to grow into the nineteenth century. Conversely, the first commentary on *Ancient Matters* was not completed until the beginning of the nineteenth or the very late eighteenth century.

At the time that *Ancient Matters* and *Chronicles* were written, the Japanese syllabaries of hiragana and katakana had not yet been developed. All writing used Chinese characters. Chinese characters can be used for their phonetic value to write words from any language. This is how English names are converted into modern Chinese today. Ancient Japanese people used Chinese characters for their phonetic value to spell out Japanese character names, place-names, and words that were imagined to have a ritual or talismanic quality. They also used phonetic characters to write down vernacular Japanese poetry. Both *Ancient Matters* and *Chronicles* include poems in Japanese, not to mention another 4,500 Japanese poems in the *Myriad Poems* anthology. The modern Japanese writing systems of hiragana and katakana originate from the practice of using Chinese characters to spell out Japanese words.

Ancient Japanese people also wrote using Chinese characters for their meanings and observing the grammar of Chinese. This written language is usually called literary Sinitic, and it was the *lingua franca* in East Asia at the time. Scholars distinguish literary Sinitic, a pan-Asian written script, from Classical Chinese, which was used in ancient China to write the Confucian Classics like *The Analects* and *The Annals of Spring and Autumn*. Using literary Sinitic, readers in China, Korea, Vietnam, and Japan could read the same materials. Thanks to this shared written register, the Confucian Classics and Chinese translations of Buddhist scriptures spread throughout East Asia. Each country developed its own distinct methods for translating material written in literary Sinitic into the native vernacular language. In Japanese, this method is called *kanbun*, meaning "Han Chinese Writing." In contemporary Japan, students still learn *kanbun* in school, but almost no one in Japan composes poetry or prose in *kanbun* anymore.

In the modern era, it is customary to associate languages with nations: Vietnam and Vietnamese, Korea and Korean, etc. This custom

has led to a somewhat misguided idea that *Ancient Matters* was written in Japanese and *Chronicles* was written in Chinese. In truth,
*Chronicles* was mostly written in literary Sinitic but also includes vernacular Japanese poems. *Ancient Matters* combines literary Sinitic
with other experimental writing styles related to vernacular Japanese,
but *Ancient Matters* cannot be cleanly classified as literary Sinitic or
vernacular Japanese. Ancient Japanese readers deemed *Chronicles* as
the preferred and official version of events due to its standardized
written style. *Ancient Matters* rose in popularity in modern Japan,
when distinguishing Japan from China became a major goal of academics and politicians.

Chinese historical writing and cosmology influenced the narrative of *Chronicles*. The opening lines of *Chronicles*, which explain the
separation of yin and yang and the creation of the cosmos, are copied
from Chinese texts. Unlike *Ancient Matters*, *Chronicles* begins its narrative before heaven and earth are created. After their formation, the
kami appear and create the Japanese archipelago. The importance of
yin and yang also shapes the narrative. In *Chronicles*, Izanami does
not die. Instead, she and Izanagi come together to create the Japanese
archipelago, which they do successfully and completely. Also, in
*Chronicles*, Izanagi and Izanami are not ordered by the heavenly gods
to commence creation but rather do so of their own accord, following the natural order of yin and yang seeking to combine.

Because Izanami and Izanagi create the world on their own, and
because Izanami does not die, the narrative development of the
myth in *Chronicles* is different from *Ancient Matters*. Ō-kuni-nushi,
who completes creation in *Ancient Matters*, drops out of the main
creation narrative in *Chronicles*. He appears later, when Amaterasu's
grandson Ninigi is meant to become the ruler of the archipelago.
*Chronicles* still contains a story in which Ō-kuni-nushi must cede his
power. However, his rise to prominence is only given in *Ancient
Matters*.

The narrative style of *Chronicles* differs from that of *Ancient
Matters*. *Ancient Matters* relays events in a streamlined narrative. As

with any extended narrative, the careful reader can identify plot holes and inconsistencies, but by and large, the narrative holds together. *Chronicles* presents the reader with a main narrative and then a set of variants. The main narrative is customarily divided into eleven sections. After each of the eleven sections, *Chronicles* include some number of variants. These are called *issho*, meaning "one writing says" in Japanese. On the surface, this makes it look like the compilers of *Chronicles* assembled a narrative from a variety of different sources. Rather than make a single editorial decision about which sources to include and which to exclude, the compilers created a single main narrative and then included the different variants accounts alongside. The variants frequently conflict with the main narrative. For example, several variants describe a similar myth to that in *Ancient Matters*, in which Izanami dies giving birth to the fire kami and then is followed to Yomi by Izanagi.

It is not entirely clear why the compilers decided to include these variants. There are some cases where the inclusion of the variant seems required to understand later events, and the main narrative of *Chronicles* does not completely stand on its own. For example, the kami that are sent to take control of the archipelago away from Ō-kuni-nushi in the main narrative are descended from kami that were born when Izanagi kills the fire kami in a variant. Ancient Japanese readers adopted a variety of approaches to explain the relationship of these variants to the main narrative, such as claiming that they were accounts from the perspectives of different kami or that they referred to myths from China. In this book, the main account and the variants are differentiated using the traditional Japanese fashion. The main narrative of *Chronicles* has eleven sections. The variants are numbered and follow the section after which they appear. Variant 2 of Section 4, for example, is referred to as 4.2.

Historical emperors are described in more detail in *Chronicles* than in *Ancient Matters*. One reason is simply that *Chronicles* is much longer than *Ancient Matters*. *Chronicles* includes details about rulers all the way through Emperor Jitō, who abdicated the throne to her grandson in 697 (Jitō was female, but her title "emperor" was the same as male rulers. "Empress" is used for the wife of a male ruler). *Chronicles* includes about one century of additional information compared with *Ancient Matters*. Also, for the reigns between Kenzō and Suiko, *Ancient Matters* has only minimal information, but in *Chronicles*, these reigns are filled with extensive historical detail.

The comparison of *Ancient Matters* and *Chronicles* suggests that the primary goal of *Ancient Matters* was, as the name of the text states, to record "ancient matters" and to make it clear how those ancient matters were connected to the present. *Ancient Matters* is not concerned with providing an explanation or a recounting of relatively recent history. On the other hand, *Chronicles* attempts to provide a comprehensive history of Japan and the Japanese state all the way up to Jitō, who at the time of the text was written, had only been dead for about a decade. It is also clear that Toneri, the main compiler of *Chronicles*, was deeply invested in the legacy of Tenmu, his father. Two volumes of thirty in total are devoted to the reign of Tenmu, and Tenmu is the only emperor in *Chronicles* who receives this level of dedicated treatment. The first of these volumes details the coup, or war of righteous succession, depending on your viewpoint, that Tenmu fought to seize the throne from his nephew. Toneri's first volume about Tenmu legitimizes his rebellion. The second volume about Tenmu legitimizes his reign and records numerous activities associated with dynastic founders, such as sending away the diplomatic officials who came to mourn the previous emperor and the revision of court ranks.

Both *Ancient Matters* and *Chronicles* began circulating in print around the seventeenth century. The first two volumes of *Chronicles*, which constitute the Japanese creation myths, were printed in 1599, with the other twenty-eight volumes of the text following in 1610. However, this edition does not appear to have circulated widely, and the most popular printed edition of *Chronicles* was printed in 1669. This edition included vernacular Japanese glosses, which helped Japanese readers understand the content by providing the Japanese

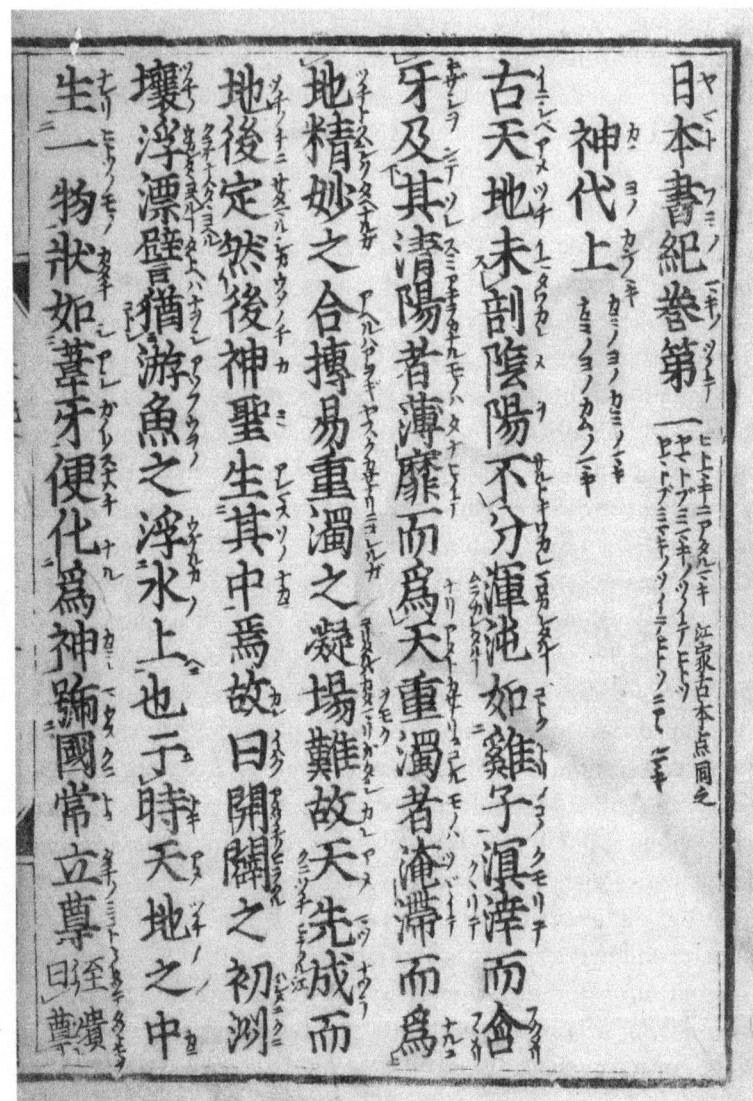

**FIGURE 1** 1669 printing of Chronicles.
The larger characters are the text; the smaller characters written vertically between the lines are the vernacular Japanese glosses. The text is the opening passage of Chronicles.
(CC BY 4.0, Ibaraki University Library)

word or words that accompanied a particular Chinese character or characters.

The glosses in the 1669 printing of *Chronicles* were based on the long history of scholarship that *Chronicles* enjoyed from the ninth through the sixteenth centuries. They also lowered the literacy level that would be required for a reader to understand the text. Additionally, while the older manuscript lineages of *Chronicles* were not complete, the 1669 edition provided the entire text from beginning to end. Modern Japanese printed editions of *Chronicles* are based on this 1669 edition. The most recent modern edition, the *Shinshaku zenyaku Nihon shoki*, goes so far as to reproduce the 1669 version alongside a modern Japanese translation so that Japanese readers can get a feel for the original.

*Ancient Matters* was first printed in 1644. Since *Ancient Matters* did not have the long reading history of *Chronicles*, there was serious debate about how to gloss the text. The most influential glossed version was the late eighteenth-century commentary *Kojiki-den* or *Commentary on an Account of Ancient Matters* by Motoori Norinaga.

While *Ancient Matters* and *Chronicles* are the oldest sources for Japanese myths, several other important texts from the eighth, ninth, and early tenth centuries also contain Japanese myths. The first of these is *Kogo shūi*, or *Gleanings from Ancient Stories*. It was translated into English in 1923 by Katō Genchi and Hoshino Hikoshirō. *Gleanings* was written by a court official named Inbe no Hironari in 807. Hironari combined the mythical creation narratives from *Ancient Matters* and *Chronicles* into a single, streamlined version. Hironari also added details about the imperial accession ritual, when the emperor would first take the throne, and regalia, or objects that were used in that ceremony. Hironari asserted that his Inbe clan had an important ceremonial function to play during this ritual. However, we should take Hironari's claims in *Gleanings* with a grain of salt, because Hironari wrote the text in order to increase the prestige of his own lineage group. His claims, which linked the ninth-century accession ritual to mythical accessions in *Ancient Matters* and

*Chronicles*, are best considered an adaptation, and not an original version.

The most contentious of the early Japanese mythical accounts is *Sendai kuji hongi*, or *Original Record of Previous Reigns and Past Matters*. *Original Record* first appeared in the historical record at a tenth-century lecture on *Chronicles*. The lecturer claimed that the author of *Original Record* was Prince Shōtoku, a quasi-mythical figure from the early seventh century. That assertion likely drew from the fact that *Original Record* ends with the death of Shōtoku and that in *Chronicles* an entry claims that Shōtoku and Soga no Umako wrote a history of the Japanese state, but that history was lost in a fire. Complicating matters further, there is a preface to *Original Record* that explicitly attributes the work to Shōtoku. However, research from the Edo Period (1603–1868 CE) demonstrated that this preface was a forgery.

The content of *Original Record* is largely a patchwork of material from *Chronicles*, *Ancient Matters*, and *Gleanings*. Because much of this material appears verbatim, it is certainly clear that one of these texts was the basis for the others. Given the comparatively late date in which *Original Record* first appears in the historical record, the majority opinion among scholars of Japanese myth is that *Original Record* is the later text and was preceded by *Ancient Matters*, *Chronicles*, and *Gleanings*. However, there is a minority opinion that holds that some content from *Original Record* predates *Ancient Matters*. Regardless, *Original Record* is an important source for the study of Japanese myth. While most of its content already appears in *Chronicles*, *Ancient Matters*, or *Gleanings*, *Original Record* provides additional information related to several early court rituals and the genealogy of the Mononobe clan, and extensive information about the genealogy for various provincial governors. These additions certainly make it seem like the text was written by someone with a connection to the Mononobe clan in order to cement their association with particular court rituals. Because the possibility that the text was a forgery was not considered until the early modern era, *Original*

*Record* enjoyed a position of high prestige in medieval Japan. For several medieval traditions of Shinto, *Original Record* was considered scripture, alongside *Chronicles* and *Ancient Matters*.

In 815, the imperial court attempted to resolve some of the contestation and uncertainty related to the genealogy of clans prominent at court who claimed descent from mythical ancestors. This effort resulted in a text called *Shinsen shōjiroku* or *New Selected Register of Lineage Groups*. *New Selected Register* has not been translated into English. This text is not written in a narrative format but rather divides the clans of Japan depending upon the degree of closeness that their mythical ancestor had to the imperial family. The clans are then listed with information concerning their mythical ancestors, sometimes including ancestry details that match *Ancient Matters* and *Chronicles*. This text is especially useful when attempting to identify historic persons who appear in *Chronicles* but may not have their full genealogical record given in that text. Of course, because the information in *New Selected Register* is self-reported, lineage groups were incentivized to exaggerate their genealogical details, and their claims must be considered carefully.

The eighth-century Japanese court also produced a series of gazetteers, texts that record the administrative divisions, local lore and stories, soil condition, and notable products from a particular region. These gazetteers are known in Japan as *Fudoki*, or *Records of Wind and Earth*, and they were created for each province of ancient Japan. Because these records contain local lore, they often refer to mythical events and legendary figures. Unfortunately, most of these works have not survived. The mythical information in these works rarely dovetails with the narratives in *Ancient Matters* and *Chronicles*, but hints at the ways in which *Ancient Matters* and *Chronicles* attempted to create a unified mythological narrative for the imperial court. The gazetteer of Izumo Province, luckily one of those remaining, is especially important in this regard because Izumo is the province associated with Susano-o, the younger brother of the sun goddess, and his alleged descendant who completed the creation of the world,

Ō-kuni-nushi. The Izumo region is also significant for its proximity to the Korean Peninsula and its appearance in a conquest narrative centering on a Yamato hero who subdues the bravest warrior of Izumo. The full consideration of these gazetteers is beyond the scope of this guide, but two extant gazetteers have been translated into English and are recommended for further study.

The oldest extant Japanese poetry collection, *Myriad Poems*, contains about 4,500 poems, most from the late seventh and eighth centuries. The poems are important for the study of Japanese myth for three reasons. First, on rare occasions, the poems refer directly to Japanese kami. Second, the collection includes poems by several legendary emperors. Finally, some of the poems written in the late seventh century were composed precisely at the moment that the Japanese imperial line had coalesced power on the archipelago and was engaging in the process of mythologizing itself. This collection contains the first usage of the phrase "kami no manima," meaning "as a god," in reference to the will of the gods and the divinity of the Japanese emperor. There is an extensive body of study on this text in Western languages, and while the full consideration lies outside the scope of this guide, there are a number of partial translations listed in the References section.

One final importance source for the study of Japanese myths, from a slightly later date, is the early tenth-century text *Engi shiki*, or a *Record of the Procedures of the Engi Era*. This court record was created in 927 to document religious and other court rituals. It includes several *norito* or Shinto prayers. These prayers predate the text, although it is not precisely clear how old they are. The Shinto prayers refer to the Japanese myths and the kami. The prayers also offer new adaptations of Japanese myth. A separate portion of *Record of the Procedures* records the information about various shrines in the Japanese archipelago, with special attention paid to the largest and oldest shrines. Because it provides information about the kami associated with shrines, *Record of the Procedures* is a useful resource for understanding myth and Shinto in ancient Japan. An English translation of the prayers is given in Philippi; an English translation of the first five volumes of *Record of the Procedures* is available separately.

## Myth and Mythology

This book distinguishes between "myth" and "mythology." In modern English, the two are sometimes used interchangeably. In this book, "Japanese myth" refers to Japanese narratives related to the creation of the world and the Japanese archipelago, and to legends of past Japanese emperors and other figures whose existence may be dubious or exaggerated. Myth also refers to local Japanese traditions and stories. In the discipline of mythology, these categories are often separated into myth, legends, and folklore, but "myth" is used in this book to refer to all three. "Mythology" in this book refers exclusively to the study of myths. For example, Japanese myth refers to the stories and narratives of the sun goddess or the legendary conqueror Yamato Take, and Japanese mythology refers to the tradition of reading, writing, and studying those stories and narratives. Myth is the object of study, and mythology is the act and process of studying it.

The word "myth" did not exist in ancient Japan. This constitutes a major difference from Greek mythology, which is the origin of the word "myth." The modern Japanese word for myth, *shinwa*, meaning "divine story," was coined at the end of the nineteenth century by scholars who adapted the Western mythological methods for studying Japanese myths. This is not to say that myths did not exist in ancient Japan, only that in the premodern and early modern eras, the terminology used to refer to myths was unstable and changed overtime. This topic is treated in more detail in Chapter 5, but before embarking on the study of Japanese myths, it is important to realize that for most of their history, these myths were not treated as myths, but rather a variety of other genres including history or scripture. For example, in premodern Japan, myths were envisioned as historical narratives explaining the legitimacy of the imperial clan's preeminent position at the Japanese court, historical repositories for stories and anecdotes about antiquity, or sources for information about the nature of the kami and the rituals used to worship them.

The definition of myth used in this book is taken from Robert Segal: a myth is a story that has some significant meaning to a group of people at a particular time. This broad definition is particularly suited to the Japanese case, where myths have served a wide variety of roles and where a narrower definition would circumscribe the actual scope and significance that these narratives have played in Japan during their history.

Two related Japanese approaches to mythology that do not have exact equivalents in English until the nineteenth century but that feature prominently in the history of reading and studying Japanese myths are theology and philology. Theology refers to the study of gods and divinity, and to the study of religious systems. One Japanese word for theology in premodern times was *Shinto*, meaning "the way of the gods." Of course, Shinto refers not only to the study of the way of the gods but also to the ritual practices in which a believer would engage. In this sense, Shinto is both a methodological perspective and a religion. In considering the history of Japanese mythology, a key point is that before modern mythological study emerged in Japan, practitioners of Shinto performed research on Japanese myths for theological purposes, that is, to understand the way of the gods.

Philology refers to the study of ancient words and texts. It is related to linguistics and focused on word meanings and origins. However, its object of analysis is not a language or system of words, but rather a specific text and the usage of words within that text. The Japanese philological tradition developed after the printings of *Ancient Matters* and *Chronicles* opened these texts up to a wider audience for study and critique. In Japanese, this tradition is usually called *kokugaku*, which translates to "national learning" or "state studies." The term dates from the eighteenth century, but at that time, several other terms for this field were also in use. During the eighteenth century, scholars in the national learning tradition performed important commentarial work on *Ancient Matters* and *Chronicles*. Scholars in this field also performed groundbreaking work on *Myriad Poems* and identified that *Original Record* was not a seventh-century historical work by Prince Shōtoku. The philological perspective centered on reading *Ancient Matters* and *Chronicles* and figuring out exactly what the ancient language used in these texts meant. Because the texts were written using Chinese characters, it also meant trying to decipher or define the correct vernacular Japanese glosses for the texts. Or, conversely, it meant justifying a refusal to define vernacular readings of the texts, in the case of philologists who believed that such work was not academically sound or viable.

## Modern Mythology Methods

There are many methods for studying and analyzing myths. *The Truth of Myth,* the keystone book for the series "World Mythology in Theory and Everyday Life," discusses these methods in detail. *Japanese Mythology: A Guide* presents a selection of theories for myth interpretation demonstrating the many ways in which Japanese myths have been understood. Each of these approaches makes its own claims for assessing the truth of myth, and some approaches make exclusionary claims that deny the viability of other methods. However, for the purposes of this book, no one method of studying myths is considered superior to any other.

One approach reads myths as literary texts. This approach to mythology focuses on written records as discrete units of analysis. For example, a scholar using a textual studies approach would study the Japanese creation myth in which Izanagi and Izanami create the world by looking at the constituent texts. The narratives from *Ancient Matters* and/or *Chronicles* would be considered on their own terms and possibly, but not necessarily, compared to identify contrasts. The ultimate objective would be the identification of how each text or narrative functions to produce a coherent worldview or exhibits certain ideological perspectives. Using this approach to interpret the Izanagi and Izanami story would lead to the conclusion that *Ancient Matters* and *Chronicles* have different mythical narratives, a conclusion that is only possible if the texts are studied independently of each other and not as a single mythical account. The literary and textual studies approach is strongly influenced by post-modern thought, which denies the existence of universal truths or meta-narratives and encourages rigorous historicization.

A competing method of textualism that rejects post-modern influence and often employs comparative analysis with other written materials assumes the existence of some larger truth. For example, a scholar might claim that literature is a carrier of universal human truths and analyze the narrative of *Ancient Matters* in order to identify those truths. The scholar could also claim that *Ancient Matters* is a carrier of timeless or fundamental truths about Japan or the Japanese people. Similarly, the approach may focus on the author as a creative entity and identify the characteristics of their work. What distinguishes this mode of textualism from post-modern textualism is that it assumes the existence of a universal human truth or of a commonly observable set of values by which a text can be read or literature appreciated. Conversely, post-modern textualism asserts that such truths and values are themselves products of certain historical moments.

Japanese mythology is closely related to the folklore tradition. Scholars of folklore focus on local legends and popular narratives. These are often derived from oral sources, and oral literature exists in a complex relationship with written literature. For example, one could be considered as the primary source and the other as derivative. Or, the focus on local traditions and oral accounts could create a binary between written and oral materials. Assuming folklore is derived from popular stories and connected to common people, in parts of the world where writing was associated with the elite, the two might exist in opposition to each other. In the Japanese case, it is frequently asserted that *Ancient Matters* was based on preexisting oral literature. A scholar of folklore might research the Izanagi and Izanami story by collecting oral accounts of these kami through fieldwork and observing regional biases or local particularities. Folklore might also look toward the eighth-century gazetteers since these texts include local narratives. In the Japanese case, this scholarship often seeks to explain the origin of the Japanese people or unique qualities of Japanese culture. Sometimes it is called "ethnology" in Japan, as a translation of the Japanese word *minzokugaku.*

One approach popular among scholars of religion is to historicize myths and any associated ritual traditions and religious institutions. The strength of the approach is that being diachronic, it shows how Japanese myths have changed overtime. A scholar using a history of religion approach would consider how the Izanami and Izanagi creation story appears in original texts and then was adapted in later periods. Furthermore, they might identify how those adaptations connect to trends in intellectual history and dominant religious practices at the time. A scholar employing this approach might also analyze Japanese mythology overtime, tracing how the study of Japanese myths has changed and identifying trends, influences, and innovations in the field. A closely related avenue of study might be assessing how the Shinto religion has changed overtime.

An opposing approach to the history of religion might focus on the continuities within a religious tradition or commonalities across world religions. In this approach, rather than focusing on the manifestation of myth or religion at particular historical moments, the scholar focuses on commonalities and broader observations present in multiple accounts and across historical periods. A scholar using this approach might consider the Japanese creation story in various versions and identify motifs, such as the emphasis on uncleanliness versus purity, to suggest larger conclusions about the character of Japanese religion generally. These common elements, as important features of Japanese myth, might also be related to some more fundamental or elementary features of religion generally. This approach can used to speak hypothetically about the nature of Japanese myth or religion in the distant past before textual sources were available. It can also be used to generalize about the development of religious traditions across the world.

One important and popular model of mythological study closely related to religious study is comparative mythology. Comparative mythology or comparative approaches analyze Japanese myth alongside one or more other mythical traditions. The approach can be used for multiple objectives. The comparison can be illustrative and used as a tool for better understanding both Japanese myths and whatever mythical traditions are used as references. Alternatively, comparative mythology can be used to identify potential influences on Japanese myth, perhaps from other parts of Asia or even further afield. Comparative mythology can be used to make a larger statement about the nature of myths, religion, and their connection to humanity or the human experience. In the same vein, a proposed theory about the nature of myths might use comparative mythology to demonstrate its efficacy. A scholar employing a comparative approach may compare the Japanese creation story with creation stories from Asia to identify potential cultural influences, or with the other parts of the world to understand the nature of creation myths generally, or simply as an exercise to better understand Japanese myths.

The full utility of the comparative approach is most clearly demonstrated when evaluating multiple mythical traditions. Because this book is focused on Japanese myths and mythology, comparative mythology is under-represented here, and readers are encouraged to follow up with *The Truth of Myth* and other books in the "World Mythology in Theory and Everyday Life" series. The series editors, Tok Thompson and Gregory Schrempp, present five "axes of comparison" in *The Truth of Myth* that make comparison across mythical traditions more fruitful: time, space, quantity, quality/kind, and relation/cause. One of the comparative axes is applied in each of the five chapters of this book to encourage comparison.

The comparative approach is related to anthropological approaches. Anthropologists have long studied myth with the objective of understanding its role in human society. Early work in Japanese mythology centered on a debate between naturalists, who associated myth with nature, and ritualists, who associated it with early religion. Both approaches attempted to understand what role or function myth played in human society, and their explanations often related to the human experience with nature and the connection between magic, science, and religion. Using a naturalist approach for studying the Izanami and Izanagi myth might note the role that Izanami plays by allowing humanity to tame fire or the connection between her death by fire and the birth of kami connected to crops, recalling slash-and-burn agriculture. A ritualist approach might focus on the actions used to lure the sun goddess out of the heavenly rock cave and treat these actions as early examples of Shinto practice.

One of the most influential mythological methods is called structuralism. This approach, popularized by the French anthropologist Claude Lévi-Strauss (1908–2009), understands myths in terms of fundamental paradigms, called structures. These structures are not observed in terms of narrative, distinguishing structuralism from the other approaches discussed here. Rather, a structuralist would break myths down into their most simple parts, such as "gods create world" or "boy cries because he wants his mother." Then, the structuralist identifies patterns that emerge in these simplifications, called "mythemes." Mythemes are often understood in terms of binary oppositions like cleanliness and filth or darkness and light. Early structuralist approaches asserted that these structures were common to the human experience and could be observed in mythical traditions across the world. Later structuralist approaches restricted analysis to Japanese myths and instead focused on what distinguished them from other traditions.

A psychoanalytic approach to myth study, popularized by the Swiss psychologist Carl Jung (1875–1961), also analyzes myth based on the assumption of a shared human experience. A psychoanalytic approach might observe archetypal figures that appear in Japanese myth. Connecting those archetypes with similar figures and other mythical traditions provides insight into the human psyche. It might also provide points by which a unique Japanese psyche can be distinguished. Jung believed that humanity shares a collective unconscious and that mythical narratives, as humanity's oldest stories, provide one avenue for accessing that collective unconscious. More recently, the approach has been adopted by some evolutionary psychologists who use a comparative psychoanalytic study of mythical traditions to discover or observe central truths about human society and the human condition. The claims toward universal human qualities align this approach more closely with structuralism and naturalism and in opposition to textualism and the history of religions.

One final modern mythological method, rapidly growing in popularity in the twenty-first century, is neuro-centrism. This approach is closely associated with the more contemporary approaches used by modern psychoanalysts or evolutionary psychologists. Neuro-centrists assume that the human brain is the totality of the human person and the organ that differentiates Homo sapiens from other varieties of humanoids such as Neanderthals. In neuro-centric mythology, the defining attribute of the human brain is its capacity to create stories and narratives. These stories served an important function by bringing early humans together into larger groups. Allowing many humans to work together toward a common cause distinguished Homo sapiens from the smaller bands of Neanderthals and other humanoids and allowed Homo sapiens to change their natural environment on an unparalleled scale. Myths, as the oldest human stories, are studied by neuro-centrist scholars in terms of their capacity to bring human beings together through uniting belief.

## Book Contents

The book is divided into five chapters. The first four chapters are organized around major themes in Japanese myths: the creation of the world, the myths centered in the Izumo region, the founding of the Japanese empire, and the mythical exploits of select emperors. The mythological perspectives in each chapter progress chronologically because mythologists of later eras built their theories on the work of the scholars who preceded them. Mythology in the first chapter is from around the turn of the twentieth century, and in the fourth chapter, from turn of the twenty-first century and later. Finally, the fifth chapter addresses the study of *Ancient Matters* and *Chronicles* in premodern Japan.

Chapter 1 retells the myths of the creation of the world, the creation of the Japanese archipelago by the kami Izanagi and Izanami, Izanagi's trip to the Land of Yomi and fight with Izanami, the birth of Amaterasu and Susano-o, the fight between Amaterasu and Susano-o, and the expulsion of Susano-o from heaven. The mythological perspectives discussed in Chapter 1 are anthropological and sociological. These include early debates between naturalist and ritualist interpretations, the French, Vienna, and American schools of anthropology and sociology, comparative mythology, and structuralism.

Chapter 2 retells Susano-o's descent to Izumo, his slaying of the eight-headed snake, the trials of the kami Ō-ana-muji, Ō-ana-muji's renaming to Ō-kuni-nushi, Ō-kuni-nushi's completion of the creation of the Japanese archipelago, and Ō-kuni-nushi's surrender of the Central Reed Plain Land to the heavenly kami. The mythological perspectives discussed include the tri-functional hypothesis of Georges Dumézil (1898–1986), historical and political interpretations of Susano-o, the relationship of Susano-o with Korea, Jungian psychological interpretations, the Hero's Journey, and literature study of Ō-kuni-nushi.

Chapter 3 retells the descent of Amaterasu's grandson, Ninigi, to the Central Reed Plain Land, Ninigi's marriage, the voyage of Yama-sachi-hiko to the Palace of the Sea God, the foundation of the Japanese empire by the first mythical emperor, Jinmu, and the pacification of the Miwa kami by Emperor Sujin. The mythological perspectives discussed include mythical influences from the South Pacific, foundation myths in comparison with Korean myths,

Jungian psychology, theology and religious history, folklore associated with the Miwa kami, and intertextual methods using Chinese literature.

Chapter 4 retells the conquests of Yamato Take (sometimes called Yamato Takeru), the mythical subjugation of the Korean peninsula by Empress Jingū, the exploits of the legendary Emperor Yūryaku, and the reigns of the historical emperors Tenmu and Jitō. The mythological perspectives discussed include intellectual history, post-modern religious history, new interpretations of Dumézil, work by historians of ancient Japan, myth symbolism in anthropological and literary approaches, literary and linguistic studies of *Ancient Matters* and *Chronicles*, philosophical consideration of myth as a symbolic form, myth in post–World War II Japan, and updated structuralist treatments of Japanese myths.

Chapter 5 summarizes mythology in Japan before 1900. This includes treatment of *Chronicles* as a state history, traditional Japanese poetry written about mythical figures, Buddhist and Confucian interpretations of Japanese myths, various traditions of Shinto, and eighteenth- and nineteenth-century philology (national learning). These interpretations are distinguished from those appearing in Chapters 1–4 because prior to 1900, mythologists in Japan did not use "myth" as a conceptual category to orient their study. For this reason, "mythology," as it existed before 1900, incorporates genres like history, poetry, and theology.

At the end of the book, a list of references is divided into translations of primary sources, secondary sources mentioned in this book, and further reading in English on Japanese myths. A glossary of kami describes the major kami in the retellings in this book and their relationships to each other.

# 1

# The Yamato Cycle

## The Yamato Myths

### Creation of the World and Seven Generations of Gods

In *Chronicles*, it says that in the beginning, heaven and earth and yin and yang had not yet divided, and so were mixed together in a swirling mass. Within the depths of that mass, a bud sprouted. The lighter and brighter elements of the mass rose and formed heaven. The darker and heavier elements sank and formed earth. Hence, heaven formed first and earth afterward. After that, various kami began to appear.

When heaven and earth burst into being, the land floated like fish on the surface of the water. Then three kami symbolizing the separation of the land from the water came into being. The first was like a budding reed. He was called Kuni-toko-tachi, meaning "land always standing." The next was called Kuni-no-sa-tsuchi, meaning "thin strip of land." The third was called Toyo-kumu-nu, meaning "richly watered swamp." Because they were associated with the power of yang, these three kami were all male.[1]

---

[1] The first paragraph of *Chronicles* draws heavily from Chinese sources; it is sometimes interpreted as a preface providing a global creation story as context for a local creation story appearing in the second paragraph.

**TABLE 1** First Gods across Sources

| Source | First God | Second God | Third God | Fourth God | Fifth God |
|---|---|---|---|---|---|
| *Ancient Matters* | Ame-no-mi-naka-nushi | Taka-mi-musuhi | Kamu-musuhi | Umashi-ashikabi-hikoji | Ame-toko-tachi |
| *Chronicles* 1 | Kuni-toko-tachi | Kuni-no-sa-tsuchi | Toyo-kumu-nu | | |
| *Chronicles* 1.1 | Kuni-toko-tachi | Kuni-no-sa-tsuchi | Toyo-kumu-nu | | |
| *Chronicles* 1.2 | Umashi-me-hikoshu | Kuni-toko-tachi | Kuni-no-sa-tsuchi | | |
| *Chronicles* 1.3 | Kami-ashi-me-hikoji | Kuni-soko-tachi | | | |
| *Chronicles* 1.4 | Kuni-toko-tachi | Kuni-no-sa-tsuchi | Ame-no-mi-naka-nushi | Taka-mi-musuhi | Kamu-musuhi |
| *Chronicles* 1.5 | Kuni-toko-tachi | | | | |
| *Chronicles* 1.6 | Ama-toko-tachi | Kami-ashi-me-hikoshu | Kuni-toko-tachi | | |

*Ancient Matters* says that when heaven and earth first appeared, three kami orienting heaven and symbolizing the creative forces of the universe came into being in the High Heavenly Plain. The first was called Ame-no-mi-naka-nushi, meaning "august center of heaven." The second was called Taka-mi-musuhi, meaning "high august generative force." The third was called Kamu-musuhi, meaning "divine generative force." Then, the young land floated like oil on water, drifting about like a jellyfish. Two kami burst forth like budding reeds. The first was called Umashi-ashikabi-hikoji, meaning "fine reed man." The second was called Ame-toko-tachi, meaning "heaven always standing." In *Ancient Matters*, these five kami were known as the spirits of heaven.[2]

Next there were seven generations of kami, but the sources count the generations differently.

In *Chronicles*, the first three generations were the three kami that came into being earlier: Kuni-toko-tachi, Kuni-no-sa-tsuchi, and Toyo-kumu-nu. Then, four generations of kami were born as pairs. The first pair symbolized the formation of land and were called U-hiji-ni, meaning "muddy earth," and Su-hiji-ni, meaning "sandy earth." The second pair symbolized the separation of male and female and were called Ō-to-no-jj, meaning "great door pathway man," and Ō-toma-be, meaning "great woven mat woman." The third pair symbolized the assumption of human form and were called Omo-taru, meaning "complete face," and Kashiko-ne, meaning "beautiful apprehension." The fourth pair symbolized the union of male and female and were called Izana-gi, meaning "he who invites," and Izana-mi, meaning "she who invites."

In *Ancient Matters*, the seven generations of kami were different from the kami who had appeared before. The first two generations were Kuni-toko-tachi and Toyo-kumu-nu, who in this version had not yet come into being. They symbolize the land appearing out of

---

[2] In *Ancient Matters*, there is no creation story for heaven and earth. Rather, the myth begins with heaven and earth already existing.

**TABLE 2**  Seven Generations of Gods

| Generation | *Ancient Matters* | *Chronicles* (Main Version) |
|---|---|---|
| 1 | Kuni-toko-tachi | Kuni-toko-tachi |
| 2 | Toyo-kumu-nu | Kuni-no-sa-tsuchi |
| 3 | U-hiji-ni and Su-hiji-ni | Toyo-kumu-nu |
| 4 | Tsuno-kui and Iku-kui | U-hiji-ni and Su-hiji-ni |
| 5 | Ō-to-no-ji and Ō-toma-be | Ō-to-no-ji and Ō-toma-be |
| 6 | Omo-taru and Kashiko-ne | Omo-taru and Kashiko-ne |
| 7 | Iza-na-ki and Iza-na-mi | Iza-na-ki and Iza-na-mi |

the water. Then, five generations of kami were born as pairs. The first pair was U-hiji-ni and Su-hiji-ni, associated with earth and sand. The second pair symbolized the emergence of a reed from the soil and were called Tsuno-kui, meaning "horned peg," and Iku-kui, meaning "lively peg." The third pair was Ō-to-no-jj and Ō-toma-be. The fourth pair was Omo-taru and Kashiko-ne. The fifth pair was Izana-gi and Izana-mi.

Of the kami that came into being as the First Gods and the Seven Generations of Gods, only Taka-mi-musuhi, Kamu-musuhi, Izana-gi, and Izana-mi have major roles in later myths. Izana-gi and Izana-mi will be abbreviated to Izanagi and Izanami in the sections that follow. Izanagi is sometimes called Izanaki; the accent marks used to distinguish "ki" from "gi" in modern Japanese were not used in ancient times.

## Creation of the Japanese Archipelago

In *Ancient Matters*, the heavenly gods commanded Izanagi and Izanami to complete the creation of the land and gave them the jeweled spear of heaven so that they could accomplish this task. Izanagi and Izanami stood atop the floating bridge of heaven and thrust the spear down into the blue sea below. They swirled the spear around, making a curdling sound. When they pulled it back up and out, the salt from the brine that dripped off of the spear coagulated into an island called Ono-goro-shima meaning "self-coagulating island." They went down to the island and found a pillar erected at its center. Then Izanagi said to Izanami, "Tell me about the shape of your body."

Izanami replied, "There is a place on my body with a gap."

Izanagi said, "There is a place on my body with something extra. I'd like to take this excess from my body and put it into the gap in your body. Then we will give birth to the land. How does that sound?"

Izanami said, "That sounds good."

Then Izanagi said, "I'll go around the pillar that is on this island from the left. You go around the pillar from the right. We'll meet again after we come around."

The two kami each went around the pillar from their respective directions and circled until they met each other again. Then Izanami said, "Oh my! What a lovely young man."

Izanagi said, "Oh my! What a lovely young woman. But it would have been better if I had spoken first."[3]

The two kami consummated their marriage. First, Izanami gave birth to Hiru-ko, meaning "leech child." The child was unable to stand after three years because its bones did not ossify, and so it seemed to have no skeleton, like a leech. Izanagi and Izanami put him in a boat and cast him to the winds. Next, Izanami gave birth to the island of Awa.[4]

Given this unfortunate turn of events, Izanagi and Izanami consoled each other, saying, "Something is wrong with our children."

---

[3] In *Chronicles*, this sequence of events is reversed. There, Izanagi and Izanami first go around the pillar and exchange their auspicious greeting. Then, Izanagi complains that he should have spoken first. Then two kami go around the pillar again, and this time Izanagi speaks first. Then he asks Izanami about her body.

[4] Awa literally means "froth" but could also mean "to be ashamed" or "to regard lightly." In *Chronicles*, the island is described as the afterbirth.

They went back to heaven and told the heavenly kami what had happened.[5]

The heavenly kami performed divination to find out the nature of the problem. Then they told Izanagi and Izanami, "This happened because the female kami spoke first. Go back to the island and try again."

Izanagi and Izanami went around the pillar again just like they did before. Then Izanagi said, "Oh my! What a lovely young woman." Izanami said, "Oh my! What a lovely young man." Then she gave birth to the eight great islands of Japan.[6]

The names and birth order of the islands differ across sources.[7]

Awaji, Sado, Oki, Iki, and Tsushima use the same names in the present. Ō-yamato is the island of Honshu, Tsukushi is Kyushu, and Iyo is Shikoku. Kibiko is the Kojima Peninsula of Okayama Prefecture, which was an island in antiquity located in the powerful region of Kibi. Koshi refers to the northwestern seaboard of Honshu, present-day Niigata, Toyama, Ishikawa, and northern Fukui Prefectures. Ōshima is perhaps Yashirojima in Yamaguchi Prefecture, but there are several islands with this name in the Japanese archipelago. Azuki is Shōdoshima. Omina is perhaps Himeshima in Oita Prefecture. Chika is perhaps the Gotō Islands of Nagasaki Prefecture. Futago is perhaps the Danjo Islands of Nagasaki Prefecture.

In *Chronicles* 4.5, when Izanagi and Izanami went around again, Izanagi spoke first and said, "Oh my! What a lovely young woman." Then they were going to consummate their marriage, but they did

---

[5] This episode and the divination that follows are absent from the main version of *Chronicles*. This absence is consistent with the earlier difference that in *Chronicles*, Izanagi and Izanami are not commanded by the heavenly gods to create the land, but rather do so of their own accord.

[6] In ancient Japanese sources, the number eight is often used with the meaning of "many," but the compilers interpret the number literally.

[7] In all sources, the islands born include the major islands of Honshu, Kyushu, and Shikoku. The northernmost major island of the modern Japanese state, Hokkaido, was not part of the ancient Japanese state and so does not appear in its creation stories.

**TABLE 3** Eight Great Islands of the Japanese Archipelago

| Birth Order | Ancient Matters | Chronicles 4 | 4.1 | 4.6 | 4.7 | 4.8 | 4.9 |
|---|---|---|---|---|---|---|---|
| 0 | Awa, as mistake | | Awa, as mistake | | | | Awaji, as placenta |
| 1 | Awaji | Awaji, as placenta | Ō-yamato | Awaji | Awaji | Ono-goro-shima, as placenta | Ō-yamato |
| 2 | Iyo | Ō-yamato | Awaji | Ō-yamato | Ō-yamato | Awaji | Awa |
| 3 | Oki | Iyo | Iyo | Iyo | Iyo | Ō-yamato | Iyo |
| 4 | Tsukushi | Tsukushi | Tsukushi | Tsukushi | Oki | Iyo | Oki |
| 5 | Iki | Oki and Sado as twins | Oki | Oki and Sado as twins | Sado | Tsukushi | Sado |
| 6 | Tsushima | Koshi | Sado | Koshi | Tsukushi | Kibiko | Tsukushi |
| 7 | Sado | Ōshima | Koshi | Ōshima | Iki | Oki and Sado as twins | Kibiko |
| 8 | Ō-yamato | Kibiko | Kibiko | Koshima | Tsushima | Koshi | Ōshima |
| Others | Kibiko, Azuki, Ōshima, Omina, Chika, Futago | Tsushima, Iki, and others | | | | | |

**MAP 1** Eight Great Islands of the Japanese Archipelago.

not know how to do it. Just then, they saw a wagtail, a bird whose tail goes up and down when it sings. The two kami saw how the bird moved and were able to consummate their union by imitating it.

## Birth of Other Kami and Death of Izanami

In *Ancient Matters*, after giving birth to the land, Izanagi and Izanami gave birth to the kami who inhabited it. First, they gave birth to ten kami related to earth, trees, buildings, and the sea. The last of these two kami were charged with governance of the rivers and seas, and they gave birth to eight more kami associated with water. After that, Izanagi and Izanami gave birth to four kami of the winds, trees, mountains, and fields.

**FIGURE 2** Izanagi and Izanami Create the Japanese Archipelago. After an artwork by Kawanabe Kyosai (1831–89). Made in *c*.1870 by unknown artist and captured on film for *The Connoisseur* magazine in 1925.

In *Chronicles*, Izanagi and Izanami gave birth to the kami of the seas, rivers, mountains, trees, and fields.[8] Then they conferred together, saying, "We have already given birth to the land and its

---

[8] In the main version of *Chronicles*, Izanagi and Izanami give birth to the sun goddess, Amaterasu, together. This is a major difference from *Ancient Matters* and *Chronicles* 5.1, 5.6, and 5.11.

mountains, rivers, fields, and trees. We should give birth to a kami fit to rule this realm." Then together they gave birth to the kami of the sun, Ō-hiru-me-no-muchi, meaning "noble lady of the great sun." She is usually called Ama-terasu, meaning "heaven shining." Hereafter she is given as Amaterasu. When she was born, Izanagi and Izanami rejoiced, saying, "Of all the children we have had, this one is the greatest. She should be sent to heaven above to take charge of affairs there." Then they used the pillar of heaven to send her back upward.

Next, they gave birth to the kami of the moon, either called Tsuku-yomi meaning "moon counting" or Tsuku-yumi meaning "moon bow." Because his brilliance was second only to that of the sun, Izanagi and Izanami sent him to heaven as well, to aid Amaterasu in her governance.

Next, they gave birth to Hiru-ko, the leech child.[9] Even after three years, he could not stand, so they placed him in a boat and cast him to the winds.

Then they gave birth to Susa-no-o, meaning "raging man." Hereafter he is called Susano-o. This kami was brazen and cruel and was always weeping and wailing. He killed many of the people in the land and caused its verdant mountains to dry up. Izanagi and Izanami told him, "You are an evil kami and unfit to rule this realm. We banish you to the Land of Ne." Then they drove him out.

In *Chronicles* 5.1 and *Original Record*, Izanagi said, "I want to give birth to one who is fit to rule this realm." He took a mirror in his left hand and a kami came into being, called Ō-hiru-me. He took a mirror in his right hand and a kami came into being called Tsuku-yomi. Then he turned his head and looked behind him and a kami came into being called Susano-o. Ō-hiru-me and Tsuku-yomi were bright and beautiful, and so Izanagi sent them to heaven to shine down upon the realm. Susano-o was brazen and cruel, and so Izanagi made him descend and rule the Land of Ne.

---

[9] In *Ancient Matters*, Hiru-ko was born earlier, when the kami made a mistake consummating their marriage.

In *Chronicles* 5.2, after Izanagi and Izanami gave birth to the sun and moon, they gave birth to Hiru-ko, who could not stand on his own even after three years. This happened because when Izanagi and Izanami went around the pillar, Izanami spoke first, violating the principles of yin and yang. Next, they gave birth to Susano-o, but this kami had an evil character and enjoyed weeping and wailing all the time. Many people in the land died and its verdant mountains dried up. Izanagi and Izanami told him, "If you were to rule this land, disaster would ensue, and so you must rule the distant Land of Ne." Then they gave birth to a camphor boat. They put Hiru-ko in this boat and set it adrift.

Next, they gave birth to the kami of fire, Kagu-tsu-chi, meaning "fire spirit." But in giving birth to this kami, Izanami was burned and died. While she was dying, she lay down on the ground and gave birth to a kami of earth, Hani-yama-hime, meaning "lady of clay mountains," and a kami of water, Mitsu-ha-no-me, meaning "woman of waters." Kagu-tsu-chi married Hani-yama-hime, who gave birth to an agriculture kami, Waka-musuhi, meaning "young generative force." Silkworms and mulberry trees grew from Waka-musuhi's head, and the five grains sprouted from his navel.[10]

In *Chronicles* 5.4 and *Ancient Matters*, the kami born when Izanami was dying resembled bodily fluids that she excreted. Izanami threw up, and this became a kami of metal smelting, Kana-yama-hiko, meaning "lord of metal mountains." Izanami urinated, and this became a kami of water, Mitsu-ha-no-me. Izanami defecated, and this became a kami of earth, Hani-yama-hime.

In *Chronicles* 5.5, when Izanami died, she was buried in Arima Village, Kii Province. The residents there venerate her spirit. The Hananoiwaya Shrine in the Arima District of Mie Prefecture marks Izanami's grave.

---

[10] The five grains can vary by source but might refer to wheat, barley, barnyard millet, foxtail millet, and beans.

In *Chronicles* 5.6, when Izanagi and Izanami had given birth to the land of eight great islands, Izanagi said, "A morning fog hangs over these lands we have made." Then he exhaled to blow the fog away, and his breath became the kami of the wind, Shi-naga-tsu-hiko, meaning "lord of long breath." Izanagi became hungry and a rice kami was born, called Uka-no-mi-tama, meaning "soul of rice storage." Then they gave birth to the kami of the sea, Wata-tsu-mi, meaning "sea spirt"; the kami of the mountains, Yama-tsu-mi, meaning "mountain spirit"; the kami of the trees, Kuku-no-chi, meaning "spirit of trees"; and the kami of the earth, Hani-yasu, meaning "clay peace."

When the fire kami was born, Izanami died from the burns. Izanagi was beside himself, saying, "Why did my beloved have to die for the sake of just one child?" Then he crawled alongside the corpse and wept. His tears fell and became a kami, called Naki-sawa-me, meaning "crying swamp woman."

Then Izanagi drew his ten-span sword and cut the fire kami into three pieces. The blood that coated Izanagi's sword produced kami of swords, thunder, shattered stone, and mountain valley torrents. First, the blood that dripped from Izanagi's sword blade became the myriad stones along the riverbank of heaven and the ancestors of the sword kami Futsu-nushi, meaning "slicing master." The blood that dripped from the sword guard became the sword and thunder kami Mika-no-haya-hi, meaning "vigorous swift spirit," and Hi-no-haya-hi, meaning "fire swift spirit." Mika-no-haya-hi was the ancestor of the kami Take-mikazuchi, meaning "brave vigorous spirit" or "brave august lightning." The two kami Futsu-nushi and Take-mikazuchi would later be sent from heaven to earth to subdue the unwieldy kami there. The blood that dripped off Izanagi's sword tip became the kami of the shattered stone, and the blood that dripped off the sword pommel became the kami of mountain valley torrents.

In *Ancient Matters*, the blood from the tip of Izanagi's sword spattered on the rocks and produced the kami of stone splitting. The blood from the guard of his sword spattered on the rocks and produced the kami of thunder, including Take-mikazuchi. The blood from the hilt of the sword dripped through Izanagi's fingers and produced the kami of mountain valley torrents. The body of the fire kami produced eight mountain kami, starting with the highest peaks and going downward toward the edge of the range.

Izanagi wanted to meet Izanami again, and so he followed her to Yomi, the land of the deceased gods. When he arrived, she came out from the door of the funeral hall where she had been laid to rest and greeted him. Then Izanagi said, "My dear, we have not finished creating the land. Please, come back with me."[11]

Izanami replied, "I wish you had come sooner! Alas, I've already eaten the food of Yomi. But seeing you here makes me wish to return. Let me confer with the kami of this land about the situation. In the meantime, I beg you, do not look upon me." Then Izanami went back into the funeral hall.

Izanami was gone for a long time, and Izanagi could not wait any longer. He broke off the large tooth from the end of the comb that was stuck in his left hair bun and turned it into a torch and then looked inside the hall to see what was going on. When he saw Izanami, maggots were squirming and oozing out of her corpse, and on her body, there were eight types of thunder. When Izanagi saw them, he was terrified and fled.

Izanami then came forth and said, "You have shamed me!" She sent the ugly hags of Yomi to chase him down. While he fled, Izanagi untied the black vine that was holding his hair back and threw it to the ground, where it turned into grapes. The hags stopped to eat the grapes while Izanagi continued his flight. When the hags finished, they continued chasing him, and so he pulled out the comb that was stuck in his right hair bun and threw it to the ground, where it turned into bamboo shoots. The hags stopped to pick the sprouts, and in the meantime, Izanagi fled. Izanami then sent the eight thunder

---

[11] This statement appears in *Ancient Matters*. In the main version of *Chronicles*, Izanami does not die and so the couple complete the creation of the land without incident.

kami that had been on her body and the armies of Yomi to catch him. Izanagi drew his ten-span sword and waved it behind him while he ran away.

In *Chronicles* 5.6, Izanagi also urinated on the side of a tree, and this turned into a great river, slowing down his pursuers.

In *Ancient Matters*, when Izanagi reached the foot of the pass that marked the entrance to Yomi, he took three peaches that he found there and threw them at his pursuers, who scattered and fled. Izanagi said to the peaches, "Just as you have saved me, so save any mortal from the central reed plain land who falls into peril." Then he named the peaches Ō-kamu-zu-mi, meaning "great divine spirt."

At last Izanami herself came after him. Izanagi picked up a massive boulder that would require 1,000 men to move and used it to block off the pass that marks the entrance to Yomi. Then Izanagi and Izanami each stood on one side of the boulder and spoke to each other, ending their marriage. Izanami said, "My dear husband, if you leave me, every day I will strangle 1,000 people of your land."

**FIGURE 3** Entrance to Yomi, Shimane Prefecture. (CC 3.0, Chief Hira. Wikipedia Commons)

Izanagi replied, "My dear wife, if you do that, every day I will build 1,500 huts used for giving birth." This is the reason that the human population continues to grow. The path marking the entrance to Yomi is in the land of Izumo, present-day Shimane Prefecture.

## Birth of Amaterasu and Susano-o (Third Version)

In *Ancient Matters*, Izanagi said to himself, "I've been in an awful, unclean land, and must purify myself." He went to the mouth of the river in Tachibana, Himuka, present-day Miyazaki Prefecture, and was going to perform ritual bathing. When he disrobed, twelve kami were born from the articles of clothing he threw down and from his walking stick.

Then Izanagi said, "Upstream, the current is too fast for bathing, and downstream, it is too weak." So, he went into the middle stream, and in doing so produced the kami Yaso-maga-tsu-hi, meaning "spirit of many disasters," and the kami Ō-maga-tsu-hi, meaning "spirit of great disaster." These two kami came into being due to the pollution that Izanagi brought back with him from the land of Yomi. In order to correct the influence wrought by these two evil spirits, Izanagi then produced the kami Kamu-nao-bi, meaning "divine corrective spirit;" Ō-nao-bi, meaning "great corrective spirit"; and Izu-no-me, meaning "righteous woman."

When Izanagi bathed in the depths, he produced two kami: Soko-tsu-wata-tsu-mi, meaning "spirit of the deep sea," and Soko-tsu-tsu-no-o, meaning "man of the deep seaport." When Izanagi bathed at a medium depth, he produced two kami: Naka-tsu-wata-tsu-mi, meaning "spirt of the middle sea," and Naka-tsu-tsu-no-o, meaning "man of the middle seaport." When Izanagi bathed at the surface, he produced two kami: Uwa-tsu-wata-tsu-mi, meaning "spirit of the upper sea," and Uwa-tsu-tsu-no-o, meaning "man of the surface seaport." The three kami of sea spirits are worshipped by the Muraji of Azumi as their patron deity, in present-day Fukuoka.

The three kami of the seaports are those venerated in the Sumiyoshi Grand Shrine, in present-day Osaka.

Then, when Izanagi washed his left eye, he produced the kami Amaterasu. When he washed his right eye, he produced the kami Tsuku-yomi. When he washed his nose, it produced the kami Take-haya-susa-no-o, known as Susano-o. Izanagi was overjoyed and said, "I have given birth to so many children, but finally have three whose esteem surpasses that of all the others." He took off his necklace and bestowed it upon Amaterasu, saying, "You shall rule the High Heavenly Plain." Then he told Tsuku-yomi, "You shall rule the night." Then he told Susano-o, "You shall rule the ocean."

In *Chronicles* 5.11, Izanagi said, "Amaterasu shall rule the high heavenly plain. Tsuku-yomi shall share rule of heavenly affairs with her. Susa-no-o shall rule the ocean."

After Amaterasu had settled in heaven, she heard that in the Central Reed Plain Land below there was a kami named Uke-mochi, meaning "food preserver." She ordered Tsuku-yomi to go and investigate.

Tsuku-yomi received his orders and immediately went to see Uke-mochi. When they met, Uke-mochi turned her head to face the land and grain came out of her mouth. Then she turned her head to face the sea, and fish came out of her mouth. She turned her head to face the mountains and game animals came out of her mouth. She prepared food from all of these sources and placed them on one hundred tables of offering as a feast for Tsuku-yomi. He, however, was furious and said, "How disgusting! How can you feed me things that you threw up from your mouth?" And so, he drew his sword and slew her.

Tsuku-yomi went back to heaven and told Amaterasu what had happened. Amaterasu responded angrily, "You are an evil kami. I never want to see you again." This is the reason that the sun and the moon are estranged.

Later, Amaterasu sent Ama-no-kuma-hito meaning "heavenly offering presenter person," to see how things had developed.

Uke-mochi was already dead, but cows and horses came forth from the crown of her head, foxtail millet from her forehead, silkworms from her brows, barnyard millet from her eyes, rice from her stomach, and barley and beans from her genitals. Ama-no-kuma-hito collected these foods and brought them back to Amaterasu. When she saw them, Amaterasu declared, "These things shall serve as sustenance for the people of the world." She took the silkworms in her mouth and reeled them into thread; this was the beginning of silk making.

In *Ancient Matters*, Izanagi produced three noble children when he bathed to purify himself after escaping from the land of Yomi. He gave each child a charge. Amaterasu and Tsuku-yomi carried out their duties as he had entrusted them to do, but Susano-o did not perform the administration of his realm. Instead, he wept and wailed, even after he had grown up and his beard hung down to his chest. His crying was so bad that it caused the verdant mountains to wither and the water from the rivers and seas to dry up. In response, the cries of rampaging kami filled the land like summer flies, and calamity ensued.

Izanagi said to Susano-o, "Why don't you rule the land that I entrusted you with? Why are you always crying?"

Susano-o replied, "I want to go to the Land of Ne, the land of my mother. This is why I cry."

Then Izanagi said angrily, "You cannot stay in this land!" and drove him out.

## Amaterasu and Susano-o

When Susano-o received the order from Izanagi banishing him to the Land of Ne, he said, "Father, before I go, I want to give my regards in person to my older sister, Amaterasu."

In *Chronicles*, Izanagi replied, "Granted." Then, having completed his divine task, Izanagi prepared to leave this world. He built a hermitage for himself on the island of Awaji and hid himself away. It is also said that he went up to heaven and reported the outcome of his creation efforts and then stayed in the Lesser Palace of the Sun.[12]

When Susano-o ascended to heaven, the seas churned and the mountains and rivers cried out, and all the land shook. Amaterasu was startled when she heard this disturbance and said, "Surely my brother comes with bad intentions. He must be planning to take over my lands." She untied her hair, wrapped it into buns on the sides of her head like a warrior, and then wrapped each with a string of beads. She also wrapped beads around her arms. She put a one-thousand-capacity quiver on her back and hung a five-hundred-capacity quiver at her side, strapped on an arm protector that thundered when struck by the bowstring, nocked an arrow, raised her bow, planted both feet into the ground all the way to the thigh, and then kicked the earth about as if it were snow. Then she issued a fierce shout and stamped her feet, demanding of Susano-o, "Why have you come?"

Susano-o replied, "I have no evil intentions. Our father asked why I was always weeping and wailing, and I told him I wanted to go to the land of our mother. He said that I could not stay in my land and drove me out. I wanted to give you my regards in person before my departure."

"But how can I know that your intentions are pure?" Amaterasu asked.

The two kami decided to test Susano-o's intentions by taking an oath and producing children together. Sources differ on who produced which children.

In *Ancient Matters*, Susano-o proposed, "Let us make an oath and produce children."[13] The two kami took positions on opposite sides of the tranquil river of heaven and made their oaths. Amaterasu

---

[12] *Ancient Matters* says that Izanagi dwelt in Taga in Awaji. The Izanagi-jingū shrine in the Taga area of Awaji City claims to mark this location.

[13] In *Ancient Matters*, Susano-o declares his victory and rages afterwards, linking his later bad behavior to this oath.

asked Susano-o for the ten-span sword that he wore at his side. Then she broke the sword into three pieces, rinsed them in a heavenly well, chewed them up, and spat them out. The misty spray she blew out produced three kami. First was Ta-kiri-bime, meaning "lady of mist." She is also called Oki-tsu-shima-hime, meaning "lady of the deep sea island." Next was Ichi-ki-shima-hime, meaning "lady of the island of devoted veneration." She is also called Sa-yori-hime, meaning "lady of divine possession." Last was Tagitsu-hime, meaning "lady of rushing waters."

Susano-o asked Amaterasu for the long string of beads wrapped around her left hair bun. These he rinsed in a heavenly well, chewed up, and spat out. The misty spray he blew out produced a kami named Masa-katsu-a-katsu-kachi-haya-hi-ame-no-oshi-ho-mimi, meaning "Truly winning, I win, swiftly winning spirt, divine spirit of heavenly great rice ears." This kami is usually called Oshi-ho-mimi for short.

Then Susano-o asked for the beads strung on the wrap securing Amaterasu's right hair bun. He chewed them up and spat them out, and the misty spray he blew out produced a kami named Ame-no-hohi, meaning "heavenly rice ear spirit." Susano-o then asked for the beads strung on the wrap holding back Amaterasu's hair. He chewed them up and spat them out, and the misty spray he blew out pro-duced a kami named Ama-tsu-hiko-ne, meaning "heavenly lord." Susano-o then asked for the beads strung around Amaterasu's left arm. He chewed them up and spat them out, and the misty spray he blew out produced a kami named Iku-tsu-hiko-ne, meaning "lively lord." Finally, Susano-o asked for the beads strung around Amaterasu's right arm. He chewed them up and spat them out, and the misty spray he blew out produced a kami named Kumano-kusu-hi, meaning "miraculous spirit of Kumano."

Then Amaterasu said to Susano-o, "The five male children were produced from my beads and therefore belong to me. The three female children were produced from your sword and therefore belong to you." The oldest of the female children, Ta-kiri-bime, dwells in the Oki-tsu-miya shrine. Ichi-ki-shima-hime dwells in Naka-tsu-miya shrine. Tagitsu-hime dwells in the He-tsu-miya shrine. All three live in Munakata, and they are venerated by the Kimi of Munakata as their patron deities.

Ame-no-hohi and Ama-tsu-hiko-ne are the ancestors of a number of lineage groups who work as provincial officials and other dignitaries.

Then Susano-o said to Amaterasu, "Because my intentions were pure, I had three female children, and have won the contest." Then he raged with victory.

In *Chronicles*, Amaterasu asked Susano-o, "How can I know that your intentions are pure?[14]

Susano-o replied, "Let us make an oath together. If the children I produce are female, then you will know that my intentions are impure. If the children I produce are male, then you will know that my intentions are pure."

Amaterasu demanded and took Susano-o's ten-span sword, broke it into three pieces, rinsed it in a well of heaven, and chewed it up. In the midst of the breath she exhaled, three female kami were born: Ta-kiri-bime, Tagitsu-hime, and Ichi-ki-shima-hime.

Susano-o appealed for the strings of beads wrapped around Amaterasu's hair buns and arms. These he rinsed in a well of heaven and chewed up. In the midst of the breath he exhaled, five male kami were born: Oshi-ho-mimi, Ame-no-hohi, Ama-tsu-hiko-ne, Iku-tsu-hiko-ne, and Kumano-kusu-hi.

Then Amaterasu decreed, "Originally, the beads were mine, and so these five male kami are all my children. The ten-span sword was yours, and so these three female kami are also yours." Then she bestowed them upon Susano-o. These kami are venerated by the Kimi of Munakata as their patron deities.

---

[14] In *Chronicles*, the conditions of victory are set before the oath takes place, and there is no casual connection implied between Susano-o's victory in the oath and his later evil conduct. This exchange also emphasizes Amaterasu's superiority thorough use of verbs like "decreed," "appealed," and "demanded."

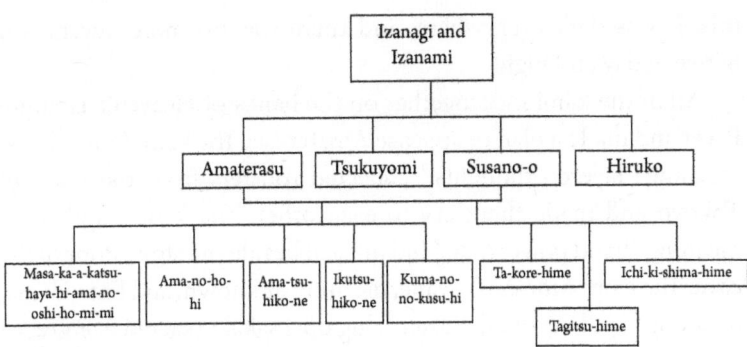

**FIGURE 4** Children of Amaterasu and Susano-o.

After this, Susano-o's behavior was truly deplorable. Amaterasu had set up rice paddies in heaven, but Susano-o double planted the seedlings in the spring, ruining the neatness of the rows. Then he broke down the ridges around the paddies, which let all the water out. In the autumn, he released horses into the paddies and made them roll around inside. When Susano-o saw that Amaterasu was planning to celebrate the feast of first rice, he secretly defecated in the feast hall and spread his excrement all around. Amaterasu made excuses for him and said, "This looks like excrement, but it must just be vomit that my brother threw up when he was drunk. As for damaging my rice paddies, he must have thought there was a better use for the land."

And yet Susano-o's behavior grew even worse. When he saw Amaterasu weaving the clothing of the gods in the sacred weaving hall, he flayed a horse backwards, cut a hole in the roof of the hall, and threw the horse inside. Amaterasu was so surprised that she hurt herself with the weaving shuttle.

According to *Ancient Matters*, when Susano-o threw the horse into the hall, a weaving woman accidentally stabbed herself in the genitals with the weaving shuttle and died.

Amaterasu was furious and immediately withdrew to the rock cave of heaven, closed the stone door, and stayed inside. Because of this, it was dark everywhere, and there was no more alternation between day and night.

All of the kami met together on the banks of Heaven's Tranquil River and made a plan to appease Amaterasu. The kami Omoi-kane, meaning "layered thoughts," collected roosters from the Land of Tokoyo and made them cry to each other. The kami Ta-jikara-o, meaning "hand power man," hid himself beside the stone door of the cave. The kami Ame-no-koyane, meaning unknown, and Futo-dama, meaning "opulent ritual master," dug up a sakaki (sacred evergreen) tree from Mt. Kagu. They hung an innumerable span of beads from its upper branches, an eight-span mirror from its middle branches, and blue and white streamers from its lower branches. Then they prayed that Amaterasu would come out. The kami Ame-no-uzu-me, meaning "heavenly headdress woman," hung vines from her sleeves, took a wreath as her headpiece, started a fire, and overturned a stock tank in front of the cave. Then she stripped, revealing her breasts and genitals, and danced as if she were divinely possessed. When the other kami saw this, they all burst into laughter.

Inside the rock cave, Amaterasu heard the commotion outside and said, "Because I am concealed inside this cave, it should be dark out there. How can Ame-no-uzu-me be having a such jovial celebration?" Then Amaterasu cracked open the door and peeked outside.

Ame-no-uzu-me said to her, "We are celebrating because we found a kami that is even more brilliant than you! Take a look!" Ame-no-koyane and Futo-dama had taken a mirror and stood it up facing the rock door. Amaterasu could see it through the crack, and being curious, she opened the door further and started to come out.

Then suddenly, Ta-jikara-o grabbed her by the hand and pulled her all the way out of the cave. Ame-no-koyane and Futo-dama quickly pulled a rope behind her blocking the entrance to the cave. "Please do not go back in," they implored her. And so, the High Heavenly Plain and the Central Reed Plain Land were filled with light once more.

The many kami conferred with each other after this and decided to fine Susano-o 1,000 tables of offerings in atonement for his crimes. They also pulled out the nails on his hands and feet and all of his hair. After this, they banished him from heaven.

According to *Chronicles* 7.3, the various kami denounced Susano-o for his bad behavior and told him that he could no longer live in heaven or in the Central Reed Plain Land. They banished him to the Land of Ne and chased him out. When they did, there was torrential rain. Susano-o bound grass into a hat and raincoat and begged the various kami to give him shelter.

All of the kami rejected him, telling him that he was banished as punishment for his evil deeds. He was unable to find shelter from the wind and rain and descended to earth in bitterness. In the present, one avoids entering the house of another while wearing their hat and raincoat. If they do, then purification rites must be performed.

After this, Susano-o said, "The various kami have banished me, and I will depart forever. How could I leave without seeing my older sister first?" Then again he shook the heavens and earth and ascended to heaven. Amaterasu and Susano-o made an oath, etc.[15]

According to *Ancient Matters*, Susano-o asked the agriculture kami Ō-getsu-hime, meaning "great food lady," for the food that he needed to provide for the offering.[16] And so Ō-getsu-hime pulled food out of her nose, mouth, and anus; prepared it in various fashions; and presented it all to him. Susano-o saw where she got the food from and assumed that she was polluting the food that was to be used for his offerings. Then he killed her. Various crops came from her corpse: silkworms from her head, rice from her eyes, millet from her ears, beans from her nose, wheat from

[15] *Chronicles* 7.3 reverses the order of events, with Susan-o going to heaven and confronting Amaterasu after he has been banished for his bad behavior.

[16] The episode with Ō-getsu-hime appears only in *Ancient Matters*; it is similar to the episode in *Chronicles* 5.11 with Uke-mochi.

her genitals, and soybeans from her anus. Kamu-musuhi collected the seeds from these products.

The Shinto prayer for the Great Exorcism of the Sixth Month was recited annually at the ancient imperial court, and it has a list of sins that seem related to the Susano-o myth. According to this prayer, Amaterasu proclaimed that her grandson, Ninigi, was to rule the Japanese archipelago and expel the evil deities from the land. Then she made Ninigi descend and rule. The people who came into existence in this land committed heavenly and earthly sins. The heavenly sins were breaking down the ridges between rice fields, filling in the irrigation ditches for rice fields, destroying the irrigation canals, double planting the seedlings, setting up stakes for claiming fields, skinning animals alive, skinning animals backwards, and defecating.[17] The earthly sins were cutting the flesh of the living, cutting the flesh of the dead, leprosy, boils, sex with one's mother, sex with one's child, sex with a mother and then their child, sex with a child and then their mother, bestiality, disasters caused by crawling insects, disasters caused by heavenly kami, disasters caused by flying birds, cursing someone's livestock and causing them to die, and cursing other people through use of incantations. When these sins appear, the leader of the Nakatomi Clan recites this prayer, and the heavenly kami blow all these sins away.

## Mythological Perspectives

### Comparative Axes: Space (Thompson and Schrempp)

In *The Truth of Myth*, Thompson and Schrempp suggest that spaces and places in myths, including their organization, spatial layout, occupants, relative centrality, and distinguishing characteristics, are useful for considering similarities and differences between

---

[17] Presumably the last of these refers to defecating in a sacred place and polluting it.

mythical traditions. In the Japanese case, the spatial layout of the world is primarily given in the Yamato cycle, with some elaboration in the Izumo Cycle which is discussed in Chapter 2. The world is organized into a High Heavenly Plain (or in *Chronicles*, sometimes simply heaven), a central reed plain land (the Japanese archipelago), a sea plain, Yomi, the Land of Ne, and Tokoyo. Movement between these realms is a major feature of the mythical narratives. Besides the High Heavenly Plain and the central reed plain land, there is some confusion with regards to spatial organization, but the central reed plain land is generally the focal point, and travel to other realms involves going to the central reed plain land first. For example, Susano-o goes from heaven to the Land of Ne, but only after passing through the central reed plain land.

Scholars disagree on whether Yomi and Ne are the same. Both locations are connected to Izumo Province. Izanami clearly goes to Yomi, but at the end of her narrative sequence, Izanagi blocks the way to Yomi, suggesting that no one else may go there. It is usually taken for granted that the souls of the dead go to Yomi, but there is nothing in the myths of *Ancient Matters* or *Chronicles* that indicates that to be the case. Similarly, it is usually assumed that Yomi is under the earth, but the language in *Ancient Matters* does not explicitly specify this. Regarding the Land of Ne, Susano-o says he wants to go to the land of his mother, but in truth he has no mother as Izanami was dead before he was created by Izanagi's bathing. Later, the kami Ō-ana-muji will go to the Land of Ne and confront Susano-o. As Ō-ana-muji leaves, he will pass by the entrance to Yomi. Hence, the entrances to these two lands are in the same place, but they may or may not be the same location. The word "ne" could mean "root," evoking an underground space, or by the same token, it could refer to the distant tip, like of a tree root, suggesting a land at the far extremes of the universe.

One of the most important features of Japanese mythical spaces is that they are assigned specific rulers. The natural order proceeds only when the legitimate and appropriate ruler governs their respective space. "Quality/Kind" is another of Thompson and Schrempp's comparative axes, and the quality of order vs. disorder maps onto spaces in Japanese myths very cleanly. Susano-o's failure to govern his assigned space leads to disorder, and chaos reigns when Amaterasu hides in the rock cave. Izanami is seemingly promoted to ruler of Yomi, and in Chapter 2 of this book, Susano-o will seem to be the ruling authority of the Land of Ne. The ruler of the sea plain, the kami Wata-tsu-mi, will appear in Chapter 3. The rulership of the central reed plain land is contested, and its legitimate governance is linked to power drawn from other realms, often in the form of a bride. The kami Ō-kuni-nushi takes over the central reed plain land after taking a bride from the Land of Ne. Later, Oshi-ho-mimi is assigned to rule the central reed plain land, and he marries the daughter of the heavenly kami Taka-mi-musuhi. Oshi-ho-mimi's grandson, Yama-sachi-hiko, marries a princess from the sea plain, as does his son.

## Naturalism and Social Anthropology (Takayama, Takagi, Anesaki)

The Japanese creation myths and the conflict between Amaterasu and Susano-o are some of the most heavily studied Japanese mythical narratives. An 1899 debate on the nature of Susano-o as a deity constituted the first modern study of Japanese myths. We could call this debate the beginning of Japanese mythology. The debate occurred between three key figures who approached the question of Susano-o from two different theoretical perspectives. On one side, Takayama Chogyū (1871–1902) and Takagi Toshio (1876–1922) argued for a naturalist interpretation of Susano-o as a storm god. This school of thought, heavily influenced by German and English mythologist Max Müller (1823–1900), imagined that myths were derived from natural phenomena. By this interpretation, the conflict between Amaterasu and Susano-o was based on the rivalry between storm and sun. On the other side, Anesaki Masaharu (1873–1949) argued that myth was linked to ritual and social practice, an anthro-pological framework for interpreting myth inspired by the work of Edward Burnett Tylor (1832–1917) from England.

For Müller, mythology was one piece of a broader pursuit that also included linguistics and religion. Müller was active in the nine-teenth century, when Indo-European studies was a major academic topic of interest. Franz Bopp (1791–1867) and other linguists demonstrated the shared linguistic background for Indo-European languages, including Sanskrit, Greek, Persian, Latin, German, and English. This linguistic connection fostered interest in language as a shared aspect of human experience and myths as a possible way to identify connections from before the Indo-European languages split up. Müller used linguistic parallels such as the names of deities to posit the development of myths and religion as a corollary shared aspect of human experience. Analysis and comparison of myths from around the world could reveal common core functions of myth and religion for humans.

Based on a study of the Indian *Rigveda*, Müller concluded that ancient people worshipped nature, especially the sun. Myths resulted from the transformation of the relationship that early humans had with nature into narrative form. Words that originally described abstract aspects of nature evolved into the concrete names of deities with distinct features and personalities. Identification of this process, by which a metaphorical description becomes rigid and fixed, led Müller to declare that myth was "a disease of language." As noted in *The Truth of Myth*, Müller's approach is dogmatic and reductive, since all deities and mythical narratives boil down to explanations of natural phenomena. Yet, Müller's theories were enormously influential, likely because Müller combined several fashionable academic trends from the time like the study of India, philology, and an anthropological theory for cultural development. Because his work is so tightly connected to comparative linguistics, Müller's mythology can be described as both linguistic and natural-istic. Several vectors introduced Müller's work to Japan, including

Buddhist exchange students who studied Sanskrit with Müller, Japanese scholars who visited England, and Japanese Unitarian theologists who cited Müller in their work.

In Japanese mythology, Müller's influence appears most prominently in a March 1899 essay by Takayama Chogyū, "Myth and History in the Divine-age Volumes of *An Account of Ancient Matters*." This essay marks the starting point for modern mythology in Japan. Takayama proposed, as might be guessed from the title, that the first volume of *Ancient Matters* was split between myth and history. The mythical portion began with the creation of the High Heavenly Plain and ended with Susano-o's banishment, roughly corresponding with the content of this chapter. The historical portion began with Susano-o's actions on earth in Izumo, discussed in the next chapter. Takayama argued that the content up to Susano-o constituted nature worship of the sun and was similar to myths of the "Aryan peoples," by which he meant Indo-Europeans. Susano-o was a storm god like the Indian deity Indra. In Indian mythology, Indra has power over lightning and thunder and is associated with storms and weather, with similarities to the Norse god Thor. Takayama interpreted the conflict between Amaterasu and Susano-o as a clash between sun and storm. The storm, Susano-o, was temporarily victorious in blotting out the sun, as Amaterasu retreated to the heavenly rock cave. However, Susano-o would then be driven away, just as a storm blows out, and the sun would return, just as the High Heavenly Plain and the Central Reed Plain Land are lit again once Amaterasu leaves the cave.

The historical portion of *Ancient Matters* based on Takayama's theory identifies the origins of the Japanese people. Once Susano-o is driven out, he descends from heaven to Izumo in western Japan, where he has children who are later incorporated into the early Japanese state. Takayama suggested that Susano-o's descendants were the Izumo people. Humans associated with Amaterasu and the imperial court were the "Tenson" people; "tenson" means "heavenly grandson," a reference to the kami Ninigi, Amaterasu's grandson.[18] Takayama proposed that both the Izumo people and the Tenson people originated from the sea, because the myths in *Ancient Matters* contain numerous references to the ocean such as Onogorojima, where Izanami and Izanagi coupled, and Izanagi's ritual bathing, which he performed after leaving the land of Yomi. Furthermore, Takayama argued that the absence of North Asian natural phenomena such as snow in Japanese myths, combined with similarities between Japanese myths and Polynesian myths, meant that the Japanese people had arrived at the archipelago from the south and were thus related to Polynesians. Citing a theory that Polynesians had originated in southwest Asia, Takayama further claimed that Polynesians had learned of Indra and Indo-European mythology from the Dravidians of South Asia, creating a contact hypothesis for the similarities between the myths in *Ancient Matters* and the Vedas.

Takayama's death at 31 prevented him from applying Müller to Japanese mythology more thoroughly, and that role fell to Takagi Toshio. Takagi reviewed Takayama's article only a few months after its release and then, in November and December of 1899, published "Theory of Storm God Susano-o." Takagi argued that deities were based in nature, illustrated by the three kami born together, Amaterasu (sun), Tsuku-yomi (moon), and Susano-o. Takagi dissected Susano-o's full name, Take-haya-susa-no-o, as "vigorous swift raging man," to reveal Susano-o's origin in a natural phenomenon: violent winds or roaring seas. Furthermore, Takagi noted, deities that originate from the breath—that is, from a nose or mouth—often end up being wind gods. This held true for Shi-naga-tsu-hiko, whose name means "long breath," and who originates from Izanagi exhaling. Takagi also noted that this matches the Pangu myth. Pangu was a Chinese creation deity whose breath created the wind and

---

[18] Izumo and the conflict between Izumo and the heavenly kami is discussed in more detail in Chapter 2.

whose eyes turned into the sun and moon. The similarity of this myth with the birth of Amaterasu, Tsuku-yomi, and Susano-o was noted in Japan as early as the thirteenth century.

In the same 1899 article and in his later work, Takagi addressed criticism of Müller's naturalism with striking openness, suggesting that mythological interpretation based on anthropological theories of ritual and social relations also needed to be considered. In his 1904 *Comparative Mythology* (*Hikaku shinwa gaku*), the first-ever book-length study on Japanese mythology, Takagi attempted to integrate Müller's work into a larger interpretive framework. Takagi rejected the idea that deities were only a "disease of language," as Müller had claimed. Takagi also rejected that all deities originated with natural phenomena. Rather, he claimed, worship of the sun and natural phenomena were one foundation that explained the origins of deities and mythical narratives. However, they were not necessarily the explanation for all deities in all myths around the world. Despite this openness, Takagi's opinion of Susano-o as a storm god, Amaterasu as a sun goddess, and their conflict as the story of a naturally occurring phenomena did not change. Ultimately, Takagi would come to regard Susano-o as a creation deity from Izumo. Susano-o's connection with Izumo is discussed in Chapter 2.

Takagi's openness to other approaches probably derived from his engagement with Anesaki Masaharu. Anesaki fiercely attacked Takayama shortly after the publication of Takayama's March 1899 article with "Legendary Myths of Susano-o" in August 1899. Anesaki accused both Müller, in his interpretation of Indra as a rain god, and Takayama, in his interpretation of Susano-o as a storm god, of bias in their choice of source materials. For example, Anesaki noted that Susano-o broke down the ridges around Amaterasu's paddies and damaged the irrigation management, which was plausible for a storm god. However, Susano-o also made horses lie down in the fields, which has nothing to do with water. When Takayama surveyed the source, he did not incorporate these horses into his explanation of Susano-o.

Anesaki also criticized Takayama for limiting his analysis of Susano-o to *Ancient Matters*. A full study of the god's characteristics would need to examine Susano-o in *Chronicles* and other ancient sources as well. Doing so made the storm god thesis questionable. For example, one variant of *Chronicles* claims that Amaterasu had three good fields in heaven and Susano-o had three fields prone to drought. Anesaki noted that this myth is very difficult to reconcile with the idea of Susano-o as a god of rain and storms.

Anesaki asserted that the Susano-o myths were better described as myths about the origins of human events rather than myths about natural phenomena. For Anesaki, Japanese myths fell into several categories. The early creation myths of Izanagi and Izanami referred to natural phenomena. However, the conflict between Susano-o and Amaterasu was linked to the issue of purity, a major focus of native Japanese religion. Susano-o contaminated the sacred weaving hall and, in other accounts, the feast of first rice. The purity stressed in the myths accorded with and explained the origins of the feast of first rice ritual and other Shinto practices. Similarly, Amaterasu hiding away in the heavenly rock cave and being lured out by Ame-no-koyane and Futo-dama looked like worship. Anesaki noted that the descendants of Ame-no-koyane and Futo-dama, the Inbe and Nakatomi clans, were associated with priesthood. Since the emperor was the descendant of Amaterasu, Anesaki argued that the myth was meant to explain the origin of emperor worship. Susano-o's punishment, in which he is fined in units of offering tables and has his nails and beard clipped, is also linked to some ancient religious practice. Susano-o's killing of the eight-headed serpent to save Kushi-ina-da-hime, discussed in Chapter 2, is linked by Anesaki to other world myths of human sacrifice and maiden rescue such as Perseus and Persephone. Put shortly, Anesaki looked to primitive religion as the origin of myths and identified them as an early stage in a given civilization's social and religious development.

Anesaki's main influence for this religious interpretation of myth was Edward Burnett Tylor. Tylor's interpretive model is generally called anthropological. At the time, the discipline of anthropology was heavily invested in studying so-called primitive societies with the objective of understanding fundamental aspects of the human experience and how societies develop. In contrast to Müller's linguistic approach, Tylor argued that animism—a belief that natural phenomena, animals, plants, and other objects possess souls—was the basis for all religions. As Tylor believed that all human beings were created with equal capacity for development and growth, the study of so-called primitive societies allowed the researcher to look back in time. Furthermore, comparative mythology could reveal common factors for the development of both religion and science in human societies. This was because, as discussed in *The Truth of Myth*, Tylor imagined myth as a kind of "primitive science" that explained the world for "savage" peoples, but that was abandoned when savage culture developed into civilized culture. In Japan, Anesaki applied Tylor's theory to identify features of primitive Japan linked to particular historical and cultural features, and beyond that, in order to identify motifs that were common to all human societies.

Ironically, Tylor himself was the first modern proponent of Susano-o as a storm god. In 1877, twenty-two years before Takayama's pioneering article, Tylor wrote a brief paper "Remarks on Japanese Mythology." A Japanese man living in London, Baba Tatsui (1850–1888), translated some of *Ancient Matters* for Tylor. Tylor identifies Susano-o as the God of Winds. However, true to form, alongside these "nature-myths," Tylor also picks out "special episodes, and mention of ideas and customs of considerable interest." These include Izanami's visit to Hades and eating of food there, which Tylor parallels with a story from New Zealand, and the paper streamers used to lure Amaterasu out of her cave, because they are an item used for ritual worship. That is to say, while Tylor admitted the existence of nature myths and nature deities, his primary interest was in ritual worship, festivals, and other social activities, or as he put it, "episodes which may help to throw light on other branches of mythology and religion."

In the long run, Takayama and Takagi's thesis that Susano-o was a storm god became the dominant hypothesis, and ultimately, even Anesaki eventually adopted it. This is also the case for early English-language scholarship. Edmund Buckley, in *The Shinto Pantheon*, identified Susano-o as a storm god as early as 1896, three years before Takayama. William George Aston (1841–1911), the first translator of *Chronicles*, wrote in his 1905 book *Shinto: The Way of the Gods* that there were problems with Buckley's thesis but that it was "substantially correct." Most strikingly, Anesaki wrote in his 1930 English-language *History of Japanese Religion* that "the details of his [Susano-o's] atrocities against his sister in heaven remind us strongly of storm-gods in other mythologies."

## Sociological Approaches (Matsumoto, Ebersole)

Matsumoto Nobuhiro (1897–1981) was a Japanese mythologist and pioneer of Southeast Asian studies in Japan. In his early years, he was heavily influenced by French sociological treatments of myth and scholarship on Polynesia. Initially interested in China, Matsumoto's studies took him to Paris, where he met anthropologist Marcel Mauss (1872–1950), a specialist in Polynesia. Under Mauss' tutelage, Matsumoto published *Essai sur la Mythologie Japanaise*, a foundational work in the French study of Japanese mythology, in 1928, and a Japanese translation in 1931. The influence of Mauss, and Mauss' uncle Émile Durkheim (1858–1917), appeared in the connection of myth to ritual, especially present-day ritual, and the social function, often a creation of social cohesion, provided by that ritual. For Durkheim, myth was part of the religious system, with myths using words to express the social cohesion that rituals accomplished by their performance. Myths and rituals thus functioned to create and maintain social solidarity and social identity. For this reason, Durkheim's approach to myth is especially useful for ethnology, the study of ethnic groups and identities. In Japan, ethnology became a major influence on mythology, especially in the work of Matsumoto and other mid-twentieth-century mythologists.

Matsumoto's early study of Japanese mythology identified parallels between Polynesian myths and Japanese myths, and Matsumoto argued that Japanese ethnic origins were thus based on people movements from the South Seas. For Polynesian myth, Matsumoto relied on Roland Dixon's 1916 *Oceanic Mythology*, where Dixon proposes two essential kinds of Polynesian myth. Dixon called the first the Genealogical or Evolutionary Type. Evolutionary referred to a self-evolving cosmos, in which a void or mixture called "po" in Polynesian existed, then successively light, heat, and dampness. These combined to create substance and form, which then solidified into earth and heaven. Heaven would be personified as male and earth as female. At this point, the evolution ends and all the natural forces, along with numerous deities, are born. While there is no single exemplar, in general, in Polynesian myths, first gods appear individually signifying each stage of the evolution of the universe. Then two gods appear as husband and wife, and these two gods give birth to all things. Matsumoto includes examples from New Zealand, among others.

For Japanese myths, Matsumoto applied this Polynesian typology to the seven generations of gods. These deities were similar to New Zealand myths in which the early gods, born from the void and before the creation of heaven and earth, had names related to the growth of trees, land coming into being from water, and buildings. Umashi-ashikabi-hikoji, who in Japanese is related to a reed, paralleled the growth of trees. Matsumoto argued that U-hiji-ni and Su-hiji-ni, the gods of earth and sand, referred to the process of land coming into being from the water. Iku-kui referred to thrusting pegs or poles into the ground. Kashiko-ne referred to a building. Finally, Izanagi and Izanami referred to the surface of the ocean from which land would emerge. Most important for Matsumoto was that the genealogical type, in both Polynesia and Japan, ended with a male and female couple. Izanagi must then relate to heaven and Izanami to earth, Matsumoto suggested, and their union would result in the birth of all things.

Dixon called the second kind of myth the Creative Type. In this pattern, first the gods live in heaven above and below them is only a vast ocean. Then, the gods throw a rock down. This becomes the earth, to which the beings from heaven above descend, and then human beings appear. Matsumoto compares this type with an Okinawa creation myth in which the sun god orders two deities to go to an island and create innumerable other islands. In another myth from Okinawa, the sun god orders a deity to create islands, and that deity throws rocks and trees down from heaven, which become islands. Then that deity goes back to ask for the seeds of humans and is given one man and one woman; Matsumoto asserted that in antiquity, Okinawan and Japanese myths were the same; and so the Okinawan stories were variants of the Izanagi/Izanami story. Thereby, Japanese myths were related to myths from Polynesia and the South Seas. Izanagi and Izanami standing on the floating bridge of heaven and dipping a spear was a variation of throwing a stone. Matsumoto also noted the similarity of this narrative to the New Zealand hero Maui using a hook to pull land from the sea. He noted the Izumo Gazetteer myth of pulling land using ropes as further evidence of the connection between Japan and Polynesia; this myth is given in Chapter 2. These numerous similarities led Matsumoto to propose a South Seas origin for the Japanese people, who moved into Okinawa and the Japanese archipelago from the south.

A similar application of Durkheim's sociological theory to Japanese myths is given by American historian of religion Gary Ebersole, who has interpreted Amaterasu's retreat into the heavenly rock cave as a depiction of the double burial ritual practiced by the ancient Japanese court. In this ritual, the corpse of the deceased would first be laid out in a tomb for a temporary burial; legendary temporary burials described in *Chronicles* sometimes lasted over one year, though the chronology is not factual. After some time had passed, the corpse would be relocated to a permanent burial location.

The temporary burial is also reflected in Izanagi's initial visit to Izanami after her death, as Izanami implies that the gods of Yomi might assent to her returning to life. The temporary burial was, after all, temporary. Ebersole argued that rituals surrounding double burial, including attempts to recall the soul to the body, are reflected in the efforts of the kami to bring Amaterasu back out into the world.

## The Vienna School (Oka)

One major influence on Japanese ethnology and mythology was Oka Masao (1898–1982), who adapted the "cultural strata" (*Kulturschichten*) theory developed by Wilhelm Schmidt (1868–1954). The underlying principle of the theory is that all the elements of human activity: political, social, economic, religious, etc., come together to form a culture complex or set of culture layers. Moreover, these layers overlap as a society passes through history. A society would have a primitive culture layer going back to the days of hunter-gatherers, a primary culture layer from early agriculturalists, a secondary culture layer, and so on. Each culture layer could have different cultures of marriage and kinship, religious beliefs, and so on.

The unique circumstances created by the overlapping of these layers for a particular culture explained ethnic difference. And just as these culture layers might overlap, a myth could contain elements from multiple layers. Comparing culture layers from different regions but the same strata might reveal connections between people who otherwise appear to be unrelated, again linking these culture layers to ethnic groups. The focus on ethnicity was a hallmark of the Vienna School and German-language anthropology at the turn of the twentieth century, and these theories are referred to as ethnologic interpretations of myth. In contemporary anthropology, sociology, and mythology, the use of "cultural layers" is no longer accepted because the focus on a society's progression through the strata of culture layers is too prescriptive, and because the culture layers themselves erase meaningful differences within a culture group. However, the theories were extremely influential in the first half of the twentieth century.

After finishing graduate school in sociology, Oka studied under the most famous Japanese ethnologist, Yanagita Kunio (1875–1962), then travelled to Vienna, and studied directly with members of the Vienna School. His 1933 doctoral dissertation, "Kulturschicten in Alt-Japan" (Cultural Strata in Old Japan), attempted to apply Schmidt's theory of culture layers to Japanese prehistory. The completed dissertation, over 1,100 pages in length, concludes with an attempt at synthesizing Old Japanese culture into seven layers based on societal organization, mythology, religion, sacrifices, burial customs, language, technology, and emergent local cultures. The summary of Oka's research is given in the table below; some items refer to categories he created for his dissertation such as "human sacrifice type 10." For space, the last column of emergent local cultures has been omitted.

As seen in the third "Mythology" column, Oka believed that Japanese myths had been built up in layers. These began with early myths devoted to the moon, then newer myths about the seas, and then finally myths about the sun. Oka's process depended on comparing mythical narratives with logical and naturalistic functions. For example, in analyzing Amaterasu, Oka noted that there are many stories with Amaterasu as the main character, but only the heavenly rock cave associates the character Amaterasu with the natural function of the sun. Nor does she appear as a supreme being or creation deity. Rather, she is primarily a political, hero god, most notable for her status as the progenitor of the imperial family. Unlike other nature deities, she also has descendants. Oka argued that the original sun deity was male, and as revealed in the alternative name Ō-hiru-me, "woman of the great sun," that Amaterasu was actually the wife of the great sun, i.e. the sun god. The sun god is Taka-mi-musuhi, Oka claimed, as the two are often mentioned side by side.

**TABLE 4** Oka Masao's Cultural Strata

| Layer | Society | Mythology | Religion | Sacrifice/Offering | Burial | Language | Prehistoric Chronology (Tech) |
|---|---|---|---|---|---|---|---|
| 1 (oldest) | Coming-of-age rituals for boys and girls (abstinence, rebirth, removal of teeth) | Lunar Myths (elixir of life, immortality)) | Original moon people or original moon woman cult, animism, female shamanism 1 | Primitive head offering, primitive field fruits offering | Crouched burial (?) | ? | Mesolithic |
| 2 | Plant-based, secret alliance oriented, small family, exogamous, maternal (secret initiation for boys and girls, removal of teeth) | Lunar myth ideology Cosmogonic myth? | Thing (*mono*)-belief (animism), soul (*tama*) belief (souls, dead and ancestor cults), skull cult (?), mysterious visitor (*marebito*) belief (skull cult, female shamanism 1 and 2 | First field fruits offering, blood offering, human sacrifice type 10, 11, or 12 (?) | Crouched burial | Papuan; North Halmahera | Polished stone axe, knobbed club, bone culture, house sunk into the ground with a gable roof, dog, wild boar, Jōmon thick (*atsude*) pottery, Jōmon round (*entō*) pottery, pattern pottery, Neolithic |

| | | | | | | | |
|---|---|---|---|---|---|---|---|
| 3 | Plant-based, village community, large family, exogamous, maternal (initiation for girls) | Lunar mythology 2 (water, seas, killing of agricultural goddess by the moon deity, creation of grain), cosmogonic myths 2 and 4, Izanagi and Izanami myths, Susano-o myths, marriage of the gods | Animism, agrarian-oriented magic, soul (*tama*) belief (souls, dead and ancestor cults), female shamanism 2 | Primitive rice offering etc, human sacrifice types 1–8 and 9 (?) | Crouched burial and double burial | Austro-Asian | Australian | Shoulder axe, rice, Jōmon thick (*atsude*) pottery, Jōmon round (*entō*) pottery, pattern pottery, Neolithic |
| 4 | Hunting, fishing, plant-based, warrior, paternal, public initiations for boys, tooth sharpening (legal role for mothers) | Sea myths, cosmogonic myths 4 (5?) (sun god myth?) | Soul and ancestor cult, shame cult (?), sun-analogous magic (?) | Primitive animal, fish, and field fruit offerings, human sacrifice 9? | Supine burial, water burial, fire burial (?) | Austronesian | Australian | Square axe 1, long axe, stilt house, rice, Jōmon thin (*usude*) pottery, beads, Neolithic |

**TABLE 4** Oka Masao's Cultural Strata (Continued)

| Layer | Society | Mythology | Religion | Sacrifice/Offering | Burial | Language | | Prehistoric Chronology (Tech) |
|---|---|---|---|---|---|---|---|---|
| 5 | Plant-based, pigs, husbandry, large family, paternal (legal role for mothers) | Ideology of heavenly realm mythology (sun god myth?) | Deity (*kami*) belief, ancestor cult, medium (*ichiko*) shamanism (*yudate*) | Pig sacrifice (?) | Supine burial 2 | Tungusic, Manchurian | Altaic | Square axe 2, pigs, Yayoi pottery (potter's wheel), smooth ceramics, Neolithic |
| 6 | Nomadic, horse-breeding, militaristic, large family, paternal, lordship | Heavenly realm mythology, cosmogonic myth 1 (and 5?), Lunar mythology | Deity (*kami*) belief (sky deities), ancestral hero cult, medium (*ichiko*) (forge) shamanism | Horse consecration, human sacrifice 12 | Supine burial 2, Burial graves | Mongolian | Altaic | Square axe 2, horses, iron, bronze, Yayoi pottery (potter's wheel), smooth ceramics, Chalcolithic |
| 7 | Chinese and Korean High Culture | | | | | Chinese characters | | Proto-historic |

Presumably, Oka said, the two were originally equals, but Taka-mi-musuhi gradually faded away in importance. The suggestion that Izanagi and Izanami gave birth to the sun kami on earth and then sent her to heaven is illogical, so this is probably a newer myth created by linking what were originally separate Izanagi/Izanami myths and the "younger" sun myth of *Ancient Matters* and *Chronicles*. This creates three layers: older creation myths about Taka-mi-musuhi and Amaterasu, Izanagi and Izanami myths with which those older myths fused, and then the younger sun myths in which Amaterasu is the main actor and progenitor of the imperial clan. This explains why in the younger creation myth in *Ancient Matters*, the heavenly gods command Izanagi and Izanami had to create the world. This version was a fusion of two separate layers of myth. The original layer was preserved in the main version of *Chronicles*, in which Izanagi and Izanami create the world of their own accord.

Perhaps the reason that Oka's culture layers approach was so influential in Japan was its comprehensive quality. Comparing the variants of myths between *Ancient Matters*, *Chronicles*, and other texts to determine what the original form of the myth was or whether the narrative order needed to be adjusted was commonplace among Japanese mythologists from the eighteenth century. The discovery, in the nineteenth century, of Jōmon period (10,000 BCE–300 BCE) and Yayoi period (300 BCE–300 CE) artifacts in Japan launched the field of archeology, but linking those discoveries with mythical narratives proved difficult. Comparative mythology studies suggested ways that myths might travel between regions or spread between people groups, and anthropology hypothesized about societal and kinship organizations, coming-of-age rituals, and food sources for societies (hunting, agriculture, etc.). Both anthropology and religion analyzed the role of sacrifices and burials in societies. Linguists in the early twentieth century were busy searching for the next great discovery that could potentially link non–Indo-European languages, especially Finnish/Estonian, Hungarian, Turkish, Mongolian, Korean, and Japanese, into a single family. Japanese linguists were also avidly pursuing linguistic connections with Southeast Asia, South Asia, and the islands of the South Seas. Oka was the first, for Japan, to bring all these disciplines and observations together and integrate them into a systematic and comprehensive theory. The deterministic quality in which an ideal society progressed through these cultural layers ultimately rendered Oka's conclusions untenable, but the notion that the meaning and interpretation of myths can be linked to archeological, linguistic, and other historically relevant data remains influential in Japan today.

## The American School (Mishina)

While Matsumoto Nobuhiro argued for a southern origin for Japanese myths, Mishina Shōei (1902–1971) proposed an affinity with the north, especially Korea. Mishina studied history at Kyoto Imperial University before moving to Yale in 1937. During his time in the US, Mishina met Robert Lowie (1883–1957), then a professor of anthropology at the University of California, Berkeley. Lowie was himself a student of Franz Boas (1858–1942) and a specialist in Native American cultures. Presumably Lowie's influence led Mishina to apply Boas' notion of the "culture area" to Japanese mythology. A culture area referred to a geographic space whose people shared set of cultural elements, including kinship, language, social organization, and material culture.

Unlike the culture strata of the Vienna School, Boas' culture areas did not stack to form layers, nor was there a prescribed movement from primitive to primary and secondary culture. Boas vocally rejected theoretical approaches that incorporated an evolutionary element, in which a culture group would progress from primitive to civilized. *The Truth of Myth* describes this as Boas' most important contribution, as it oriented American anthropology away from the evolutionary models, reconstructions of the past, and race-based theories of development, and toward participant observation, cultural diffusion, and cultural relativism. Boas was also interested in folklore, because he argued that commonalities between folk tales in different folk groups revealed patterns of dissemination. Folk tales might indicate a single culture area, and they could spread from one culture area to another. Anthropological work in the American School focused heavily on the indigenous peoples of North America, and early figures predating Boas wrote extensively on kinship systems, including dual organization, in which an individual might, for example, belong to both a tribe and a clan. A larger group might be split between two exclusive groups, called a moiety. Naturally, Boas and his followers incorporated research on kinship systems into the theoretical framework of the culture area.

Based on the Japanese creation myths, Mishina argued that ancient Japan was also a dual organization society in which the heavenly gods and earthly gods signified two moieties of ancient Japanese society. Ancient Japan was organized into lineage groups, called "uji," which sometimes are described as clans in English-language scholarship. For example, Nakatomi, Fujiwara, and Mononobe were distinct *uji* in the sixth century. The highest-ranking member of an *uji* was charged with the worship of the patron kami of the clan. Mishina argued that the patron kami of the *uji*, and by extension, the clan members, were split into two moieties based on whether the deity was a heavenly kami or an earthly kami. The heavenly kami referred to the kami introduced in the myths from this chapter, such as Amaterasu and Ame-no-koyane. The earthly kami referred to the kami descended from Susano-o and other kami that populate the Japanese archipelago. Mishina surveyed the usage of the terms "heavenly kami" and "earthly kami" in *Ancient Matters* and *Chronicles* and noted that the words often appear in the phrases like "child of an earthly kami" or "child of a heavenly kami." Based on these phrases, Mishina argued that the real meaning of "heavenly kami" and "earthly kami" was not a distinction between kami, but rather a distinction between kinship groups. Among all the *uji* of ancient Japan, some were descended from heavenly kami and some from earthly kami. Based on that distinction, Mishina proposed that the clans in ancient Japan were assigned different societal roles. In other words, Mishina interpreted Japanese myths as the explanations for the societal schema that existed in ancient Japan.

## Dema Deities (Obayashi, Yoshida)

A major comparative theory for interpreting the myths of Uke-mochi and Ō-getsu-hime relies on the concept of a Dema Deity, pioneered by German ethnologist Adolf E. Jensen (1899–1965). Jensen's studies took him to Seram, the largest island in Maluku Province, Indonesia, where he encountered the Hainuwele myth. According to this myth, a man found a coconut, an item that he had never seen before, and was instructed in a dream to plant it. When the coconut grew into a tree, the man climbed the tree to harvest from it but cut himself in the process. Some days later, he found a girl where the blood from his cut had splattered onto the tree blossoms. He named the girl Hainuwele. Whenever Hainuwele defecated, valuable objects came out. Later, at a dance, instead of presenting the traditional areca nut to the male participants, Hainuwele distributed valuable items that she had excreted. This continued for some days until the men became disgusted at how she was producing the items and buried her alive. Her father later exhumed the corpse, cut it into pieces, and buried the body parts in new locations. The parts grew into various useful plants, including tubers, a staple crop for the people of Seram Island. Jensen suggested that this myth corresponded with a more general culture based on simple plant cultivation and differed from the origin myths for hunter-gatherer civilizations and those centered on grains, which often involved a theft or gift from heaven. Jensen identified other societies in which a murder and burial resulted in the creation of tubers, and further research led him to propose the existence of Dema Deities: divine figures who provide for humans, often through their bodies.

Ōbayashi Taryō (1921–2001) and Yoshida Atsuhiko (1943–) proposed that the myth of Ō-getsu-hime in *Ancient Matters* and

Uke-mochi in *Chronicles* are Hainuwele-type myths. Much like Hainuwele, both kami excrete items of value, are killed by someone angered by the way in which they produce these items, and then sprout food from their corpses. Of course, there are several major differences, namely that Ō-getsu-hime and Uke-mochi produce grain from their corpses, not tubers. Uke-mochi also produces horses and silkworms. Those differences notwithstanding, both Ōbayashi and Yoshida suggested that the presence of Hainuwele-type myths in *Ancient Matters* and *Chronicles* meant that there was some kind of cultural exchange with the cultural area inhabited by cultivators of basic, non-grain foods, i.e. the South Seas, Indonesia, and Southeast Asia. Ōbayashi proposed that the Hainuwele myth was first altered by people from Southern China and Southeast Asia

**FIGURE 5** A Dogū (Jōmon Period Statuette). Japan, 1000–300 BCE
Metropolitan Museum of Art, Open Access

who employed slash-and-burn or swidden agriculture, then introduced by those people to western Japan in the late Jōmon period, between 4,000 and 2,500 years ago. Yoshida, following Oka, proposed that in the middle Jōmon, around 5,000 years ago, a tuber-growing culture came to the archipelago and spread. Yoshida linked the spread of this Hainuwele-type myth to the dogū, figurines that have been excavated in large numbers from Jōmon sites. These figurines often depict females and have one limb broken off, seemingly intentionally. For Yoshida, the dogū were a depiction and recapitulation of the fate of Uke-mochi and Ō-getsu-hime.

## Structuralism (Lévi-Strauss)

One of the most influential mythological approaches is structuralism. Structuralism proposes that by breaking myths down into their parts, the mythologist can engage with them on a deeper level than narrative. Comparing parts allows the identification of patterns, similarities, tensions, and substitutions within myths, either for a single mythical tradition or across mythical traditions. French anthropologist Claude Lévi-Strauss (1908–2009) played an instrumental role in developing this mode of analysis. Lévi-Strauss drew his initial inspiration from structural linguistics, which broke language down into constituent parts of words and sounds and analyzed the relationship between them. Structural linguistics asserted language was a system of signs. For example, the sign "tree" is made up of the word, "tree," and a tree, real or imagined, to which the word "tree" refers. Importantly, signs do not have inherent meaning; they are arbitrary and hold meaning because of shared understanding. The word "tree" is not itself tree-like or tree-ish. Signs have meaning because they exist in a system with other signs. "Tree" means something because it is not "bush" and it is not "flee." As such, language forms a structured system. Lévi-Strauss was also influenced by linguistic theory that viewed words in terms of binary oppositions, like hot and cold. As *The Truth of Myth* notes, Lévi-Strauss' approach centered on exposing tension between binary oppositions and the socially agreed upon ways they were expressed.

When Lévi-Strauss expanded linguistic analysis to myths, he proposed breaking the myth down into constituent parts. Words are made up of phonemes, and Lévi-Strauss defined myths as being made up of mythemes, the smallest unit of a myth. For example, the mythemes "Oedipus marries his mother," "Oedipus kills his father," "Antigone buries her brother Polynices in defiance of its prohibition," and "Eteocles kills his brother Polynices" are four mythemes from the Oedipus myth. Once the mythemes had been isolated, Lévi-Strauss analyzed them out of chronological order to identify the structure of the myth. "Oedipus marries his mother" and "Antigone buries her brother Polynices" do not occur in sequence, but they both illustrate a transgressive over-appreciation of family relations. Another way to put this is that for structuralist mythology, the plot or narrative of the myth is less important. The actual structure of the myth is revealed by the patterns in mythemes. Finally, because meaning is determined by a structured system, the patterns have meaning in relation to binary elements. The over-appreciation of family relations is revealed by corresponding mythemes that reveal the under-appreciation of family relations: "Oedipus kills his father" and "Eteocles kills his brother." This binary reveals a tension in Ancient Greek culture, and according to Lévi-Strauss, the myth functions to mitigate, displace, or resolve this tension.

Most of Lévi-Strauss' mythology focuses on indigenous people's myths from North and South America, but strikingly, Lévi-Strauss also discussed Susano-o. Based on a variant from *Chronicles* where Susano-o is created by Izanagi along with Amaterasu and Tsukuyomi when Izanagi escapes from Yomi, Lévi-Strauss summarized that Susano-o was given rule of the earth. However, though Susano-o was in the prime of his life, he neglected his duties and wept and wailed because he wanted to follow his mother to the Land of Ne. Izanagi drove him away, but before he went, Susano-o visited heaven and defiled it. Amaterasu shut herself away in the rock cave and Susano-o was banished to the other world, which he reached after many trials and tribulations.

Lévi-Strauss introduced the Susano-o myth as an example of "the crying baby" and compared it with a myth from Amazonia. In the Amazonia myth, a black jaguar kills his pregnant, cheating spouse, and when he opened the corpse, a baby jumped out into the water. After being captured, the baby cried incessantly, and only the owl could calm him by telling him the story of his birth. At that point, the baby resolved to avenge his mother and set out to kill all the jaguars and then rose into heaven to become the rainbow. Because the sleeping humans did not hear his cries, their lifespans were shortened. Lévi-Strauss noted similar myths from the South American Chimane and Mosetene peoples, in which a child abandoned by his mother never stops crying. The tears change into rain, and then the child becomes the rainbow. Lévi-Strauss noted that in *Chronicles*, Susano-o's banishment from heaven is accompanied by torrential rain. Susano-o seeks shelter, but his request is refused. Later, Susano-o kills a giant snake, and in some South American myths, the rainbow is a snake. Lévi-Strauss gave one additional crying baby myth from the Cashinawa people, in which a pregnant woman went off to fish. A storm broke out and the baby she was carrying disappeared only to reappear some months later as a large child. The child cried incessantly and was thrown into the river. The river dried up instantly, and then the child disappeared up into the sky.

Structural analysis of these myths identifies mythemes in which a crying child has in some capacity been abandoned by his mother. The child reaches the age of maturity but continues crying and causes a cosmic, usually meteorological, disruption resulting in a rotten or polluted world. The structure of these myths is a hero who refuses to become socialized or grow up, and who remains obstinately attached to nature and the feminine. At a deeper level, for

Lévi-Strauss, this attachment recalled the maternal incest seen in the Oedipus myth, in which the hero returns to the maternal fold. The problem or tension is between the binaries of feminine and masculine, nature and society, and defilement and cleanliness. Elsewhere in his analysis, Lévi-Strauss discussed myths connecting the rainbow to the origin of diseases, and the South American and Japanese myths support the association of the rainbow with some kind of rotten or defiled state. While not the core of his discussion, Lévi-Strauss admitted his own belief that Japanese and American myths have some common source material that goes back to Paleolithic times. In that ancient past, myths spread among peoples of Asia, then some of those people migrated to North and South America.

Lévi-Strauss' account reveals the full potential of structural analysis for identifying universal human truths. Within a tradition, a structural analysis can reveal important sources of tension within that culture. For the Japanese case, for example, we could identify a similar mytheme for Hiru-ko, who like Susano-o, does not mature or socialize. Hiru-ko was born because Izanami spoke first, linking him to the feminine, and he is cast to the winds, thus being returned to nature. In later myths not given here because they are not in *Ancient Matters* or *Chronicles*, Hiru-ko returns as the adult god Ebisu, patron of fishers and good fortune. In Chapter 2, Susano-o will reappear as an adult father figure. We could interpret these myths structurally to conclude that in Japanese myths, banishment transforms the socializing act of ensuring masculine dominance and mitigates a recurring tension of matriarchal society and powerful women. That binary is similarly reflected in episodes such as Amaterasu changing her appearance to that of a man before confronting Susano-o, etc. Alternatively, we could attempt to analyze myth structures across cultures. For example, Lévi-Strauss identified connections between Japan and the Americas. At their most basic level, the common structures in world myths would indicate universal human experience.

# Other Major Topics

## Shinto Sects and the First Gods

With the exceptions of Taka-mi-musuhi and Kamu-musuhi, the kami that appear before Izanagi and Izanami play no major role in the myths that follow. However, Shinto scholars often attached incredible power to these figures due to their position at the beginning of the narrative. Kuni-toko-tachi was often counted as the founder of the Japanese imperial reign because he is the first kami according to *Chronicles*. Ame-no-minaka-nushi, whose name literally means "master of the center," was imagined as an all-powerful figure at the axis of the universe. These developments were especially marked in the Watarai, Yoshida, and Suika sects of Shinto and provided a metaphysical element to Japanese religious beliefs that is difficult to extract from the base myths as they are written in *Ancient Matters* and *Chronicles*.

## Hiru-ko and Ebisu

The Seven Lucky Gods continue to be celebrated in contemporary Japan as bringers of good fortune, and while six of these gods are of Indian and Chinese origin, Ebisu is a native Japanese kami. The two main shrines to Ebisu disagree on whether Ebisu is Hiru-ko or Koto-shiro-nushi, an oracle god discussed in Chapter 2. However, the Hiru-ko belief is more widespread. Worship of Ebisu appears in medieval Japan and suggests that Hiru-ko returned to Japan after being cast adrift. Depictions of Ebisu usually show him with one leg folded under him because Hiru-ko could not stand. He is a patron kami for fishers and is usually shown holding a large fish.

## Seafoam

One consequence of greater knowledge about the outside world during Japanese history was that the interpretations of the creation myths given here had to change to match the shape of the new world. The statement in the creation myth that the froth of the seawater formed other islands was used in the late eighteenth century to explain where Europe, Africa, and the Americas came from after Japan learned of their existence.

## Central Reed Plain Land

The Central Reed Plain Land is the phrase used for the lower islands (Honshu, Shikoku, and Kyushu) of the Japanese archipelago in the *Ancient Matters* and *Chronicles* myths. Izanagi does not explicitly assign one of his children to rule this land, and in myths where Izanami dies, the couple does not even finish creating it. Later in the mythical narrative, the kami Ō-kuni-nushi will complete creation and rule over this land, but the language in *Ancient Matters* specifies that he is not a legitimate ruler. The human beings who populate this land are referred to when Izanagi and Izanami divorce, but their creation is not specified in the mythical narrative. Rather they exist, like the rocks and trees, to be ruled over. Later commentators have suggested that perhaps the creation of humans was lost or omitted from the narrative. Alternatively, because *Ancient Matters* and *Chronicles* were written to legitimize the emperor, they do not bother discussing content that is not directly related to imperial rule.

## Heavenly Rock Cave

The myth sequence around the heavenly rock cave is widely studied for both its naturalist qualities and its ritualistic qualities. The former includes a storm covering the sun or a solar eclipse, and the latter might refer to luring the sun back in winter; the use of paper streamers; sacred ropes, and sakaki trees; and the divine possession dance known as kagura. Kagura exists in different variants around the Japanese archipelago and is still performed at Shinto shrines today. Of the myths in *Ancient Matters* and *Chronicles*, the Heavenly Rock Cave is one of the most readily associable with contemporary Shinto practice.

# 2

# The Izumo Cycle

## The Izumo Myths

### Susano-o Slays the Eight-Headed Snake

Susano-o descended from heaven to the land of Izumo in western Japan and landed near the banks of the Hii River. Izumo is present-day Shimane Prefecture; the Izumo Grand Shrine to Ō-kuni-nushi stands in the western part of the prefecture. Smaller shrines to Susano-o, Kushi-ina-da-hime, and the other kami in the Izumo Cycle are spread throughout Shimane Prefecture. Suga, where Susano-o built his shrine, means "refreshed." Note that in Japanese, the word *miya* means both "shrine" and "palace."

In *Chronicles* 8.4, when Susano-o first came down from heaven, he came with his son, I-takeru, meaning "much bravery," and they first landed in Silla, on the Korean Peninsula.[1] However, Susano-o said, "I do not wish to dwell in this land," and so he built a clay boat and crossed over the sea to the east, arriving in Izumo on the banks of the Hii River. When I-takeru descended from heaven, he brought tree seeds with him, but he did not plant them in Korea and instead brought them over to Japan. Beginning in Kyushu, I-takeru planted trees all throughout the eight great islands of the Japanese archipelago.

---

[1] The mother of I-takeru is unknown.

This kami now lives in Ki Province, known as the land of trees, present-day Wakayama Prefecture.

In *Chronicles* 8.5, Susano-o said, "The lands of Korea are rich in gold and silver.[2] The land that my descendants rule will need wood to build boats so its people can cross over to Korea." And so, Susano-o pulled out his beard and scattered it, and it became cedar. He pulled out his chest hair, and this became cypress. The hair from his buttocks became yew. The hair from his eyebrows became camphor. Then Susano-o declared, "Cedar and camphor should be used for making boats. Cypress should be used for shrines. Yew should be used for coffins." Susano-o's children, I-takeru, Ō-ya-tsu-hime, meaning "great house lady," and Tsuma-tsu-hime, perhaps meaning "lumber lady," also planted tree seeds. The three kami passed through all the land and arrived in Ki Province.

When Susano-o arrived at the banks of the Hii River in Izumo, from upstream, he heard the sounds of weeping and wailing. According to *Ancient Matters*, he also saw chopsticks floating downstream. When he went upstream to investigate, he found an old man and an old woman, who were sobbing as they consoled a young girl standing between them. Susano-o inquired, "Who are you, and why are you crying like this?"

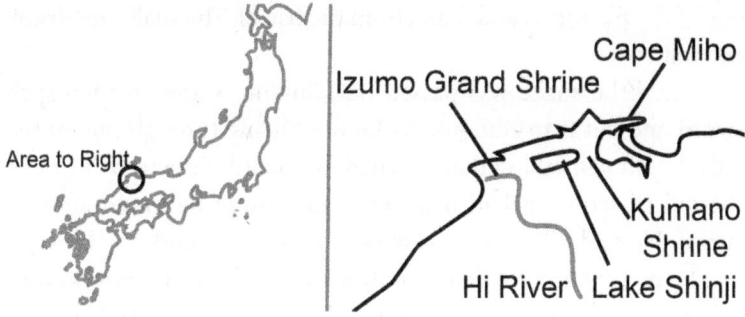

**MAP 2** Izumo Area.

[2] This account is a foreshadowing of the Korean conquest myth of Empress Jingū, discussed in Chapter 4.

The old man said, "I am an earthly kami called Ashi-na-zu-chi, meaning 'leg rubbing spirit.' My wife here is called Te-na-zu-chi, meaning 'hand rubbing spirit.' This girl is our daughter, Kushi-ina-da-hime, meaning 'miraculous rice ear paddy lady.'[3] We are crying because in the past we had eight daughters. Every year, a giant eight-headed snake comes and swallows one of them. Soon this girl will be swallowed as well, and there is nothing we can do about it."

Susano-o said, "If you let me marry your daughter, then I will save her from the snake."

The two kami asked, "What is your name?"

Susano-o replied, "I am Susano-o, younger brother of Amaterasu, and I have just come down from heaven."

The two kami answered, "Help us and she is yours."

Susano-o first changed Kushi-ina-da-hime into a comb and inserted her into his hair bun. Then, he had the two parents brew eight barrels of very powerful saké. They built eight platforms, and around each platform, a fence with a gate. Then Susano-o placed one barrel of saké atop each platform.

At last, the giant snake appeared. It had eight heads and eight tails, and its eyes glowed red like fiery lanterns. It was covered in moss, with trees growing on its back, and crimson blood oozed from its underside. When the snake saw the saké, each of its heads went to one of the platforms and drank from the barrel. The snake got drunk and fell asleep.

While the snake was passed out, Susano-o drew his ten-span sword and cut it to ribbons. As he was slicing through one of the tails, he hit something that notched his sword. Susano-o cut open the tail to see what had happened, and inside he found another sword. He said, "This is a divine sword. I should send it to heaven," and he presented it to the heavenly kami. This sword is now known as Kusa-nagi, meaning "grass mower." Later, the sword would be presented to Yamato Take, and it is one of the three imperial regalia,

---

[3] The names of the two parents refer to their consoling of their daughter. Kushi-ina-da-hime's name contains a pun on "comb," into which Susano-o later changes her.

**FIGURE 6** Susano-o Slays the Eight-Headed Serpent. Tsukioka Yoshitoshi, c.1887. From the series Nihon ryakushi Wikipedia Commons.

symbols of the reign of the emperor. It is now kept at the Atsuta Shrine in Nagoya. The sword that Susano-o used to kill the snake is held in the Isonokami Shrine in Nara.

Having dispatched the snake, Susano-o transformed Kushi-ina-da-hime back into a woman and searched for a place for them to get married. He finally settled on a place called Suga in Izumo, where he said, "Being here makes me feel refreshed." He built a shrine there to consummate his marriage. Clouds rose when he built the shrine, and so he wrote the first Japanese poem.

> Eight-fold clouds rise at
> the eight-fold hedge of Izumo.
> To enclose my wife,
> I've built this eight-fold hedge.
> Oh, this eight-fold hedge!

Susano-o named Kushi-ina-da-hime's parents as caretakers of his shrine and bestowed upon the two of them the title Ina-da-no-miya-nushi, meaning "master of the shrine of Inada."

Sources differ on the descendants of Susano-o and Kushi-ina-da-hime. The fullest account of Susano-o's descendants is in *Ancient Matters*. *Chronicles* abbreviates the list and simply says that the two gave birth to the kami Ō-ana-muji, later titled Ō-kuni-nushi, meaning "great land master." Of the descendants given in *Ancient Matters*, one named O-mizu-nu, meaning "master of flood waters," is notable because he is probably the same kami as Ya-tsuka-mizu-o-mizu-no, meaning "many handbreadths deep flood master." Ya-tsuka-mizu-o-mizu-no is a creation deity in the *Records of Wind and Earth of Izumo*, a collection of Izumo stories and folklore from the early eighth century.

In *Records of Wind and Earth of Izumo*, Ya-tsuka-mizu-o-mizu-no decreed, "The land of Izumo, where eight-fold clouds rise, is a young land, like a thin cloth. It was the very first land that was created, and so it was made very small. Therefore, I will sew on more land to expand it."

He continued, "When you look at the cape of Silla on the Korean peninsula, is there not an excess of land there?" Then he took up his plough, flat as a maiden's chest, thrust it into the land of Silla like plunging a knife into the gills of a great fish, and sliced away a hunk of land as if filleting a fish. He tied a heavy rope to this hunk of land, pulled as if uprooting a kudzu plant, yanked as if towing a boat up a river stream, and screamed, "Come on!" Then he sewed the new land onto Izumo. The land from this stitching goes from Mt. Kozu to Cape Kizuki. He inserted a stake so that the land would not drift; this is Mt. Sahime, on the border of Izumo and Iwami Provinces. The rope he used to tow the land is now the long beach at Sono.

Ya-tsuka-mizu-o-mizu-no pulled land from around the Japanese archipelago three more times and sewed it onto Izumo in the same way that he did with the land from Korea.

"Now I have finished pulling land," he said. Then at Ou Shrine, Ya-tsuka-mizu-o-mizu-no thrust his staff into the ground and said, "Ou," meaning "It is done!" Therefore, this land is called "Ou." The Ou Shrine is situated on the eastern edge of the district office and is on a small hill within a rice paddy.

## Travails of Ō-ana-muji/Ō-kuni-nushi

According to *Ancient Matters*, Ō-ana-muji had eighty older brothers. All of the brothers ultimately surrendered their claims to the Central Reed Plain Land to Ō-ana-muji, who became Ō-kuni-nushi. The reason is as follows. The eighty brothers all wanted to marry Ya-kami-hime of Inaba, the eastern part of present-day Tottori Prefecture. And so, the eighty brothers all traveled together to see her. They made Ō-ana-muji carry their luggage and follow along behind them.

On the way to Inaba, the brothers ran into a rabbit that had lost its fur coat. They told the rabbit that it should first bathe in the ocean, then climb to an exposed mountain ridge and let the wind blow over its body. But when the rabbit did what the brothers had suggested, the salt dried up its skin, which then chapped and split from the wind. The rabbit was lying on the ground, writhing in agony, when Ō-ana-muji came upon it and asked, "Why are you laying there crying?"

The rabbit said,

"I was on Oki Island and I wanted to cross over to this land, but there was no way for me to do so. So, I tricked the sharks into helping me. I told them, 'I want to know who has more relatives: you or me. In order to count your family, line up everyone from this island to Keta. I will run across and count as I go. Then we will know who has the larger family.' Once they had all been tricked into lining up, I ran across and counted, but just as I reached this shore, I said, 'I have tricked you!' and the very last shark caught me and completely tore off my fur coat. Because of this, I was crying when your eighty brothers came upon me, and they told me to bathe in the sea water and then lie down exposed to the wind. But when I did as they had instructed, my flesh split apart."

Ō-ana-muji told the rabbit, "Quickly go to the river and bathe there. Then, pick the flowers there and scatter them on the ground and then roll around in them. If you do this, your fur coat will be as it was before."

The rabbit did as instructed and his fur coat was restored. Then he told Ō-ana-muji, "None of your eighty brothers will marry Ya-kami-hime. Though you only carry their bags, in the end, you'll be the one to marry her."

Just as the rabbit had foretold, Ya-kami-hime told the eighty brothers, "I'm not going to marry any of you. I'm going to marry Ō-ana-muji."

Ō-ana-muji's eighty brothers were furious and hatched a scheme to kill him. When they reached Mt. Tema in the land of Hahaki, they told him, "There's a red boar on this mountain. We'll go to the top and drive it down to you. You wait here and catch it when it comes down." Then the brothers went up the mountain and found a boulder that resembled a boar. They heated it in a fire until it was red hot, and then rolled it down the mountainside. Ō-ana-muji caught the boulder and died instantly.

Ō-ana-muji's mother was devastated. She went to heaven and begged Kamu-musuhi to help her. Kamu-musuhi sent Kisa-kai-hime, meaning "lady of the scraping shell," and Umu-kai-hime, meaning "lady of the assembling shell," to bring Ō-ana-muji back to life. Kisa-kai-hime scraped Ō-ana-muji off of the boulder and collected the pieces of him; then, Umu-kai-hime took them for reassembly. She spread his mother's milk onto the pieces of his body, and Ō-ana-muji transformed into an attractive young man.

Ō-ana-muji's eighty brothers saw that he was back and so they tricked him into coming into the mountains. There, they split a large tree apart at the trunk and inserted a wedge to hold the forked trunk apart. They forced Ō-ana-muji into the gap of the tree trunk and then pulled out the wedge so that the tree would snap shut. Ō-ana-muji was crushed and died instantly.

Ō-ana-muji's mother was devastated again. She went to look for him, and when she found him, she cut down the tree, took him out, and brought him back to life again. Then she told him, "Your brothers are never going to let you live." She secretly helped him escape to the land of Ki, where he stayed with the kami Ō-ya-biko, "lord of great buildings."

But his eighty brothers pursued him, and when they caught up to him, they all nocked arrows to their bowstrings and demanded that he be handed over. Ō-ya-biko helped Ō-ana-muji escape by passing through the fork of a tree. He said to Ō-ana-muji, "You must go to the Land of Ne and consult with Susano-o. Surely that great kami will know what to do."

Ō-ana-muji did as instructed and went to the Land of Ne, where he found the dwelling of Susano-o. Susano-o's daughter, Suseri-bime, meaning "lady of rage," came out of the house to meet him, and the two immediately fell in love and pledged themselves to each other. Then she went back into the house and told her father, "There's a handsome kami outside."

Susano-o went outside to meet Ō-ana-muji and declared, "From now on, you shall be known as Ashi-hara-shiko-o, meaning 'ferocious man of the reed plain.'" He invited Ō-ana-muji into his house and made him sleep in a chamber full of snakes.

Suseri-bime gave Ō-ana-muji a scarf of snake charming and said, "When the snakes come and try to bite you, wave this scarf three times in the air and it will drive them off." Ō-ana-muji did what she asked and the snakes calmed down, and he slept safely through the night.

The next night, Susano-o put Ō-ana-muji in another chamber, this one filled with centipedes and hornets. Suseri-bime gave Ō-ana-muji a scarf of centipede and hornet charming and told him the same thing as before. Again, he was able to emerge unscathed.

Then, Susano-o fired a whistling arrow into a wild field and told Ō-ana-muji to go get it. Once Ō-ana-muji had gone into the field, Susano-o set the field on fire from all directions.

While Ō-ana-muji tried to figure out what to do, a mouse came and told him, "Come hide inside my hole where there is plenty of space." Ō-ana-muji stamped on the ground there and fell through into an underground space, where he stayed until the fire above burnt out. Then the mouse brought Ō-ana-muji the whistling arrow. The mouse's children had nibbled on the arrow's feathers.

Suseri-bime prepared her mourning clothing and came crying. Her father Susano-o was sure that this time Ō-ana-muji was dead, but he still went out to the field to confirm. Just then Ō-ana-muji came strolling up with the arrow, which he gave back to Susano-o.

Finally, Susano-o invited Ō-ana-muji into his house and asked him to pick the lice from his hair. Ō-ana-muji got behind Susano-o and prepared to do this task, but when he looked down into his hair, he saw that it was swarming with centipedes. Suseri-bime brought him dogwood berries and red clay. Ō-ana-muji split the berries in his mouth, then put some of the red clay in his mouth, then spit them out. Susano-o saw the red, seedy mixture and thought that Ō-ana-muji was picking the centipedes out of his hair, biting them, and spitting them back out. He began to feel some affection for his new son-in-law and fell asleep.

Once Susano-o was asleep, Ō-ana-muji took Susano-o's hair and tied it to the rafters that were holding up the roof of the house. He took a boulder that would take five hundred men to move and blocked off the door. Suseri-bime jumped on his back and the two of them made a run for it. Before they left, they took Susano-o's enchanted sword, enchanted bow and arrows, and jeweled zither. But as they fled, the zither bumped against a tree, and the sound caused the ground to shake.

Susano-o heard the sound and jumped awake with a start, but because his hair was tied to the rafters, he pulled the whole roof down around him. By the time he got himself untangled, Ō-ana-muji and Suseri-bime were already far away. Susano-o chased them all the way to the pass that leads to Yomi, but there he stopped and said to Ō-ana-muji, "Use the enchanted sword and enchanted bow you carry to chase down your brothers and kill them. Chase them to the hills and defeat them, chase them to the rivers where they will be swept away. Then you will no longer be Ō-ana-muji; you will be Ō-kuni-nushi, master of the land, and Utsushi-kuni-tama, soul of the visible world. My daughter Suseri-bime shall be your primary wife, and at the foot of Mt. Uka, build your mighty dwelling. Sink its pillars down to the bedrock and stretch its roof to heaven, you rascal!"

Ō-ana-muji used the enchanted sword and the enchanted bow to hunt down his brothers. He chased them into the hills and defeated them there, and he chased them into the rivers where they were swept away. Then he began to fashion his land.

His first wife, Ya-kami-hime, was still married to him, but she was afraid of his new wife, Suseri-bime, and so Ya-kami-hime returned to her home in Inaba. She left the child she had given birth to in the fork of a tree, and so it was called Ki-mata, meaning "tree fork."

Ō-kuni-nushi, under the name Yachi-hoko, meaning "innumerable spears," then went to the land of Koshi to woo Nunakawa-hime, meaning "lady of Nunakawa." When he arrived at her house, he sang to her,

> Yachi-hoko has had difficulty
> finding a wife
> in this eight-island land.
> He heard
> that in the distant, distant
> land of Koshi,
> there is a clever woman.
> He heard
> there is a beautiful woman.
> He has come to woo her,
> not yet untying the string holding his sword,
> not taking off his mantle,
> at the door of the house where the maiden sleeps
> he stands and knocks over and over.
> He stands and raps over and over,
> while the thrush sings on the verdant mountains.
> The pheasant, too, calls,
> and the rooster crows.
> How vexing it is to hear them,
> those obnoxious birds!
> Will no one kill them
> and end their incessant noise?
> Relay this message,
> oh birds following each other in the sky.
> My purpose here, is relayed
> just as it is said here.

However, she did not open the door and instead sang to Yachi-hoko from inside the house.

> Oh Yachi-hoko!
> As a woman,

my heart is like a bird
on the sand of the beach.
Now it is my own,
but soon it will be yours.
Do not take the life of this bird!
Oh birds following each other in the sky,
relay that message.
My purpose here, is relayed
just as it is said here.

When the sun goes down
behind the deep green of the mountains,
night will fall.
Come like the morning sun,
a radiant smile filling your face.

Take my white arms
and these snow-white young breasts,
to stroke,
to gently fondle.
Take these hands, like jewels,
and cross them to make your pillow.
Stretch out your legs
and go to sleep.
Fall in love with abandon,
Yachi-hoko.
My purpose here, is relayed
just as it is said here.

Thus, they did not spend that night together, but consummated
their marriage the next evening.

Yachi-hoko's primary wife, Suseri-bime, was filled with jealousy.
Yachi-hoko was troubled and decided to move from Izumo up to
Yamato. He prepared to depart and, with one hand on the saddle and
one foot in the stirrup, sang to Suseri-bime,

When I carefully put on this jet-black clothing,
and look at my chest, like a sea duck,
even if I flutter the lapels
it does not fit.
I cast it off, slipping out
as the breaking waves slip off the cliffs.

Then I carefully put on this bright blue clothing,
and look at my chest, like a sea duck,
even if I flutter the lapels
it does not fit.
I cast it off, slipping out
as the breaking waves slip off the cliffs.

Then I carefully put on this deep red clothing,
dyed with the extract from roots
of madder from the mountains.
I look at my chest, like a sea duck,
and I flutter the lapels,
and it fits!

My dearest wife,
if we go along with everyone else,
if I am taken with someone else,
I will not weep, you say.
But being alone, like a single strand of pampas grass,
hanging your head dejectedly,
though you weep,
may your cries pass like the deep fog
that rolls through the morning sky,
my wife.

My purpose here, is relayed
just as it is said here.

When she heard his song, Suseri-bime took a wine cup, drew
close to Yachi-hoko, and raised the cup to him. Then she sang,

Yachi-hoko,
my great master of the land, Ō-kuni-nushi.
Since you are a man,
at all the island capes you pass by,
at all the seaside capes you pass by,
at every one of them,
you have a wife and come calling.

However, I am a woman,
and I have no other man than you,
no other husband than you.

Under the billowing twill fabric,
under the smooth silk bedding,
under the rustling paper linens,
take these snow-white young breasts,
and these white arms,
to stroke,
to gently fondle.
Take these hands, like jewels
and cross them to make your pillow.
Stretch out your legs
and go to sleep.
Here, drink to your health.

When Yachi-hoko heard her song, they immediately shared wine cups and renewed their vows, each put their hands on the neck of the other, and they dwell in peace to this day.

One day, when Ō-kuni-nushi was in Izumo, he met the kami Sukuna-biko-na, meaning "small lord," who came from across the sea. Sources differ on how Sukuna-biko-na arrived and whose son he was, but after he landed, he helped Ō-kuni-nushi finish creating his realm.

According to *Ancient Matters*, when Ō-kuni-nushi was at Cape Miho in Izumo, a kami came from across the waves in a boat made from the seed pod of a rough potato plant and wearing the skin of a goose. Ō-kuni-nushi asked this kami for his name, but he got no reply. He also asked his attendants if any of them knew, but they all said they did not. Then the toad said, "The scarecrow god is sure to know."

When Ō-kuni-nushi summoned the scarecrow and asked him if he knew who this kami was, the scarecrow replied, "This kami is the son of Kamu-musuhi. His name is Sukuna-biko-na."

Ō-kuni-nushi reported this to Kamu-musuhi, who told him, "This is one of my children. He was so small that he slipped between my fingers and fell to earth. Please be like a brother to him and work together to finish creating the land." And so Ō-ana-muji and Sukuna-biko-na finished creating the land together.

According to *Chronicles* 8.6, Ō-kuni-nushi was at Isasa Beach when he heard a voice from across the sea. He saw a small man riding on a boat made from the skin of a rough potato plant and wearing the feathers of a wren. Ō-kuni-nushi picked the man up and placed him on the palm of his hand to inspect him, but then the man jumped up and bit him on the cheek. Ō-kuni-nushi sent a messenger to report this to the heavenly kami. Taka-mi-musuhi replied, saying, "In total I have 1500 children. Among them there was one who was badly behaved and would not heed my instruction. He slipped between my fingers and fell to earth. The kami you met must be him. Love him and raise him."

Ō-kuni-nushi and Sukuna-biko-na worked together and created the realm. They invented ways to treat the illnesses of humans and their domesticated animals, and they formulated ritual incantations that could be used to ward off troublesome birds, wild beasts, and insects. The people of the realm continue to enjoy these blessings even into the present.

After they were finished, Ō-kuni-nushi said to Sukuna-biko-na, "Is not this land we have created well and complete?"

Sukuna-biko-na replied, "There are some places that are complete, but there are some places that are not." Then Sukuna-biko-na crossed back over the sea to the Land of Tokoyo.

Ō-kuni-nushi traveled throughout the rest of the land and finished its creation. When he reached Izumo, he said to himself, "When I started this process, the Central Reed Plain Land was vast and wild. Even the rocks, grass, and trees were out of order. However, now I have subdued them all, and everything has fallen into place. But the ruler of this land is only me, alone. Is there no one who should rule this land together with me?"

At just that moment, a divine light shone from the sea, and something floated to the shore. It said to Ō-kuni-nushi, "If it were not for me, you could not have completed the creation of the land."

Ō-kuni-nushi asked the light, "Who are you?"

It replied, "We are your spirit of fortune and your spirit of discernment."

Ō-kuni-nushi recognized the spirits and said, "Indeed you are. Where do you wish to dwell?"

The spirits said, "We wish to dwell on Mt. Miwa, in Yamato Province."

According to *Ancient Matters*, after Sukuna-biko-na had gone to Tokoyo, Ō-kuni-nushi lamented, saying, "How can I finish creating this land on my own? What spirit can create it with me?"[4]

At just that moment, a shining kami came from the sea. It said, "If you worship me, then I will help you finish creating the land. If you do not worship me, it will be difficult for you to finish it on your own."

Ō-kuni-nushi replied, "In that case, how should I go about enshrining you for worship?"

The kami said, "Worship me in the eastern range of the mountains that surround Yamato Province." This kami now dwells on Mt. Miwa.

---

[4] In *Ancient Matters*, Ō-kuni-nushi needs the spirts from across the sea to finish creating the land.

## Surrender of the Central Reed Plain Land

At last, the time came for the chosen of the heavenly kami to descend to the Central Reed Plain Land and establish his kingdom. Sources differ on four major points: whether the chosen was originally Oshi-ho-mimi or his son Ninigi; whether he was sent by Taka-mi-musuhi or Amaterasu; which kami accompanied Ninigi from heaven; and the terms of Ō-kuni-nushi's surrender, besides many other finer details.

According to *Original Record*, Taka-mi-musuhi ordered that the Central Reed Plain Land be pacified. The kami Nigi-hayahi, meaning "flourishing swift spirt," was the older brother of Ninigi, and he received this order. He rode the heavenly rock boat and descended from heaven to Mt. Ikaruga in the land of Kōchi, and from there, moved into the land of Yamato. As his rock boat flew through the sky, he looked down and saw the land, coining the phrase "Sora-mitsu-yamato," meaning "Yamato as seen from the sky." He married the younger sister of Naga-sune-hiko, "lord of long shanks," and she gave birth to a son. Then Nigi-hayahi died.

Taka-mi-musuhi told a wind kami, "My descendant Nigi-hayahi was dispatched to the Central Reed Plain Land, but he has not reported back. Something is surely amiss. You go and investigate, then report back to me." The wind kami went and came back as ordered. When Taka-mi-musuhi heard that Nigi-hayahi had died, he sent the wind kami back to retrieve the corpse, and then he mourned for seven days and seven nights. Nigi-hayahi is buried in heaven.

According to *Ancient Matters*, Amaterasu decreed, "The land of bountiful reed plains where rice ears bloom for 1500 harvests should be ruled by my son, Oshi-ho-mimi." She entrusted the realm to him and sent him down from heaven.

However, when Oshi-ho-mimi arrived at the floating bridge of heaven, he looked down and said, "The land of bountiful reed plains where rice ears bloom for 1500 years is filled with an awful racket." He went back up to heaven and reported this to Amaterasu.

In response, Amaterasu and Taka-mi-musuhi commanded all the heavenly kami to assemble on the banks of the Tranquil River of Heaven to deliberate what should be done. They asked the kami Omoi-kane what he thought, saying, "We wish to entrust rule of the Central Reed Plain Land to Oshi-ho-mimi, but that land is filled with rampaging kami. Who can we send to force them to pledge allegiance to heaven?"

Omoi-kane considered the question along with all the other kami that were assembled, then he replied, "Send Oshi-ho-mimi's brother, Ame-no-hohi." So that kami was sent to pacify the Central Reed Plain Land. But Ame-no-hohi instead gave his loyalty to Ō-kuni-nushi, and for three years, he made no report back to heaven on the progress of his mission.

According to *Chronicles*, the son of Amaterasu, Oshi-ho-mimi, married the daughter of Taka-mi-musuhi, Taku-hata-chi-ji-hime, meaning "lady of one thousand paper mulberry flags." She gave birth to a son, Ama-tsu-hiko-hiko-ho-no-ni-nigi, meaning "heavenly lord, lord of flourishing rice ears." He is usually called "Ninigi." Taka-mi-musuhi especially favored his grandson Ninigi and wanted him to become the ruler of the Central Reed Plain Land. However, that land was filled with evil kami who buzzed noisily like flies, and the grass and trees could all speak. Therefore, Taka-mi-musuhi summoned the many kami and asked them, "I want to pacify this evil spirits of the Central Reed Plain Land. Who should be sent to perform this task?"

They all replied, "Ame-no-hohi is a superior kami. We should try him." Taka-mi-musuhi then sent Ame-no-hohi to pacify that land. But when Ame-no-hohi arrived in the Central Reed Plain Land, he betrayed his charge and went into the service of Ō-kuni-nushi. Even after three years, he made no report back to heaven on his progress. Taka-mi-musuhi then sent Ame-no-hohi's son to check up on his father, but the son instead submitted to the will of his father and did not report back either.

Having accepted that Ame-no-hohi had failed in his charge, Taka-mi-musuhi met with the various kami again and asked who should be sent to pacify the Central Reed Plain Land. This time, they all said, "We should send Ame-waka-hiko, meaning 'young lad of heaven.' He is a valiant warrior." Taka-mi-musuhi gave Ame-waka-hiko a heavenly bow and arrows and sent him down to the Central Reed Plain Land.

However, this kami was also disloyal. He married Ō-kuni-nushi's daughter, Shita-teru-hime, meaning "red shining lady." Then he declared "I wish to rule the Central Reed Plain Land for myself." He never reported back to heaven.

Taka-mi-musuhi thought that it was strange that there was no report back from Ame-waka-hiko for such a long time, and so he sent a pheasant to see what had happened. The pheasant flew down from heaven and perched on a tree that was planted in front of Ame-waka-hiko's gate. One of Ame-waka-hiko's servants, Ama-no-sagu-me, meaning, "heavenly seeker woman," went and told Ame-waka-hiko, "A strange bird is perched in the tree by the gate."

Ame-waka-hiko took the heavenly bow and arrows that he had received from Taka-mi-musuhi and shot the pheasant. The arrow went straight through the pheasant all the way to heaven and landed in front of Taka-mi-musuhi. Taka-mi-musuhi picked up the arrow and said, "This is one of the arrows that I gave to Ame-waka-hiko before I sent him to the Central Reed Plain Land. It is stained with blood. Perhaps this is because Ame-waka-hiko has been fighting with the earthly kami." Then Taka-mi-musuhi threw the arrow back down to earth. The arrow hit Ame-waka-hiko square in the chest while he was lying down to rest after the Feast of First Rice. He died instantly. This is the origin of the popular phrase "Beware a returning arrow."

According to *Ancient Matters*, Ame-waka-hiko went down from heaven and married Shita-teru-hime. He planned to rule the realm for himself and so for eight years gave no report back to heaven. Amaterasu and Taka-mi-musuhi again asked the heavenly kami,

"Ame-waka-hiko has not made a report for a long time. Who should we send down to find out why this is?"

Omoi-kane and the other kami said, "Send a pheasant."

Amaterasu and Taka-mi-musuhi decreed to the pheasant, "Go find Ame-waka-hiko. When you find him, tell him, 'You were sent to the Central Reed Plain Land to make all of the rebellious kami pledge their allegiance to heaven. Why have you not given us any report back for eight years?'"

The pheasant went down from heaven and landed on the tree outside Ame-waka-hiko's gate. Then the pheasant repeated the message that had been given to it by Amaterasu and Taka-mi-musuhi.

Ama-no-sagu-me heard the message that the pheasant repeated and told Ame-waka-hiko, "That bird has an inauspicious cry. You should shoot it."

Ame-waka-hiko took the bow and arrows that had been given to him by the heavenly kami and shot the pheasant dead. The arrow passed through the pheasant, reversed its direction in midair, then continued flying backwards all the way up to heaven, landing on the banks of the Tranquil River of Heaven right in front of Amaterasu and Taka-mi-musuhi. Taka-mi-musuhi picked up the arrow and saw the blood on it, then said, "This is an arrow that I gave to Ame-waka-hiko." He showed it to all of the other kami and then decreed, "If Ame-waka-hiko has been faithful to his charge and used this arrow to shoot the evil kami, then it shall not hit him. But, if Ame-waka-hiko has betrayed us, then may this arrow be his undoing." He then pushed the arrow back through the hole in the sky that it had made in its flight to heaven. Ame-waka-hiko was lying down in his bed when the arrow came and hit him in the chest, killing him.

Ame-waka-hiko's wife, Shita-teru-hime, wailed in grief at the death of her husband. Her cries resonated with the wind, which carried them all the way to heaven. Ame-waka-hiko's father, previous wife, and children heard Shita-teru-hime's cries and came down to earth. There they built a tomb for him and performed the temporary internment.

According to *Chronicles*, Ame-waka-hiko's father heard Shita-teru-hime's cries and knew that Ame-waka-hiko had been killed. He sent a swift wind down to carry Ame-waka-hiko's corpse up to heaven, and then he built a tomb in heaven for the temporary internment.

According to *Chronicles* 9.1, Ame-waka-hiko's wife and children in heaven came down to earth to collect his body and bring it back to heaven.

The various sources assign different roles for the funeral ceremony to different species of birds.

When Ame-waka-hiko had been alive, he was good friends with the earthly kami Aji-suki-taka-hiko-ne, meaning "gathering plowing high lord." Aji-suki-taka-hiko-ne was also the brother of Ame-waka-hiko's wife on earth, Shita-teru-hime. Aji-suki-taka-hiko-ne bore an uncanny resemblance to Ame-waka-hiko. Because they looked similar, when Aji-suki-taka-hiko-ne came to pay his final respects to his deceased friend, Ame-waka-hiko's wife and children from heaven exclaimed in surprise, "Our lord still lives!" They clung to Aji-suki-taka-hiko-ne and wept.

Aji-suki-taka-hiko-ne was furious. He said, "My friend is dead, and I came to mourn his passing. How dare you confuse me for a corpse!" He drew his ten-span sword and cut down the tomb. According to *Chronicles*, the tomb fell from heaven and became Mt. Moyama, meaning "mourning mountain," in Mino Province, present-day Gifu Prefecture. According to *Ancient Matters*, Aji-suki-taka-hiko-ne kicked the tomb, which flew to Mino Province and became Mt. Moyama.

Shita-teru-hime then composed a song about her brother, Aji-suki-taka-hiko-ne, because he was angry about being mistaken for Ame-waka-hiko. Or, in *Chronicles*, she wrote the song because her brother, Aji-suki-taka-hiko-ne, shined so brilliantly that his light filled two mountain valleys. *Chronicles* also says that the people who came to mourn Ame-waka-hiko broke into song. In any case, the song went,

> Like beads strung together
> on the neck,
> on the ankles,
> of the young weaver maiden
> in heaven,
> his light spans two valleys,
> Aji-suki-taka-hiko-ne.

Then, Shita-teru-hime sang,

> At the shallows crossed
> by the country woman
> (in far-off heaven),
> at the depths of the rocky riverside,
> she strings her net.
> Like drawing the gaps of the net closed,
> draw near, draw close,
> at the depths of the rocky riverside.

After this, the heavenly kami dispatched Take-mikazuchi, who was descended from the gods created when Izanagi killed the fire god Kagu-tsu-chi. In some sources he is accompanied by the sword kami Futsu-nushi, and in others, by a boat god named Ame-no-tori-fune, meaning "heavenly bird boat."

According to *Chronicles*, Taka-mi-musuhi again assembled the various heavenly kami and asked them who should be sent.[5] The kami all said, "Futsu-nushi, son of Iwa-tsutsu-no-o and Iwa-tsutsu-no-me, should be sent."

At that time, the kami Take-mikazuchi was living in the heavenly rock cave, and when he heard that Futsu-nushi was to be sent to pacify the Central Reed Plain Land, he came out of the cave and

---

[5] There is a narrative inconsistency because the kami that are sent were born when Izanagi killed the fire god, but that event does not happen in the main version of *Chronicles*.

said, "Is Futsu-nushi the only hero to be found in heaven?" And so he was sent to earth as well. The two kami departed and arrived at Itasa Beach in the land of Izumo.

In *Chronicles* 9.1, Amaterasu arranged for her son, Oshi-ho-mimi, to marry the daughter of Taka-mi-musuhi, and for the two newly-weds to descend to the Central Reed Plain Land. However, when Oshi-ho-mimi reached the floating bridge of heaven, he looked down and said, "This land is still wild and unruly." He returned to heaven and explained why he had come back. Amaterasu dispatched Take-mikazuchi and Futsu-nushi to the Central Reed Plain Land to drive out the unruly kami. They left heaven and descended to the land of Izumo.

In *Ancient Matters*, Amaterasu again asked the heavenly kami, "Who should we send now?"

Omoi-kane and the other kami said, "You should send the kami Itsu-no-ohabari, meaning 'fierce sword swing,' who was born when Izanagi slew Kagu-tsu-chi. He dwells in the heavenly rock cave at the upper reaches of the Tranquil River of Heaven. If he cannot go, then send his son, Take-mikazuchi. Since he has dammed up the river, the overland pass to his dwelling is flooded, so we should send a sailor kami to ask him about it."

When asked, Itsu-no-ohabari agreed to send his son, Take-mikazuchi, to pacify the Central Reed Plain Land. The boat kami Ame-no-tori-fune was ordered to accompany him.

The two descended to Izasa Beach in the land of Izumo. When they arrived, they unsheathed their ten-span swords, stood them upside down, and sat upon the tips. Then they questioned Ō-kuni-nushi, saying, "Amaterasu and Taka-mi-musuhi sent us to question you. They want to bestow the Central Reed Plain Land that you rule upon their descendant. How do you respond?"

Ō-kuni-nushi said, "I cannot say right now. First you must ask my son, the oracle kami Koto-shiro-nushi, meaning 'master of exchanged words.' Right now, he's gone to Cape Miho to fish and has not returned."

The kami went to Koto-shiro-nushi and asked what he was going to do. Koto-shiro-nushi said, "Who are we to say no to the heavenly kami?" Then he stepped on the bow of his boat and overturned it, made it into an eight-fold hedge of brushwood among the ocean waves, and hid himself inside it.

Take-mikazuchi then asked Ō-kuni-nushi, "We've finished speaking with your son Koto-shiro-nushi. Do you have any other sons?"

Ō-kuni-nushi said, "I have one other son you must see, Take-mi-na-kata, meaning 'fierce direction of the waters.' He is the only other son with whom you must speak."

At just that moment, Take-mi-na-kata came upon them carrying a boulder on his fingertips that it would take one thousand men to move. He said, "Who comes to our land speaking in such soft tones? I challenge you to a contest of strength. Let me take your arm first." Take-mikazuchi reached out his arm for Take-mi-na-kata to take, but Take-mikazuchi changed his arm into an icicle, and then again into a sword blade. Take-mi-na-kata was scared and backed off.

Take-mikazuchi then reached out and took Take-mi-na-kata's arm as if plucking a young reed. He crushed it in his hand, ripped it off, and threw it away. Take-mi-na-kata fled to Lake Suwa in the land of Shinano. Take-mikazuchi pursued him and was about to kill him when Take-mi-na-kata said, "Please spare my life. I submit. I render the Central Reed Plain Land unto the heavenly kami in accordance with their command."

The heavenly kami went back to Ō-kuni-nushi and said, "Your sons have submitted. What will you do?"

Ō-kuni-nushi said, "I will submit like my sons before me."

According to *Chronicles*, Ō-kuni-nushi took the broad-bladed halberd that he had used to pacify the land and handed it to the heavenly kami. He told them, "I used this to bring the land under my dominion. If the son of heaven uses it to rule, no one will dare oppose him. Now, I will depart for a distant land." Then he disappeared. The two kami went back to heaven and reported the results.

**FIGURE 7** Izumo Shrine (Izumo Taisha). Wikipedia Commons.

According to *Chronicles* 9.2, when the heavenly kami first confronted Ō-kuni-nushi, he said, "I have doubts about the authenticity of your claim."

Futsu-nushi went back to heaven and reported what Ō-kuni-nushi had said to Taka-mi-musuhi. Taka-mi-musuhi sent Futsu-nushi back to Ō-kuni-nushi with the message, "I understand your concerns. Allow me to spell it out in detail. Everyday matters shall be ruled over by my grandson. You will rule matters related to the kami. We will build a shrine for you using tall, grand pillars and broad, thick boards. Also, you shall be granted rice paddies for your sustenance. The kami Ame-no-hohi will be in charge of your veneration."

Ō-kuni-nushi replied to Futsu-nushi, saying, "Day-to-day concerns will be ruled over by the imperial grandchild. I will disappear and rule over the things unseen. I present you with this kami, Ku-na-to, meaning 'road fork,' who will attend to your needs in my absence." Then he disappeared.

Futsu-nushi traveled the land guided by Ku-na-to and subjugated all of the evil kami. The leaders of the earthly kami, Ō-mono-nushi, meaning "great object master," and Koto-shiro-nushi, assembled all of their followers. Then they led them up to heaven to pledge their allegiance and loyalty to the heavenly kami.

Taka-mi-musuhi told Ō-mono-nushi, "If you marry an earthly kami, then I will presume that you still have evil intentions. Therefore, I ask you to marry my daughter. Lead all of the earthly kami in submitting to the rule of my grandson." Then Taka-mi-musuhi sent them all back to earth.

In *Ancient Matters*, when Ō-kuni-nushi surrendered, he said, "May my shrine endure as long as the palace of the heavenly descendants who shall rule this land. Plant the pillars of my shrine in the bedrock and raise the roof beams to the high plain of heaven. I will conceal myself there. If Ō-mono-nushi is assigned as the vanguard of your army, then none of my 180 children will resist you." Then he built a shrine for himself in Izumo, built a fire, and spoke a blessing.

The Shinto prayer of the Provincial Lord of Izumo, which was recited annually in the imperial court, has a slightly different version of the Ō-kuni-nushi myth. It says that when the heavenly kami Taka-mi-musuhi and Kamu-musuhi entrusted the Japanese archipelago to Ninigi, the distant ancestor of the Provincial Lord of Izumo, Ame-no-hohi, was sent from heaven to inspect the land. He saw that the land was full of unruly kami and sent his own son, Ame-no-hina-dori, along with Futsu-nushi, to pacify Ō-kuni-nushi and force him to surrender. Ō-kuni-nushi attached his spirit to a great mirror, which was enshrined at Mt. Miwa. His sons Aji-suki-take-hiko-ne, Koto-shiro-nushi, and Kaya-naru-mi were given to Ninigi to serve as his protectors. The Izumo Provincial Lord recited this prayer every year to commemorate the service of his ancestors to the imperial court. The head priest of the Izumo Shrine still holds the title of Provincial Lord of Izumo today.

## Mythological Perspectives

### Comparative Axes: Quality/Kind (Thompson and Schrempp)

A fundamental component for many of the mythological perspectives described here and in Chapter 1 is a distinction of quality/kind between heavenly and earthly kami. *The Truth of Myth* suggests that moiety systems, social organizations of society into two exclusive groups, are an example of quality/kind. Supposing the heavenly kami from Chapter 1 and the earthly kami from Chapter 2 formed two different groups, and supposing that the humans who descended from these respective groups chose their marriage partners based on that classification, then the Japanese case would correspond with a pattern observed elsewhere across the world. A major point of debate within Japanese mythology surrounds the difference in quality between the heavenly and earthly kami. On the one hand, the heavenly kami are clearly presented as superior figures, but on the other, many of the basic activities for life, such as farming, weaving, and building, seem to characterize both sets of kami. These similarities suggest that differences in quality for kami relate primarily to genealogy and descent; this is unsurprising given that lineage was the primary organizing quality for ancient Japanese society.

The identification of different, exclusive groups also creates the possibility for a liminal or interstitial figure who operates between them. Susano-o's trickster qualities are described later in this chapter, but from the comparative perspective, the most important features of Susano-o are his subversion of established order and his combination of opposite characteristics. The former includes his rejection of his father's command to rule and his spreading chaos in the High Heavenly Plain. The latter centers on the differences between his early appearance in the narrative, when he is a crying adult or a mischievous disrupter, and his later appearance, when he is a father and provides trials for Ō-kuni-nushi. Thompson and

Schrempp argue that this rejection of the established order and ability to defy classification is central to the trickster's power, though paradoxically, that power is itself dependent on the existence of an established set of classifications. That is to say, because heavenly kami and earthly kami exist as categories, Susano-o has the power to move between them.

## The Trifunctional Hypothesis (Yoshida, Ōbayashi)

The division between heavenly gods and earthly gods is more pronounced in the myths from this chapter, which see Ō-kuni-nushi surrender to Ninigi and a clear tension between the two groups. Furthermore, several myths suggest that Ninigi's acceptance as legitimate ruler of the Japanese archipelago involved not only the subjugation of the earthly deities, but also that an agreement be made between the heavenly and earthly kami.

While Mishina proposed a dual-function kinship system as the basis for distinguishing heavenly and earthly kami (Chapter 1), Yoshida Atsuhiko (1934–) and Ōbayashi Taryō (1929–2001) argued that the distinction between heavenly and earthly kami demonstrated a trifunctional hypothesis for mythological roles. The trifunctional hypothesis was proposed by linguist and religious studies scholar Georges Dumézil (1898–1986). Dumézil was a prolific scholar of world mythology, and his study of Indian, Iranian, Greek, Roman, and Norse myths led him to propose that ancient Indo-European society was broken into three groups: one associated with legal and religious sovereignty, one associated with military force and war, and one associated with agriculture and crafts. This last group was ruled over by the other two. The hypothesis is enormously influential in mythology and had pronounced impacts on the work of Claude Lévi-Strauss (Chapter 1) and Mircea Eliade (Chapter 3). *The Truth of Myth* describes Dumézil's significance in terms of Müller, whose universalist approach had fallen into academic disfavor for being overly broad and reductive. Dumézil argued that by limiting his conclusions to Indo-European myths, he could productively return to a comparative mythological approach. More importantly, Dumézil's framework highlighted connections between myth and social structure, rekindling the relationship between mythology and anthropology. Dumézil had a significant impact in Japanese mythology. Even though Dumézil did not originally intend for his hypothesis to apply to non–Indo-European myths, several Japanese scholars have fruitfully applied it, especially Yoshida, Ōbayashi, and Hirafuji Kikuko (1972–).

Yoshida learned directly from Dumézil, and his studies culminated in his 1974 *Japanese Myths and Indo-European Myths* (Nihon shinwa to in'ō shinwa). Predictably, Yoshida assigned legal and religious sovereignty to Amaterasu. In *Chronicles*, Izanagi and Izanami agree to produce a ruler when they give birth to Amaterasu, and she was patron kami of the imperial clan. Moreover, Amaterasu is closely associated with rituals. For example, when Susano-o goes berserk, Amaterasu is weaving the clothing of the gods and preparing for the Feast of First Rice. According to Yoshida, Amaterasu also abhors violence, choosing to forgive Susano-o's initial infractions and then hiding herself away in the heavenly rock cave instead of confronting him. Taken together, Yoshida suggested that Amaterasu parallels the Hindu god Mitra, who is associated with the sunrise and was identified by Dumézil as one of four deities fulfilling the role of sovereignty within the trifunctional hypothesis.

The other three Hindu deities identified by Dumézil as fulfilling the role of sovereignty are Varuna, Bhaga, and Aryman. Yoshida linked Varuna to Taka-mi-musuhi. Varuna is a guardian of law, associated with rivers and oceans, dwells in a more distant heaven than Mitra, is willing to use violence, uses a bird as a messenger, and is usually paired with Mitra. Taka-mi-musuhi is involved in the establishment of legal authority on the archipelago, uses a pheasant as a messenger, kills Ame-waka-hiko with a cursed arrow, and often appears with Amaterasu (Mitra).

Taka-mi-musuhi's direct involvement in the mythic narrative, along with that of Amaterasu and Kamu-musuhi, is a poor fit for Varuna's supposed distance from human affairs. However, another early kami, Ame-no-mi-naka-nushi, completely drops out of the Japanese mythic narrative after creation. This led Yoshida to suggest that Ame-no-mi-naka-nushi is an inactive god, called a *deus otiosus* in religious studies. The kami's important-sounding name, "heavenly master of the center," and appearance as one of the first three gods implies that the kami is significant, but Ame-no-mi-naka-nushi has no later impact on the mythical narrative or history of worship.

Bhaga, a Hindu god of wealth, supports human affairs, so Yoshida associated Bhaga with Kamu-musuhi, who acts as a patron for Ō-ana-muji. Aryman has a close relationship to Mitra and Varuna, provides boons to worshippers, and is associated with marriage and hospitality. Yoshida associated Aryman with Taka-mi-musuhi, who arranges a marriage for Ō-mono-nushi and bestows blessings on Ō-kuni-nushi. The four Hindu deities do not perfectly align with the four kami Amaterasu, Taka-mi-musuhi, Kamu-musuhi, and Ame-no-mi-naka-nushi. However, their associated functions can be found among Amaterasu and the first three kami to appear in *Ancient Matters*.

The second piece of Dumézil's trifunctional hypothesis is the warrior role, which Yoshida assigned to Susano-o. Suggestions of similarity between Susano-o and Indra go back to the storm god interpretation first advanced by Takayama Chogyū (Chapter 1). For Yoshida, Susano-o's wild behavior and association with weaponry—such as the sword found in the eight-headed serpent and the weapons given to Ō-ana-muchi—established Susano-o as the kami who emblemized the warrior function. The sword retrieved by Susano-o would later be used by Yamato Take to conquer the Kumaso and Emishi peoples (Chapter 4). Also of note is Take-mikazuchi, who is associated with swords in both the pacification of the Central Reed Plain Land and in the Jinmu conquest narrative (Chapter 3).

The final position in Dumézil's trifunctional hypothesis is the farmer, a broad position associated with agriculture, animal husbandry, crafts, bounty and surplus, health, and beauty. Yoshida noted that many of these characteristics apply to Ō-kuni-nushi. Many of the *Records of Wind and Earth* gazetteers record legends of Ō-kuni-nushi and Sukuna-bikona in connection with agricultural production. In the myths presented here, Ō-kuni-nushi and Sukuna-bikona provide humanity with knowledge about animal husbandry and medicine, also connecting the pair with the agricultural position in Dumézil's hypothesis. Finally, Yoshida noted that Ō-kuni-nushi is called handsome by Suseri-bime, and the pair instantly fall in love. Ō-kuni-nushi also has multiple wives, leading Yoshida to suspect that the kami was unusually attractive. With Ō-kuni-nushi in the role of productivity and crafting, Amaterasu in the role of political and priestly sovereignty, and Susano-o in the role of war, Yoshida created a parallel between Japanese myths and Dumézil's trifunctional hypothesis for Indo-European myth.

Mythology scholar Ōbayashi Taryō combined Dumézil's trifunctional hypothesis with dual function and naturalist theories of myth to create a robust and influential explanation for kami in Japanese myths. In Ōbayashi's interpretation, the dual function between the heavenly and earthly kami reflected a division in social roles among the kami themselves. For the heavenly kami, Ōbayashi focused on the narrative of Amaterasu emerging from the rock cave and Ninigi's descent (Chapter 3). In general, the kami that work to lure Amaterasu out of the cave in *Ancient Matters* are the same kami that Amaterasu orders to accompany her grandson, Ninigi, when he descends to earth to assume rule of the Japanese archipelago. Ōbayashi suggested that Ame-no-koyane, Futo-dama, Ishi-kori-dome, Tama-no-oya, Ame-no-uzu-me, and Ta-jikara-o correspond to the priestly and ritual function of the first group in Dumézil's trifunctional hypothesis. In *Ancient Matters*, Amaterasu also orders the kami Omoi-kane, who hatched the plan for luring Amaterasu out of the rock cave, to take charge of worship, and so this kami also fits Dumézil's first function.

According to Ōbayashi, the second function was also fulfilled by three kami that are assigned by Amaterasu to accompany Ninigi on his descent from heaven. Ame-no-iwa-to-wake is a personification of the heavenly rock cave, and is associated with gates and barriers, suggesting a defensive function. Ame-no-oshi-hi and Ama-tsu-kume appear in *Ancient Matters* as the vanguard of Ninigi's retinue when he descends from heaven, and each is described as being armed with bows, arrows, and swords. In the Jinmu conquest narrative (Chapter 3), both of these kami are active in helping Jinmu use military force to establish the Japanese empire. Furthermore, the descendants of the two kami, the Ōtomo and Kume clans, were associated with military matters in ancient Japan. Hence, Ōbayashi identified these three kami as fulfilling the second (military and war) function of Dumézil's trifunctional hypothesis. Combined with the kami associated with worship and ritual, Ōbayashi further argued that heavenly kami fulfill the first and second functions.

Ōbayashi's identification of the roles of the heavenly kami left the third (agricultural and productive) function of Dumézil's trifunctional hypothesis to the earthly kami. Ōbayashi associated six earthly kami with the third function. First was Ama-no-sagu-me, the woman who alerts Ame-waka-hiko to the pheasant sent from heaven to investigate his progress in subduing the kami of the Central Reed Plain Land. The other five kami are given in Chapter 3 of this book. Two of them aid Ninigi upon his descent from heaven, Saruta-hiko and Kuni-nushi-koto-katsu-kuni-katsu-nagasa. Another aids Jinmu during his conquests, Sao-ne-tsu-hiko, and the last two are encountered by Jinmu during his journey. The aid rendered by these various kami suggested to Ōbayashi that these earthly kami were subjugated by the heavenly kami. Because some of them were also in the act of fishing when met by Jinmu hints at a productive role for these figures. And of course, as earthly kami, all of these figures have some connection with the land itself. As such, Ōbayashi proposed that the difference between the heavenly kami and the earthly kami related to their respective roles as envisioned in Dumézil's trifunctional hypothesis. The heavenly kami possessed political legitimacy, ritual authority, and military force, and the earthly kami were subjugated by them. Ōbayashi separately bracketed a group of kami that seemed associated with natural forces, especially the unruly kami that were conquered in order to establish the Japanese state.

## Historical and Political Interpretations (Tsuda, Matsumura)

Because Susano-o descends to Izumo, and because Susano-o's descendant, Ō-kuni-nushi, later comes to rule the archipelago, early mythologists tended to classify these kami separately. In his 1882 translation of *Ancient Matters*, for example, Chamberlain divides the myths into Yamato, Izumo, and Tsukushi mythical cycles. The myths in this Chapter constitute the Izumo Cycle, and the Chapter 1 myths are the Yamato Cycle. The Kyushu cycle refers to the much later reigns of Chūai, Jingū, and Ōjin. The Izumo and Yamato Cycles overlap with the Earthly (Izumo) Deities and the Heavenly (Yamato) Deities. While scholars inspired by Dumézil read the surrender of Ō-kuni-nushi in terms of functional categories of deities, other mythologists imagined the narratives surrounding Susano-o's fights with Amaterasu and Ō-kuni-nushi's surrender to the heavenly gods as evidence of an ancient ethnic conflict between different groups of people. The myths discussed in Chapters 3 and 4 of this book, in which a member of the Yamato imperial family defeats a warrior from Izumo, also fed the interpretation of these myths as ethnic conflict. One of the first to adopt this perspective was Takagi Toshio, discussed in Chapter 1. Takagi first claimed that Susano-o was as storm god, but his interaction with Anesaki and the development of his mythological study ultimately led him to propose that Susano-o was originally a creator god unique to Izumo. When *Ancient Matters* and *Chronicles* were written, their authors adapted Susano-o so that he could be added to the Yamato Myth Cycle because of Izumo's importance in Japanese religious affairs.

While mythologists like Takagi tended to focus on ritual/religious factors in myth, historians framed the issue in terms of factual events. One of the most radical interpretations of Susano-o came from historian Tsuda Sōkichi (1873–1961). Tsuda proposed that Susano-o was entirely made up by the compilers of *Ancient Matters* and *Chronicles* in order to connect the Izumo myth cycle, centered on Ō-kuni-nushi, with the Yamato Myth Cycle, centered on Amaterasu. Tsuda's analysis hinged on his understanding that *Ancient Matters* and *Chronicles* were themselves historical products written at a certain moment in time and with a political objective unique to that time. According to Tsuda, the two texts created a history for the eighth-century imperial court that asserted the legitimacy of the emperor over Izumo and other areas in the empire. Put differently, Tsuda assumed that the legends and myths in these texts were untrustworthy, that the time gap between when the myths were created and the creation of these texts meant that the myths were altered, and that the multiple versions of the myths meant that different version of events existed at the time these texts were written. Furthermore, while Ō-kuni-nushi and Amaterasu have grand shrines dedicated to their worship, Susano-o's footprint outside of *Ancient Matters* and *Chronicles* is comparatively small. As such, Tsuda concluded that Susano-o was simply made up to connect the two myth cycles.

One of the most prominent Japanese mythologists of the twentieth century, Matsumura Takeo (1883–1969), took the critical appraisals of Susano-o from Takagi and Tsuda and then applied a comprehensive and comparative approach. Matsumura's study of mythology is usually divided into two periods, but as the earlier of these—sometimes called his formative period—is largely an application of Tylor and Lang similar to Takagi Toshio. Matsumura's later period is epitomized by his four-volume *Research on Japanese Mythology* (Nihon shinwa no kenkyū 1955–1958). This series is still a major resource thanks to the comprehensive collection of theories

Matsumura assembled. Matsumura's method in his later career divided mythology into "intensive" and "extensive" components. The intensive referred to comprehensive study of Japanese mythology without incorporating a comparative element. The comprehensive aspect meant that unlike his early career research, which had focused on anthropological methods, his late career research included other approaches. Then, if this intensive study was unable to render a satisfactory conclusion, he applied comparative mythology, the extensive methods, to develop his interpretations.

Matsumura determined that Susano-o had originally been an agriculture deity, but that the compilers of *Ancient Matters* and *Chronicles* had altered his character in order to illustrate his subordinate position to Amaterasu. Matsumura noted that Susano-o is only a storm god in the Yamato Cycle myths. However, in the Izumo pantheon, including the Izumo Cycle myths and content from the Izumo *Records of Wind and Earth* gazetteer, many kami were related to agriculture, rain, and water. These elements were part of Susano-o's original character as a kami related to the ethnic peoples of Izumo. In the Yamato Cycle, Matsumura explained Susano-o's characteristics using extensive components. Zeus and Poseidon, for example, were a set of older and younger brothers that could be read as an example of a powerful god from one pantheon being incorporated into a subordinate position in the pantheon of a conquering group. The relations between Odin and Loki in Norse myths and Osiris and Seth in Egyptian myths also guided Matsumura. Susano-o was given a new destructive and rebellious personality when the Izumo people were conquered by the Yamato people to demonstrate that he was not as powerful as his new sibling, Amaterasu.

Matsumura also posited an even older layer of myth for Susano-o related to folklore. Snakes are connected to rain and waterways in Japanese tradition, so Susano-o's slaying of the serpent fits Matsumura's hypothesis that Susano-o was originally an agricultural and water kami. The myth recalled the fear ancient people had of flooding and snakes. Because the snake came every year to eat a girl,

Matsumura also connected it to an ancient practice proposed by folklorist Orikuchi Shinobu (1887–1953) of the "one night wife." The practice was a ritual in which a young woman would become the wife of a kami for one night. The negative feelings that the girl's family had for this practice developed into a story of human sacrifice. Matsumura linked the sacrificial element to another practice recorded by folklorists who studied Okinawan myths of *onari-gami*. Women connected to the spirit world would serve as wives to kami associated with rice, thereby guaranteeing a bountiful harvest. As such, Matsumura concluded that the Susano-o myth was built on a preexisting set of traditions in which the shamaness invited and entertained the snake, who represented the rains needed for agricultural production.

The political reading of Susano-o advanced by Tsuda and further developed by Matsumura is widely applied among contemporary historians and historians of religion. Historian Joan Piggott, for example, suggests that *Ancient Matters* and *Chronicles* legitimated the political status quo, with Izumo kami like Ō-kuni-nushi and Susano-o subordinated to the Yamato deities just like the land of Izumo was subordinated to the Yamato court. Izumo serves as the geographical opposite of the High Heavenly Plain. Religion scholar Jonathan Stockdale notes that Susano-o is a kind of "narrative bridge" that links Amaterasu—his older sister—with the Izumo kami—who are his descendants. O-kuni-nushi being rewarded for surrendering reminded local elites that their loyalty to the Yamato court would pay off.

Tylor addressed the flooding aspect of Susano-o many years earlier, in 1877. In a very brief set of remarks, Tylor noted that once Buddhist and Chinese elements were stripped away, the remainder was a purely Japanese nature-myth. Given the obvious relationship of Amaterasu to the sun and nature, Tylor imagined that Susano-o must also have such a connection, and he proposed that Susano-o was a storm and wind god. The myth of Amaterasu hiding in the rock cave was about the sun emerging after a storm. Then, Tylor (1877) notes "we read of the Wind-god descending to earth and slaying the eight-headed and eight-tailed serpent, who is about to destroy the 'lady of the young rice field.' The monster is known to the Japanese as being an eight-mouthed river, so the story seems really that of the wind and the flood." Combining the notion of the wind with the idea of the snake as the Hii River and Kushi-ina-da-hime as a representative of rice paddies, Susano-o—if taken as a nature deity—appears to be a god of not only storms, but also flood control. In this sense, he could also be a kind of "culture hero," a figure tied to the trickster and described by Boas. A culture hero performs some laudable act to transform the world in a way that makes human habitation possible.

## Susano-o as a Liminal Figure

The cultural anthropologist Victor Turner (1920–1983) placed special value on the societal function of rites-of-passage, and his work, often categorized as symbolic anthropology, made a major impact on the mythology of Susano-o. According to Turner, a culture could be understood by making sense of its symbols. Symbols functioned within a society to influence people's beliefs and practices, and they helped connect individuals within society and resolve disputes between them. The meanings of symbols are assigned and reinforced in displays—such as rituals—and in narratives—such as myths. One of the most important rituals for Turner was the coming-of-age or rite of passage, in which an individual took on a new role within society with new rights, privileges, and responsibilities. Based on earlier work, Turner split coming-of-age rituals into three phases: before, during, and after. He called the middle phase "liminal." At this in-between moment, an individual would be in a state of not-belonging and exist within a margin or threshold. For myths, Turner associated this liminal state with trickster figures. Trickster figures exist on the margins or boundaries of society and operate without an easily identifiable set of norms for their actions. At the same time, their transgressive activity highlights the borders and boundaries of acceptable behavior, boundaries that the fully formed, adult individuals in society would be expected to follow.

Many aspects of the Susano-o myths fit the description of a liminal, trickster god. Susano-o was born as a heavenly kami, but his descendants are earthly kami. In *Ancient Matters*, he refuses to accept the charge of governance given to him by his father and exhibits childish behavior, including wanting to return to his mother, so he is banished. In *Chronicles*, he defies social norms and lashes out, so he is banished. When Susano-o ascends to heaven, the space itself shakes and groans, expressing the disorder and chaos that accompany the kami. After his oath with Amaterasu, Susano-o breaks multiple taboos, including destroying Amaterasu's rice fields, defecating in the feast hall, and flaying a horse backwards and throwing it into a sacred space. After being banished from heaven, he wanders between the worlds of heaven and Izumo, in some versions asking for lodging from the gods, and in others, stopping briefly in Korea. Each of these actions can be readily associated with proscribed activities. Susano-o's longing for his mother and his oath with Amaterasu suggest an incest taboo, discussed later in this chapter. His ascent to heaven is a violation of geographical borders, the destruction of the fields is an assault on agricultural productivity, and the defecation and flayed horse demonstrate the pollution of a sacred space. Finally, Susano-o's wandering reinforces his status as a liminal figure, border breaker, and general agent of chaos.

One major question for Susano-o's classification as a trickster god is whether his actions are truly chaotic or in fact reveal some kind of deeper social order. Cultural anthropologist Mary Douglas (1921–2007) proposed that notions of dirt, impurity, and pollution are not primarily related to hygiene or sanitation, but that they reveal a classification system that orders the world. While these systems are culturally specific, the function of dirt is universal, making Douglas' approach a kind of symbolic structuralism. Douglas' hypothesis has been broadly influential in Japanese mythology by introducing the concept that Susano-o's actions, which constitute impurity, function to define their opposite. A similar claim was made in Japan in the ninth century in *Gleanings*, whose author asserted that Susano-o's mythical actions were the origins for a category of deeds called Heavenly Sins. These sins are spelled out in the Shinto prayer for the Great Exorcism of the Sixth Month (Chapter 1). Many mythologists have since connected the myths of Susano-o with the emphasis on purification rituals that characterize Shinto beliefs.

Another approach for systematizing Susano-o's chaotic actions is to focus on the political dimension of Japanese myths. Anthropologist Yamaguchi Masao (1931–2013) has argued that, given the connection between Amaterasu and the imperial family, Susano-o's trickster status was heavily mediated by ideas and demands of kingship. While trickster deities in other cultures might bring about social change or positive benefits by challenging the rules, within the Japanese mythical narrative, Susano-o is always presented in a subordinate position to Amaterasu. The restoration of order is brought about by other kami who lure Amaterasu back out of the cave, and the seeds for agricultural products created when Susano-o kills Ō-getsu-hime are collected by another kami and presented to Amaterasu. Similarly, the divine sword that Susano-o finds when he kills the eight-headed serpent is sent back to heaven; later in the narrative, Amaterasu will bestow it upon her grandson, Ninigi. Yamaguchi suggested that the Japanese myths encompass a binary dichotomy of order vs. chaos, sacred vs. profane, court vs. provinces, and others, in which Susano-o expresses the negative aspects and Amaterasu the positive ones. Within the system, the myths ensure that Amaterasu's dominion and power are reinforced.

In a similar vein, mythologist David Weiss has suggested that the political motivations for subsuming Susano-o to Amaterasu in Japanese myths also explain Susano-o's apparent reform after his descent to Izumo, when the trickster elements of his personality disappear. This inconsistency is precisely what led Takagi to suggest that the trickster Susano-o who appears in the Yamato Myth Cycle was a later construction. Weiss suggests that Susano-o appears as a stand-in for regional elites, and that this function was similarly dependent on the binary relations observed by Yamaguchi. Similarly, we could note that Susano-o defeats the serpent by using his wits, so his division into a trickster god within the Yamato Cycle and an agriculture and water god in the Izumo Cycle is not entirely clean. For Weiss, Susano-o's liminality is the most critical part of his nature because that liminality was applied to Korea during the period of Japanese colonization in the twentieth century.

## Susano-o and Korea

One perennial issue for the interpretation of Susano-o is his relationship with Korea. As seen in Chapter 1, in several versions of the Susano-o descent narrative, the kami first goes to Korea, then crosses over to Japan. The proximity of Izumo to the eastern coast of the Korean peninsula, the presence of Korea in the Izumo Cycle of myths, and archaeological evidence that Izumo was a distinct polity from the Yamato suggest that Izumo might have been a Korean settlement. Ancient Korea was divided into three major kingdoms and one confederation of smaller states. One of these kingdoms, Silla, was on the eastern coast, facing Izumo. The land-pulling myths of the Izumo *Records of Wind and Earth*, given above, imply a close connection between Silla and Izumo.

Twentieth-century history poses a major complication to further study of Susano-o and Korea. Japan went to war with Qing China in 1895 and Russia in 1905 in large part to assert its own influence over Korea. In 1910, Japan formally colonized Korea and ended the Chosŏn (Joseon) dynasty. That is to say, the moment that Japanese mythology began to develop as an academic discipline corresponded with Japanese imperial expansion into Korea. Japanese mythologists in this period tended to understand Japanese myths in a way that legitimized or justified this imperial expansion and imagined ancient Japan as a mixed-race empire ruled by the imperial clan, a mirror for the modern twentieth-century empire. The colonial legacy makes this topic extremely thorny, especially for scholars working in Japan and Korea. Because the issue is contentious, it is especially important to recall that the meanings assigned to myths can vary, as shown by the many mythological interpretations explained in this book. The interpretations presented in this section are not historical fact, and they are presented not because the author endorses them, but because they reflect an important historical moment. Moreover, these interpretations amply demonstrate how the politics of the day can influence the work of scholars who claim to being doing objective research. Or in other words, they demonstrate how myths can influence everyday life.

One mode of research on the connection between Korea and Japan based on Japanese myths was euhemeristic, that is, it treated the actions of the kami as metaphors or explanations for human actions. For example, Izanagi and Izanami dipping the spear into the ocean could be a metaphor for people using boat poles to cross over to the Japanese archipelago. This approach is named after the Greek mythologist Euhemerus, and it characterizes Confucian inspired research on Japanese history and mythology from around the seventeenth century. In modern Japan, historians infused the older euhemeristic readings with positivism, a belief that historical facts can be ascertained through the rigorous study of documentary evidence. In 1890, historian Hoshino Hisashi (1839–1917) published an article based on Japanese myth that asserted that Japanese and Koreans had shared ancestry. In truth, Hoshino was not the first to make this claim, but he was the first to use rigorous positivistic methods. Hoshino concluded that Susano-o first descended to Korea and then migrated to Japan, and that the place "Soshimori" named in the myth corresponded to an actual location on the Korean peninsula connected to the Korean words "so" (cow) and "head" (mŏri). The sea plain, which Izanagi assigns Susano-o to govern in *Ancient Matters*, must refer to the Korean peninsula, and ancient Japan and ancient Korea must have been part of the same realm,

Hoshino reasoned. When Japan annexed Korea in 1910, Hoshino argued that the ancient realm was being restored, thus legitimizing Japanese imperial expansion based on the interpretation of myth.

Closely related to Hoshino's theory was an argument made by linguist Kanazawa Shōsaburō, whose 1929 book became the defining and authoritative work arguing for Korean and Japanese shared origins. Kanazawa had originally proposed this argument in 1910, heavily influenced by Hoshino. In 1929, Kanazawa's linguistic acumen had increased, and he modified Hoshino's argument based on historical linguistic evidence rather than connections between mythical places and modern Korean. Most importantly, Kanazawa argued that Soshimori actually resolved to the name of a country, "Sohori," that was used throughout Northeast Asia, and referred to a capital city. This even influenced the name of the first mythical Japanese capital, Kashihara, which Kanazawa argued was based on the combination of "ku" for "big" and "so-ho-ri," a transformation of "shi-ha-ra." Ultimately, this meant that Soshimori referred to the capital city of Silla, Kyŏngju. Kanazawa identified several other mythical Japanese place names and uses linguistic evidence to conclude that Japanese and Korean were part of the same language family, making Japanese and Korean people part of the same ethnic group.

There are three major takeaways from the colonial-period scholarship on Susano-o and Korea. First is the usage of euphemistic and historical linguistic models for myth interpretation. Like the other methods for doing mythology presented in this book, these approaches have strong points and weak ones, and represent one fraction of a much larger continuum for doing mythology. Second is the influence that the conclusions of these methods had on later Japanese mythology. In particular, the culture areas used by Mishina and the culture strata used by Oka, both discussed in Chapter 1, were influenced by colonial ideology. That ideology derived directly from the mythological approaches discussed here. Although Mishina and Oka did not adopt the theory of shared ancestry between Japanese and Koreans, their imagination of Korean and

Japanese antiquity did not develop in a bubble. Finally, as Weiss has documented, colonial Japanese euhemerist and historical linguistic treatments of Susano-o demonstrated the power and functions of mythology. Mythology provides an opportunity to create an ancient tradition that legitimizes actions in a different time period, and it allows mythologists to invent traditions and selectively edit cultural memory in order to promote ideologies that have only tenuous connections to the original context from which myths emerged.

## Psychological Interpretations of Japanese Myth (Yoshida, Kawaii, Yuasa)

Susano-o's behavior and the vividness of the Izumo Cycle myths are an especially rich subject for psychological methods of myth interpretation. Broadly speaking, these methods can be divided into Freudian and Jungian approaches. For Freud, myths, along with dreams, were a space in which taboo desires and strong fears could be expressed. Or as described in *The Truth of Myth*, Freud's association of psychological repression with the development of human society reflected a search for the human origin story, a myth of human society's beginnings. Freud's Oedipus Complex, which established gendered sexuality, is named for a Greek myth, but in truth, the Oedipus story only became a myth, that is, became a story that explained something, in the hands of Freud. As noted in Chapter 1 of this book, structural analysis by Claude Lévi-Strauss identified Susano-o's desire to return to the land of his mother and his inability to grow up as an incestuous wish. Other mythologists have taken the sexual taboos surrounding Susano-o further, noting his incestuous relationship with his sister Amaterasu, the violence of his inserting the flayed horse into the chamber causing a woman to injure her genitals, the retreat of Amaterasu in response to the traumatic visit of Susano-o, and an erotic dance used to lure her out again. Later, Ō-kuni-nushi fights and defeats his father-figure and direct ancestor Susano-o in order to elope with Susano-o's daughter, his relative several generations removed. The most prominent of Japanese psychological mythologists, Kawai Hayao (1928–2007), suggested that Susano's incestuous longing for his mother was displaced onto his sister. This explains not only his desire to see and have children with her, but also the breakdown in social relations that resulted from their breaking of an incest taboo.

Kawai, a prominent and award-winning clinical psychologist, was more inspired by Jung than Freud. For Jung, myths and dreams were expressions of the collective unconscious, a repository of human knowledge and experience shared by all humans through evolutionary processes. Jungian psychology used this collective unconscious to explain how myths in different parts of the world that had no contact with each other, for example, Greece, Scandinavia, and Japan, all had similar mythical trickster figures, like Hermes, Loki, and Susano-o. In Jungian mythology, these figures represent archetypes whose expression goes beyond individual psychology or single cultures, and the study of mythology provided a vehicle by which one could glimpse fundamental and archaic prototypes of human existence. *The Truth of Myth* notes that objective evidence of the kind of transcendent reality and universal collective unconscious Jung proposed has never been identified. Perhaps the popularity of Jung in Japan drew precisely from the fact that Japanese mythologists were generally uninterested in universal phenomena anyway. For example, Kawai did not use Jungian mythology to identify archetypes in Japanese myths that connected to a broader human experience. Instead, Kawai imagined he could uncover the fundamental and prototypical Japanese experience, and he limited the scope of his findings to Japanese people. This application was largely due to an assumption on Kawai's part that Japanese people were psychologically different from Westerners on a fundamental level, and so Jungian and other psychological methods that were developed by Westerners could not be directly applied to the Japanese case. Kawai's goal was essentially to use myths to expose the roots of the Japanese psyche.

Jungian psychological approaches to Japanese myths and Susano-o came to a head in a 1983 symposium between Kawai, Yoshida Atsuhiko, and philosopher Yuasa Yasuo (1925–2005). Kawai argued that the key to understanding Susano-o was the kami's transition between the mother complex archetype and the old man or senex archetype. As noted in other interpretations, Susano-o's statement to Izanagi that he misses his mother, combined with his childlike behavior, suggested to Kawai that Susano-o had a mother complex, an unresolvable desire for his mother that resulted in his inability to achieve complete maturity. Based on this archetype, the child would seek a return to the safety and comfort of the maternal womb. Later, when Susano-o appears in the Land of Ne, he has transformed into the archetype of the old man, a helpful figure in Jungian psychology that emerges as a kind of mentor and guardian figure. In this interpretation, Susano-o aids Ō-ana-muji by putting him through trials that will allow Ō-ana-muji to grow and mature into Ō-kuni-nushi, his ideal self. When Ō-kuni-nushi passes his trials, Susano-o grants him the assistance, demonstrated by the weapons, that Ō-kuni-nushi needs to fulfill his quest. Of course, for Kawai, the identification of these Jungian archetypes was important because it could be reframed in a context that explained the unique nature of the Japanese psyche. Kawai argued that the spaces in which Susano-o's transformation occurred, heaven and the underground, were both ruled by women, Amaterasu and Izanami. This led Kawai to propose that Japan was characterized by a preference and pre-dilection for mothers. Separately, Susano-o also was related to the "absent center" of the Japanese psyche, a mythological interpretation unique to Kawai discussed in Chapter 3 of this book.

In the same 1983 symposium, Yoshida focused on the Susano-o's lack of independence from women. This was reflected at each stage of his life. First, as a child, Susano-o was unable to separate himself from his mother, Izanami, and it became the source of chaos and disorder. Then, he was unable to develop an identity apart from his older sister, Amaterasu, and he consumes himself with acting out against her. Finally, in the Land of Ne, Susano-o is unable to let go of his daughter, Suseri-bime, who has come of age herself and is ready to begin a new life apart from him. In this sense, Susano-o is always defined by the women around him. Yoshida noted that the inability of a young man to separate from his mother and enter male society was identified by Lévi-Strauss among indigenous people of the Americas. However, to explain this similarity, Yoshida deferred to Jungian psychology rather than structuralism and cultural contact, proposing that Susano-o reflects the anxiety, housed in the collective unconscious, of being unable to separate oneself from the Jungian archetype of the Devouring Mother. This archetype describes a mother figure who is overbearing, controlling, and prevents her children from establishing independent selves. Importantly, for Jung, the archetype can be present in anyone, even if they are not a mother, and for a male, the Devouring Mother could manifest as an inability to separate oneself from the safety and security of the mother. Yoshida proposed that this issue was part of the collective unconscious, and specific cultural features resulted in the issue being expressed in myth in different ways. Yoshida also aligned his observation with the Japanese preference and predilection for mothers proposed by Kawai.

Yuasa took the opposite position of Yoshida and focused on Susano-o's growth and maturation. In Yuasa's interpretation, Susano-o's defeat of the eight-headed serpent was a victory over the Great Mother, an archetype examined in-depth by Jung's disciple Erich Neumann (1905–1960). In Neumann's application of Jungian archetypes, the Great Mother is defeated by a Hero, which evokes the emergence of a free, individual ego from unconscious forces. Prior to defeating the serpent, Susano-o was in thrall to the Great Mother archetype, but his ultimate victory allowed him to transform into the Wise Old Man archetype and bless Suseri-bime's marriage to Ō-kuni-nushi. As such, Susano-o represented the maturation process of consciousness and the development of masculinity. In line with Neumann and Jung, and in contrast to Kawai and Yoshida,

Yuasa argued that this narrative of heroic overcoming and male socialization had a universal quality and went beyond a single ethnic tradition.

Ultimately, Kawai, Yoshida, and Yuasa did not reconcile their respective positions. This kind of individualistic interpretation characterizes the significant body of Jungian interpretations of Japanese myths that followed this 1983 symposium. These materials, only available in Japanese, are too numerous to summarize here precisely because—aside from the central guidelines of archetypes and the collective unconscious—there is little holding them together. Hirafuji has suggested that the inability of this scholarship to develop and build on itself is perhaps related to the therapist-client quality that psychological study of myths tends to evoke. In these interpretations, Japanese myths are the framework for a broader therapeutic method, not the actual research subject.

## Joseph Campbell and the Hero's Journey

Jung's proposal that myths were connected to the human psyche at a fundamental level had a major impact on Joseph Campbell (1904–1987), one of the most influential Western mythologists. Jung's archetype of the hero symbolizes overcoming obstacles to achieve goals. In myth, the hero travels, confronts a monster, struggles against being killed, captures a treasure or severs an organ, then returns. That journey is a symbol, for Jung, of the process of self-actualization and the victory of the conscious mind over the unconscious. Jung positioned the hero archetype among many others, including the mother, represented by the dragon or monster that the hero fought. Campbell, however, focused almost exclusively on the archetype of the hero and their relationship to coming-of-age rituals and rites-of-passage. Other mythologists, notably Lord Raglan (1885–1964), preceded Campbell in focusing on the hero, but Campbell's interpretation as published in his 1949 *The Hero with a Thousand Faces* is by far the most influential.

Campbell imagined that all mythical narratives were later variations of a single original story; a monomyth. Over time, this story acquired different "masks" in different cultures and historical moments, but the core story was the same, consisting of departure, initiation, and return. Within these three broader categories, Campbell identified five or six common motifs such as "supernatural aid" and "atonement with the father," though these motifs might not be exactly the same or present in any given myth. More important was that comparison of myths from around the world had the potential to reveal the monomyth about an individual who could, through their heroic journey, experience the shared humanity that gave rise to the monomyth and then harness that power to transform their world.

Campbell used two examples from Japanese myths in *The Hero with a Thousand Faces*, both with the category of "Return," when the hero escapes peril to come back to their home. Campbell puts Izanagi's return to the Central Reed Plain Land from the Land of Yomi in "The Magic Flight." If a hero wins their prize with the blessing of the gods, then their return is supported by their supernatural patrons, but if the hero claims their prize by defying the powers that be and incites the resentment of the gods or demons, then a pursuit of the hero naturally follows. In some varieties of these narratives, the hero tosses behind them various objects that create obstacles for their pursuers. Alongside Jason and the Argonauts using the dismembered body of Absyrtus to delay King Aeëtes, Campbell retells the story of Izanagi fleeing from Izanami in *Ancient Matters*. Izanagi's use of his headdress, comb, and peaches fits the broader description of using objects to delay one's pursuers. Campbell was also especially interested in the final exchange between Izanagi and Izanami, which in his retelling, is a story about humanity's relationship with death. Campbell interprets Izanami's instructions to Izanagi not to look at her as an attempt to preserve his innocence of death, his confrontation with his own mortality. When that was lost, Izanagi drew on his will to live in order to place the boulder, a veil allowing humans to overcome the existential crisis brought on by our inevitable demise.

Instead of a pursuit, in some mythical narratives, Campbell notes that the outside world must arrive to rescue the hero and bring them back from their adventure, which he calls "Rescue from Without." Campbell recounts the narrative from *Ancient Matters* in which the gods come together to lure Amaterasu out of the heavenly rock cave, with special attention to the *shimenawa*, the rope used to close the cave behind her, and to the other objects used to draw her out—the mirror, sword, and tree. The sun retreats every night, just as life retreats for sleep, but the *shimenawa*, a common sight at Shinto shrines, prevents the sun from disappearing entirely. Campbell likens the story to Little Red Riding Hood, who is rescued from the belly of the wolf by the huntsman. Campbell is especially interested in the motif of the sun as a goddess and not a god, which he suggests is an archaic form of a once widespread myth. The mirror used to lure Amaterasu out of the cave is a symbol of the world and represents divinity reveling in the glory of its creation. The sword appears in other myths as a thunderbolt. Finally, the tree represents the wish for the sun to return, and Campbell parallels the tree in the Japanese myth with the trees used by Christians at winter solstice. Ame-no-uzu-me's dance is Carnival, a celebration of the coming renewal. Finally, the *shimenawa* and the Christian cross both symbolize the boundary between the death and resurrection.

Campbell does not discuss any other Japanese myths in *The Hero with a Thousand Faces*. However, in surveying Japanese myths, the transformation of Ō-ana-muji into Ō-kuni-nushi might be single easiest narrative to fit to the hero's journey. Meeting the rabbit begins Ō-ana-muji's departure from normality, the "Call to Adventure." Unfortunately, Ō-ana-muji is unable to complete his calling of marrying Ya-kami-hime and vanquishing his brothers, though his "Refusal of the Call" is based on circumstance rather than a rejection of duty by the hero. This results in his being killed, and his "Supernatural Aid" appears in the form of Kamu-musuhi, who twice resurrects him. Ō-ana-muji then goes through the "Crossing of the First Threshold," passing through the tree into the Land of Ne, the

"Belly of the Whale." In the Land of Ne, the tests given to Ō-ana-muji by Susano-o constitute "The Road of Trials," and Suseri-bime is the "Meeting with the Goddess" who will give the hero items to aid them in the future; in this case, the scarves that protect Ō-ana-muji during his trials. Thus, he confronts Susano-o, "Atonement with the Father," which takes on the double-meaning as Susano-o is not only a symbolic father but also Ō-ana-muji's actual ancestor. Ō-ana-muji realizes that he must trap Susano-o in order to vanquish him, "Apotheosis," then makes off with Susano-o's weapons and Suseri-bime, the "Ultimate Boon." He escapes from the Land of Ne during his "Magic Flight," accidentally waking Susano-o with the stolen zither and initiating a chase narrative. Finally, Ō-ana-muji performs the "Crossing of the Return Threshold" when he goes past the pass leading to Yomi, where Susano-o pronounces him "Master of the Two Worlds." Ō-ana-muji, now Ō-kuni-nushi, returns to his world and uses his newfound power with the "Freedom to Live," in this case, to defeat his brothers and assume his rightful place as ruler of the Central Reed Plain Land.

Campbell has the unusual distinction of being influential in the popular study of myth and largely disregarded in academic mythology. As detailed in *The Truth of Myth*, many of Campbell's examples are taken from legends, popular fiction, and other non-mythic sources, and the universal themes and motifs Campbell identifies have been entirely disproven or at least impossible to substantiate. The vague quality of the stages on Campbell's hero's journey, "Supernatural Aid," for example, also makes the theory unsuitable for rigorous comparative mythology. This vagueness also lends Campbell's interpretations the veneer of universality.

## Literary Interpretations of Ō-kuni-nushi (Orikuchi, Kōnoshi)

Many Japanese mythologists are literature scholars. This is in part because *Ancient Matters* and *Chronicles* are written down, and in part because the Western notion of "literature," focusing especially on fiction and poetry, did not become widespread in Japan until the late nineteenth century. Prior to that, the word used for "literature" in Japan (*bungaku*) simply meant things that were written down. When literature departments began to be created at Japanese universities around the turn of the twentieth century, these departments were staffed with and inherited methods from scholars of things that were written down, and *Ancient Matters* was positioned as the first work of Japanese literature.

The key feature distinguishing literary interpretations of myths is the treatment of myth as a story with a plot, characters, and setting, as opposed to a model for historical events or a resource for understanding religious history. Literary accounts tend to be more particular about textual sources, for example, noting how differences between *Ancient Matters* and *Chronicles* demonstrate that they are different stories with different plotlines. Recent literary studies often center on "text," and may even ascribe active qualities to it, for example, claiming that the text acts, expresses, or evokes, rather than claiming that an author wrote a text to achieve some purpose.

One of the most prominent scholars of classical Japanese literature was Orikuchi Shinobu. In truth, Orikuchi was also a linguist, folklorist, novelist, and poet, and he studied folklore with Yanagita. However, Orikuchi also published extensively on Japanese literature, especially the eighth-century poetry collection *Myriad Poems*. His later theories, especially about the centrality of the "visitor" (*marebito*) and its connection to the kami, brought him into conflict with Yanagita. Orikuchi's body of scholarship is massive. The 1965–1968 *Collected Works of Orikuchi Shinobu* spans thirty-one volumes, each around five hundred pages. In Japan, Orikuchi even has his own field named after him: "Orikuchi Studies" (*Orikuchi-gaku*). Even a brief summary of Orikuchi's work would be very long, so the focus here is restricted to his theory of sensuality, called *iro-gonomi*. The theory continues to be influential in the study of classical Japanese literature, including *The Tales of Ise* and *The Tale of Genji*.

Orikuchi's theory of sensuality argued that in ancient Japan, people with many romantic partners, especially men with multiple wives, were seen as model citizens. Among kami, Orikuchi identified Ō-kuni-nushi as the first example demonstrating his theory of sensuality. Ō-kuni-nushi's traveling the country and wooing women was an integral part of governance. In order to bring the country together, Ō-kuni-nushi needed to call all the kami in Japan into his court, and the best way to accomplish this was to marry the shrine priestesses who served those kami.

Furthermore, the competence of the ruler—or in Orikuchi's words, the measure of their virtue—relied on how effectively they could manage the emotions, especially jealousy, of the numerous women in their life. In the myths from this chapter, Ō-kuni-nushi not only woos Nunakawa-hime, but then assuages his primary wife Suseri-bime when she is angry about his affairs. The ability to manage these relationships means, for Orikuchi, that Ō-kuni-nushi was an ideal ruler. Orikuchi went on to apply this theory to *The Tale of Genji*, a Japanese novel about a man with many sexual partners, and Orikuchi suggested that "sensuality" was the key theme in the novel. Also important for Orikuchi was that *The Tale of Genji* was written in a period when Buddhist and Confucian ideologies were politically influential. Both Buddhism and Confucianism look down on sensuality, and both are imports to Japan. For Orikuchi, this meant that *The Tale of Genji* was written as a kind of resistance piece centered on a uniquely Japanese virtue of sensuality. Identifying sensuality in myths thus served the argument that sensuality was a long-standing Japanese virtue.

Orikuchi's theory of sensuality is the centerpiece of a broader argument by literature scholar Kōnoshi Takamitsu (1946–) about the significance of Ō-kuni-nushi in *Ancient Matters*. Kōnoshi's text-centered model of scholarship unforgivingly rejected other interpretations of Japanese myths. To Kōnoshi, those interpretations either failed to grasp the nature of *Ancient Matters* as a text or strayed away from it in their sources. For example, rather than treating *Ancient*

*Matters, Chronicles, Izumo Fudoki,* etc. as a body of material for Japanese mythology, Kōnoshi argued that each of these written materials must be evaluated individually, as each is a different text. For this reason, Kōnoshi rejected the idea that the Susano-o and Ō-kuni-nushi narratives comprised an Izumo Cycle. Kōnoshi's method also involved a painstakingly close reading of the text. For example, to support his claim that there is no Izumo Cycle, Kōnoshi noted that when Ō-kuni-nushi prepared to leave Suseri-bime, the exact wording is "from Izumo up to Yamato." In Japanese, usually "up" signifies movement to the capital; in modern Japan the bullet train to Tokyo is called the "up train." This meant that the Ō-kuni-nushi narrative was centered on a Yamato perspective, with the emperor as the axis of the text and the world. As such, the Susano-o and Ō-kuni-nushi content in *Ancient Matters* cannot truly be called Izumo Mythology. Based on one word, Kōnoshi attempted to overturn a century of mythological study.

Focusing on individual texts ultimately led Kōnoshi to claim that *Ancient Matters* and *Chronicles* were fundamentally different stories. *Ancient Matters* is powered by an ideology of *musuhi,* or spontaneous growth, an element seen in the names of the first kami to appear in *Ancient Matters. Chronicles* is powered by a yin-yang ideology, and the first kami that appear in that text are not *musuhi*-aligned. Most importantly, in the main version of *Chronicles,* Izanami does not die. Izanagi and Izanami come together naturally like yin and yang, not because they are ordered to create the land by the heavenly gods. Since Izanami does not die in *Chronicles,* the creation of the land is complete, and the completion of creation by Ō-kuni-nushi is not included because it is unnecessary and does not make sense within the logic of the text.

Kōnoshi's interpretation of Ō-kuni-nushi in *Ancient Matters* hinges on his conviction that the *Ancient Matters* is a single textual narrative. Hence, even though Ō-kuni-nushi's story clearly falls into three sections, these must all be connected to a central narrative thrust. The first section covers Ō-ana-muji's fight with his brothers, his visit to Ne, and his transformation into the ruler of the land. The second includes his song exchanges with Nunakawa-hime and Suseri-bime. The third describes the completion of creation with the aid of other deities. Kōnoshi highlights the first and last sentences of the first section, "All of the brothers ultimately surrendered their claims to the Central Reed Plain Land to Ō-ana-muji, who became Ō-kuni-nushi. The reason is as follows" and "Then he began to fashion his land." Kōnoshi argues that the insertion of these passages clearly links the first section to the third, and moreover, reinforces reading the sections as a single story. The most important content in the first section is the fact that Ō-ana-muji used his wits to help the rabbit, demonstrating his superiority over his eighty brothers to the reader, and that Kamu-musuhi's intervention demonstrated that the generative power of *musuhi* was actively informing the narrative. Also of note is that Ō-ana-muji was not just put back together, but "transformed into an attractive young man," indicating that his resurrected form was superior to his earlier one. In the Land of Ne, Kōnoshi emphasizes that Suseri-bime's name is semantically related to Susano-o's name. Ō-ana-muji's marriage to Suseri-bime and bringing her back to the Central Reed Plain Land, along with Susano-o's weapons, was the capture of Susano-o's power. This power allowed Ō-ana-muji to transform into Ō-kuni-nushi and to finish the creation that was left incomplete by Izanagi and Izanami.

Kōnoshi devoted significant attention to the Land of Ne, Susano-o's realm. Kōnoshi noted that the standard explanation was that "ne" meant "root." This led to a natural presumption among mythology scholars that the Land of Ne was underground. Furthermore, the Land of Yomi, where Izanami goes after her death, was also presumed to be underground. Scholars often assumed that as such, Ne and Yomi were the same place. After all, Susano-o says that he wants to go the land of his mother, and he chases Ō-ana-muji to the pass that leads to Yomi. However, Kōnoshi argued that there is nothing indicating that "the pass that leads to Yomi" necessarily leads to somewhere underground. Furthermore, there is no real evidence that the Land of Ne and the Land of Yomi are necessarily the same location; rather they have the same entrance, the "pass that leads to Yomi." "Pass" is written with the character for "slope" in Japanese, but this is only because of the relation between the words "slope" (*saka*) and "border" (*sakai*). What is actually meant is the border of Yomi, and the Land of Ne is a place beyond that border. The full name of the Land of Ne in Japanese, *ne no katasu kuni*, contains the word *su* which can mean "sandbar," suggesting a land surrounded by water like an island, not a place underground. Finally, the meaning of "root" is not meant to refer to being underground, but rather just the extreme end of something, suggesting that the Land of Ne is some extremely far-off place. This far-off place is the counterpoint to the "Central Reed Plain Land," the Japanese archipelago.

Since Ō-kuni-nushi, at the end of part one, is identified as the great ruler who will finish making the land, Kōnoshi argued that part two, his romantic escapades, is meant to demonstrate his legitimacy and authority in that role. For Orikuchi, the virtue of sensuality was a characteristic of ancient Japan, before foreign influences like Buddhism and Confucianism made monogamy the norm. For Kōnoshi, the virtue of sensuality was that it confirmed Ō-kuni-nushi's status as the kami who will finish creating the land. The "distant, distant / land of Koshi" referred to in the first poem means that Yachi-hoko (Ō-kuni-nushi) rules the entire land, from his home in Izumo to the distant Koshi and every point in between. While difficult to capture in English translation, the same poem uses honorific language for the kami and begins in the third person, as if providing an evaluation or confirmation of the status of Yachi-hoko. The perspective then switches to that of Yachi-hoko, and Nunakawa-hime replies with her own poem in response to Yachi-hoko's complaints about the birds who signal the sunrise. In the end, their marriage is consummated. In the next set of poems, Yachi-hoko assuages his primary wife Suseri-bime, who is upset that he has wives all over the land. His ability to calm her jealousy demonstrates not only the virtue of sensuality, but also confirms that he is truly "Ō-kuni-nushi," the "great master of the land."

Kōnoshi argued that parts one and two function to establish and emphasize that Ō-kuni-nushi is the kami who completes the creation of the land in part three. This creation has three stages. First, Ō-kuni-nushi "began to fashion his land" at the end of part one. Then, he combined his power with Sukuna-bikona to "finish creating his realm," and finally, the spirit later enshrined at Mt. Miwa helped him to "finish creating the land." For Kōnoshi, the significance of Sukuna-bikona was that he is the son of Kamu-musuhi, meaning that the generative power of *musuhi* is still an active force helping Ō-kuni-nushi finish creation. Moreover, Kamu-musuhi's involvement is the extension of the original order from the heavenly gods first received by Izanagi and Izanami to create the land. The god enshrined in Mt. Miwa, a mountain in the Yamato Basin near the eighth-century imperial court, meant for Kōnoshi that this mythical narrative had Yamato at its center and did not constitute a part of the Izumo Mythology. Notably, it was only with the aid of the Yamato kami that Ō-kuni-nushi was able to complete creation. Based on a literary reading of *Ancient Matters*, the entirety of events, from Izanagi and Izanami to Ō-kuni-nushi, tells the story of how the land was created. Put differently, the story tells the mythological origins of the emperor's realm, which was created through the efforts and interventions of the heavenly gods.

## Other Major Topics

### Dragon Slaying

In Jungian analysis, the slaying of a dragon is the symbolic victory of the hero archetype over the dragon and the rescue of the princess. Insofar as the princess represents something valuable and important that must be captured to secure the future, the rescue of Kushi-ina-da-hime, "miraculous rice ear paddy lady," is unusually suggestive of the importance of agriculture for the advancement of human civilization. The dragon is known for hoarding, and if the eight-headed serpent is meant to evoke the Hi River, then the power of the river, that is, its water, must be claimed by the hero in order to irrigate the fields.

## Anatomy of Kami in Shinto

In the conversation between Ō-kuni-nushi and the kami that will later be enshrined at Mt. Miwa, the mysterious kami tells Ō-kuni-nushi that he is his spirit of fortune (*saki-mitama, sachi-mitama*) and spirit of discernment (*kushi-mitama*). Spirit of discernment could also be translated as "spirit of miracles," using the same "kushi" that appears in the name Kushi-ina-da-hime. In the Jingū myth (Chapter 4), Amaterasu identifies her "spirit of violence" (*ara-mitama*) and her "spirit of peace" (*nigi-mitama*), suggesting four kinds of spirits all associated with the "soul" (*mitama*). One theory is that a kami is comprised of these four spirits. Because human beings and other things can also be kami, this anatomy applies not only to the kami described in these myths, but to all kami in the world. Debates surrounding these spirits and their relation to the human soul were especially popular in the nineteenth century in Japan, as Shinto theologians developed a metaphysical basis for the religion that was based on the myths in *Ancient Matters* and *Chronicles* and not on Buddhist, Confucian, or Daoist understanding about the nature of reality.

## The Unseen World

Another important touchstone for nineteenth-century Shinto theologians was Ō-kuni-nushi's statement to Futsu-nushi that he would retreat and rule over the realm of the unseen. The suggestion in the original text is that in contrast to Ninigi, who would rule over the Japanese archipelago and establish the foundation for an empire, Ō-kuni-nushi would rule over divine matters related to kami. While not discussed in the text of the original myths, eventually the belief that all the kami gathered in Izumo in the tenth month of the year led to a general perception that Ō-kuni-nushi was chief among the kami of Japan.

## Early Funerary Rituals

The various roles assigned to the birds for Ame-waka-hiko's funeral have led folklorists to theorize how the ancient Japanese buried their dead. However, because *Ancient Matters* and *Chronicles* are not unified in how they describe these roles, it is not possible to make conclusions with a strong level of certainty.

## The Feast of First Rice

The fact that Ame-waka-hiko was laying down following the Feast of First Rice hints that he had illicitly taken power for himself and was assuming the role of emperor. The Feast of First Rice is an important ritual ceremony in which the Japanese emperor participates to this day. Closely associated is the Daijōsai, the first Feast of First Rice following a new enthronement. During this special ceremony, the new emperor is required to spend the night in a uniquely constructed compound. Based on Orikuchi's theory of the "one night wife," the prevailing popular opinion is that the purpose of this overnight visit is so that Amaterasu can visit the new emperor and spend the night with the usually male emperor. However, the text of the myths in *Ancient Matters* and *Chronicles* does not directly support Orikuchi's hypothesis.

# 3

# Foundation Myths for the Japanese Empire

## Japanese Founding Myths

### Descent of Ninigi

The time for Ninigi to descend from heaven came at last. Sources differ on what and whom Ninigi brought with him when he came down from heaven, but they all have him land in Takachiho, a mountain on Japan's southern island of Kyushu.

According to *Chronicles*, Taka-mi-musuhi draped Ninigi with a dazzling cloak and sent him down from heaven. Ninigi pushed apart the eight-fold clouds of heaven, cleared the way ahead of him, and descended to the peak of Takachiho in Himuka, present-day Miyazaki Prefecture. From there, he crossed the floating bridge of heaven and went west, peak to peak, across a succession of hills as he searched for the land he was to rule over. After crossing through an empty land, at last, he arrived at Cape Kasasa in Nagaya, in the region of Ata, on the southwest coast of Kyushu.

According to *Chronicles* 9.1, Amaterasu was preparing to make her son Oshi-ho-mimi descend, but during their preparations, her grandson, Ninigi, was born. Oshi-ho-mimi asked Amaterasu to send Ninigi in his place, and she agreed. She then bestowed three treasures upon Ninigi: a comma-shaped jewel called a *magatama*; a large eight-span mirror; and the sword Kusanagi, which Susano-o had

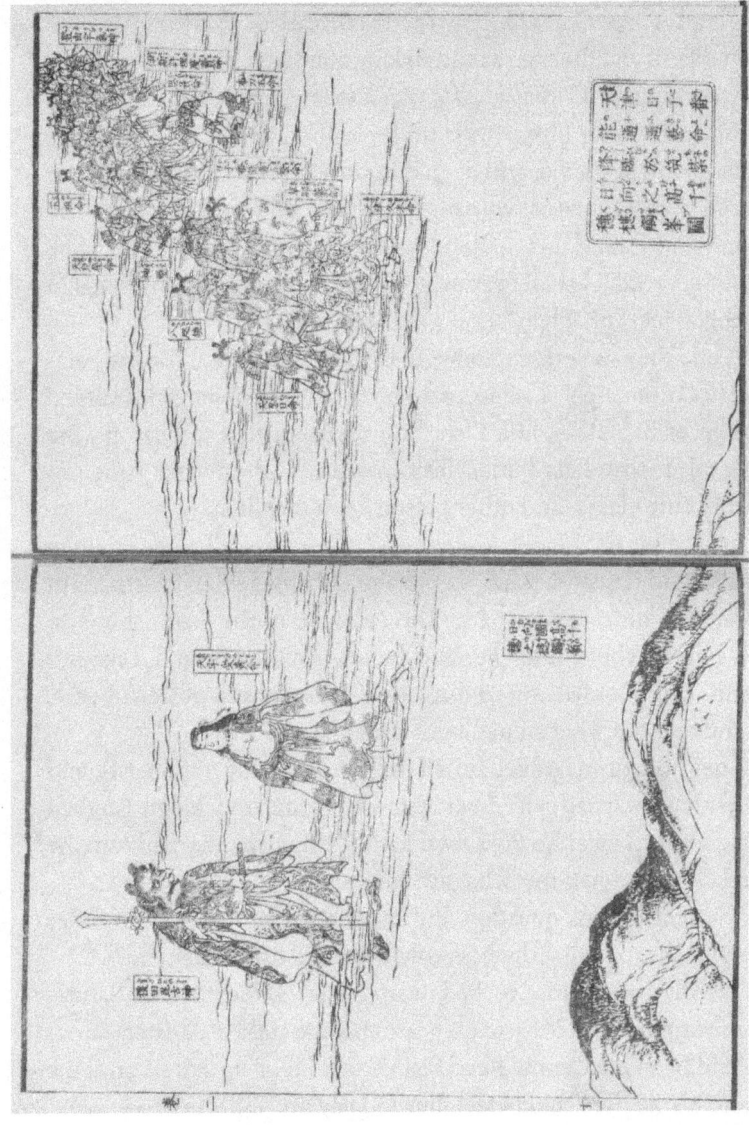

**FIGURE 8** Descent of Ninigi. Utagawa Kuniyoshi, 1860 Nihonkoku kaibyaku yurai ki, vol. 2, 10–11. National Diet Library.

found in the body of the eight-headed snake he killed in Izumo. Amaterasu told Ninigi, "You are destined to rule the abundant reed plain land where rice will grow for 1500 years of harvests. May the prosperity of your line never end so long as heaven and earth endure."

According to *Chronicles* 9.2, Amaterasu gave Oshi-ho-mimi a mirror, instructing him, "My son, look upon this mirror as if you were looking upon me, and keep it in the same room that you sleep in as an object for ritual worship." She then told the kami Ame-no-koyane and Futo-dama, "Attend on my son and protect him." She further decreed, "I shall bestow upon my son rice from my fields in the High Heavenly Plain."

While they were descending, Oshi-ho-mimi's wife, Yorozu-hata-hime (Taku-hata-chi-ji-hime), gave birth to Ninigi. Ninigi descended in place of his father, and Oshi-ho-mimi returned to heaven. The father of Yorozu-hata-hime, Taka-mi-musuhi, bestowed Ame-no-koyane, Futo-dama, and other patron kami on Ninigi.

According to *Ancient Matters* and *Chronicles* 9.1, when Ninigi was about to descend, there was a kami occupying the crossroads of heaven and blocking his path. The radiance of this kami shone to both heaven above and the land below. Amaterasu and Taka-mi-musuhi commanded Ame-no-uzu-me, "You have a powerful gaze. Go and find out what kami blocks the crossing."

Ame-no-uzu-me pulled down her top, exposing her breasts, and slid her high-waisted skirt down to her hips, then mockingly laughed as she went to face the unknown kami. When she reached him, he asked, "Ame-no-uzu-me, what are you doing?"

She ignored his question and instead asked him, "Who dares occupies the road that the heavenly kami will use to descend?"

The kami on the road replied, "I am an earthly kami named Saruta-hiko, meaning 'Lord of Saruta.' I heard that the child of Amaterasu was descending to the Central Reed Plain Land. I took up a position at the crossroads so that I could greet him and pay my respects."

Ame-no-uzu-me asked him, "Should I go down before you, or will you go before me?"

He replied, "I will go first and clear the way."

She asked, "Which way will you go, and where should the heavenly kami go?"

He replied, "The heir of the heavenly kami should go to Takachiho in Himuka. I will go to the headwaters of the Isuzu River in Ise. Since you revealed my identity, you should see me to my destination." Ame-no-uzu-me did as he requested and saw him to Ise. Ninigi bestowed the hereditary title of "Kimi of Sarume" on Ame-no-uzu-me and her descendants.[1]

According to *Ancient Matters*, later, Saruta-hiko was fishing at Azasa when he got his hand stuck in a clam and drowned. Separately, Ame-no-uzu-me was returning after having seen Saruta-hiko to Ise when she summoned all the fish of the sea and asked them, "Will you serve the descendant of the heavenly kami?"

Almost all of the fish replied, "We will."

Only the sea cucumber refused. Ame-no-uzu-me said, "See the fate of a mouth that will not speak." Then she drew a dagger and slit the sea cucumber's mouth. Even today, the mouth of the sea cucumber is split, and when Shima Province presents its offerings of fish to the imperial throne, those offerings are then given to the Kimi of Sarume. Shima Province is the southeastern part of present-day Mie Prefecture, near Ise, where Saruta-hiko drowned.

According to *Ancient Matters*, Amaterasu assigned five patron kami to descend along with Ninigi: Ame-no-koyane, Futo-dama, Ame-no-uzu-me, the blacksmith kami Ishi-kori-dome, and the jewelry-making kami Tama-no-oya.[2] Amaterasu also gave Ninigi the eight-span magatama and mirror that were used when the kami lured her out of the heavenly rock cave and the sword Kusanagi that Susano-o had found in the body of the eight-headed snake. Then she assigned the kami Omoi-kane, Ta-jikara-o, and Ame-no-iwa-to-wake,

---

[1] Kimi was a title granted in ancient Japan to rulers of provinces outside the immediate area ruled by the imperial court.

[2] These kami were involved in luring Amaterasu out of the heavenly rock cave.

meaning "lord of the heavenly rock door," to accompany Ninigi. She ordered these three kami, instructing them, "Worship this mirror as if worshipping my very soul. Omoi-kane shall be in charge of my worship."

Omoi-kane and Ninigi then set up the Isuzu Shrine and worshipped her. The kami Toyo-uke-bime, meaning "rich food lady," was enshrined at the outer shrine. Ame-no-iwa-to-wake was named kami of gates. Ta-jikara-o was enshrined in Sana District. Ame-no-koyane is the ancestor of the Nakatomi clan. Futo-dama is the ancestor of the Inbe clan. Ame-no-uzu-me is the ancestor of the Kimi of Sarume. Ishi-kori-dome is the ancestor of the Muraji of Mirror-makers. Tama-no-oya is the ancestor of the Muraji of Jewelers.[3]

When Ninigi descended, the kami Ame-no-oshi-hi and Ama-tsu-kume took up arms and served as the vanguard for his descent.

At Cape Kasasa, Ninigi encountered an earthly kami named Koto-katsu-kuni-katsu-naga-sa, meaning "matters winning land winning long and narrow." The kami represented Cape Kasasa. Ninigi asked this kami, "Is there land here?"

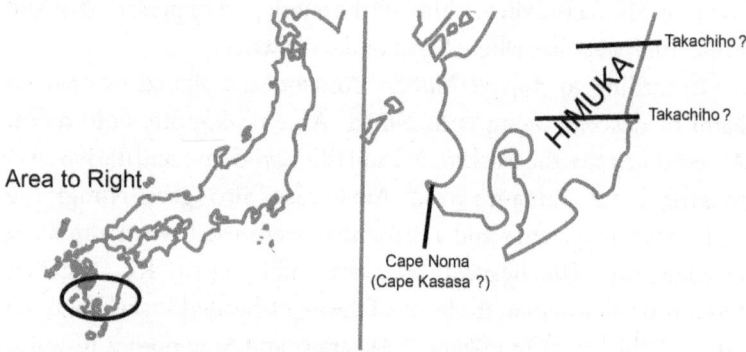

**MAP 3** Ninigi's Descent to Cape Kasasa.

---

[3] Muraji was a title granted in ancient Japan to officials in charge of clans who either produced specific goods or specialized in a type of service, including military service.

The kami replied, "There is land. Please go forth as you please." And so Ninigi continued on and dwelled there.

One day, Ninigi met a beautiful woman. He asked her, "Whose daughter are you?"

She replied, "I am the daughter of the earthly kami Ō-yama-tsu-mi, meaning 'great mountain spirit.' My name is Kamu-ata-tsu-hime, meaning 'divine lady of Ata.' I am also called Kashi-tsu-hime, meaning 'lady of Kashi,' and Ko-no-hana-saku-ya-hime, meaning 'lady of flowering trees and blossoms.' According to *Chronicles*, she said, "I am the daughter of a heavenly kami who married Ō-yama-tsu-mi."[4]

Then Ninigi asked her, "Do you have any siblings?"

She replied, "I have an older sister named Iwa-naga-hime, meaning 'Lady of Long Rocks.'" Ninigi proposed to Kamu-ata-tsu-hime on the spot, but she told him to ask her father first. When he did, her father graciously accepted Ninigi's proposal, but insisted that he marry Kamu-ata-tsu-hime's older sister Iwa-naga-hime as well.

Ninigi agreed, but when he met Iwa-naga-hime, he saw that she was very ugly and sent her back to her father. Her father was deeply shamed. He said, "I had you marry both of my daughters so that your descendants would be long-lived and hardy like the rocks and flourishing and numerous like the flowers. However, since you have only taken Kamu-ata-tsu-hime, the lifespans of your descendants will be short, like the blossoms on a flowering tree."

After only one night, Kamu-ata-tsu-hime became pregnant. This made Ninigi suspicious, and he told her, "Heavenly kami though I may be, how could you be pregnant after only one night together? The child you carry is surely not mine."

Kamu-ata-tsu-hime was enraged, and so she built a small earthen chamber and sealed off the only entrance. Then she said, "If the child I carry is yours, then it will not be hurt by the flames. If the child I carry is not yours, then it will die." She lit a fire inside the sealed

---

[4] This line is only in the main version of *Chronicles*. In *Chronicles*, there are many children of heavenly deities in the archipelago, but in *Account*, Ninigi is special as a heavenly kami.

chamber. At that moment, she gave birth to children. The older was called Ho-deri, meaning "bright flame," or Ho-no-suseri, meaning "raging flame." The younger was called Ho-ori, meaning "spreading flame," or Hiko-ho-ho-demi, meaning "lord of the emerging spirit of many rice ears." Sources also record other brothers with varying names and birth order, but they are not part of the extended narrative.

According to *Chronicles* 9.6, after the children were born, Kamu-ata-tsu-hime was proved true, and she resented Ninigi for doubting her and would not speak with him. Saddened, Ninigi wrote this poem:

> The seaweed from the depths of the sea
> draws near to the beach,
> but she has no intention of drawing near
> to our shared bed
> or emulating the mated plovers of the beach!

After a long time, Ninigi died. He is buried in E Tomb, now the Nitta Shrine in Satsumasendai City, Kagoshima Prefecture.

## Yama-sachi-hiko and the Palace of the Sea God

The older brother, Ho-deri, had a talent for fishing and was popularly known as Umi-sachi-hiko, meaning "luck of the sea." The younger brother, Ho-ori, had a talent for hunting and was popularly known as Yama-sachi-hiko, meaning "luck of the mountains." One day, they tried to exchange their talents. Umi-sachi-hiko gave Yama-sachi-hiko his fishing tackle, and Yama-sachi-hiko gave Umi-sachi-hiko his bow and arrows. However, when Umi-sachi-hiko tried his hand at hunting, he failed to shoot any game. Yama-sachi-hiko not only failed to catch any fish, but he also lost his older brother's fishhook at sea.

Since their experiment failed, the two brothers decided to return each other's talents. Umi-sachi-hiko gave Yama-sachi-hiko back his bow and arrows, but Yama-sachi-hiko had to tell Umi-sachi-hiko that he had lost his fishhook. Because he felt bad about losing the hook, Yama-sachi-hiko broke down his sword to forge an entire basket full of new fishhooks. But when he tried to give it to Umi-sachi-hiko, his older brother said, "I won't take this. I won't take anything other than my original hook."

Yama-sachi-hiko was beside himself and went to the seaside to cry.

According to *Chronicles* 10.2, while Yama-sachi-hiko was on the beach, he saw a goose caught in a trap. Being filled with sympathy, he set the goose free.

While Yama-sachi-hiko was crying on the beach, he was approached by an old man named Shio-tsu-chi, meaning "sea current spirit." The old man asked him, "Why are you crying here?"

Yama-sachi-hiko explained what had happened and the old man said, "Don't worry. Leave everything to me." Then he made a watertight basket, told Yama-sachi-hiko to get inside, and cast the basket to sea. As he pushed him off, the old man told Yama-sachi-hiko, "This basket will be carried by the ocean currents and eventually, you will reach a beach. When you arrive at the beach, get out of the basket and walk until you reach a palace. The palace is the home of Wata-tsu-mi, the kami of the sea. Outside the palace gate there is a tree next to a well. Climb to the top of the tree and wait there for the daughter of Wata-tsu-mi."

According to *Ancient Matters*, the basket floated across the surface of the water and eventually made its way to a charming little beach. According to *Chronicles*, the old man submerged the basket, and it went to the bottom of the ocean, where it arrived at a charming little beach. According to *Chronicles* 10.4, the old man took Yama-sachi-hiko to meet a giant shark that was eight meters long, a shark that the kami of the sea used as a mount. When they reached the shark, the old man asked, "How long will it take you to reach the palace of the sea kami?"

The eight-meter shark said, "I could deliver the descendant of the heavenly gods to the palace of the sea kami in eight days. However, there is a one-meter shark that the sea kami also rides, and he could make the journey in one day. I'll go to sea and tell the one-meter shark to come back here. Ride this shark and he will deliver you to a charming little beach. Follow the beach and you will arrive at the palace of the sea kami. There is a tree growing near the well by the palace gate. Climb the tree and wait there."

Yama-sachi-hiko did as instructed, and sure enough, he arrived at the palace of the sea kami. He found the tree and waited for some-one to find him. Shortly thereafter, a beautiful young woman came out of the gate and went to draw water from the well. She was star-tled to see Yama-sachi-hiko's reflection in the well water and ran back inside to tell her father, the sea kami, what had happened. The sea kami invited Yama-sachi-hiko inside and treated him with the utmost courtesy. Then he asked Yama-sachi-hiko why he had come.

Yama-sachi-hiko explained the reason he had come to the sea kami, and so Wata-tsu-mi summoned all the fish of the sea and asked them if they knew anything about the missing fishhook. The fish all said, "We have no idea. However, the seabream has a sore mouth and could not answer your summons." Wata-tsu-mi then called the seabream to the palace and they searched her mouth, where they found the missing fishhook.

Wata-tsu-mi also arranged for Yama-sachi-hiko to marry his daughter Toyo-tama-hime, meaning "rich jewel lady." It was Toyo-tama-hime who had first seen Yama-sachi-hiko at the palace well. And so happily married, Yama-sachi-hiko stayed in the palace of his father-in-law for three years. Though he wanted for nothing, in time, he began to feel homesick. Toyo-tama-hime heard his occasional sigh and told her father, "I think that Yama-sachi-hiko would like to return to his homeland."

The sea kami arranged for a shark to carry Yama-sachi-hiko back home. Before he left, Wata-tsu-mi gave Yama-sachi-hiko a set of instructions, saying, "Descendant of the heavenly gods, when you

**FIGURE 9**  Toyo-tama-hime and Tama-yori-bime. Totoya Hokkei, *c.*1826. Rijksmuseum.

give this fishhook back to your brother, lay a curse on it by calling it a hook of poverty and hunger. Then turn your back to him and throw it to him over your back. Also, I will give you two magical jewels, the jewel of the high tide and the jewel of the low tide. You can use these two jewels to torment your brother and force him to surrender."

According to *Chronicles* 10.3, Wata-tsu-mi said, "Because I am the god of the waters, if your brother makes rice paddies in high places, make yours in low places and I will see that there is not enough water for his paddies to flourish. If your brother makes his rice paddies in low places, then build yours in high places, and I will see that there is too much water and that his fields flood."

According to *Chronicles* 10.4, Wata-tsu-mi said, "When your older brother goes out to sea to fish, go to the beach and hum. When you do, I will raise a fierce wind and swift waves to drown him."

Toyo-tama-hime also stopped Yama-sachi-hiko before he left and told him, "I am pregnant with our child. I'd like you to build a birthing hut on the beach for me. On a day when the wind is fierce and the waves are high, I will come out of the ocean and use the hut to give birth."

Yama-sachi-hiko returned to the Central Reed Plain Land and gave Umi-sachi-hiko's fishhook back to him. When he did, he cursed it, just as the sea kami had instructed him. In time, Umi-sachi-hiko became poorer and poorer. The fishhook he had used to bring in a bounty from the sea was cursed, and his rice paddies never had the right amount of water to flourish. Umi-sachi-hiko confronted Yama-sachi-hiko, and Yama-sachi-hiko used the two jewels that the sea kami had given him to torment his older brother. When he raised the jewel of the high tide, the tide swelled in, drowning Umi-sachi-hiko. Umi-sachi-hiko begged Yama-sachi-hiko to save his life, and so Yama-sachi-hiko raised the jewel of the low tide and saved him.

According to *Chronicles* 10.2, after Umi-sachi-hiko had surrendered to his younger brother, he went back on his word, saying, "How can the older brother serve the younger?" Yama-sachi-hiko raised the jewel of the high tide again, and when Umi-sachi-hiko saw it, he ran and climbed a high mountain to escape the tide. However, the water kept coming. Umi-sachi-hiko then climbed a tree atop the mountain to escape, but the water kept coming. And then, when the tide overtook the tree, he surrendered to his younger brother again, this time pledging to serve him for the rest of his life. Yama-sachi-hiko raised the jewel of the low tide to send the water back to sea. Umi-sachi-hiko is the ancestor of the Hayato, who serve as guards at the imperial palace. The reason they are never far from the emperor is because of Umi-sachi-hiko's surrender. The Hayato were an ethnic group living in the far south of Kyushu.

According to *Chronicles* 10.4, when Umi-sachi-hiko surrendered, he stripped down to his loincloth, smeared clay on his hands and face, and told Yama-sachi-hiko, "For the rest of my life I will serve as your jester." Then he performed a dance. First, he walked around on his tip toes like he did when the water reached his feet. Then, he raised his feet up, taking big steps, like he did when the water reached his knees. Then, he pretended to be sloshing about as if the water had reached his thighs. Next, he twisted his waist, pretending that the water had reached his hips. Then, he put his hands on his chest, simulating the water coming up to his sides. Finally, he put his hands over his head and flapped them about, as he did when the water came to his neck. Even now, the Hayato perform this dance at the imperial palace.

Later, on a day that the wind and waves were high, Toyo-tama-hime came out of the ocean just as she had promised, riding a great turtle. She was accompanied by her younger sister, Tama-yori-hime, meaning "spirit drawing lady." They met Yama-sachi-hiko at the birthing hut that he had built on the beach, and then Toyo-tama-hime told him, "I'm going to go inside to give birth. Whatever you do, do not look inside."

Yama-sachi-hiko could not resist and tried to secretly spy on her. When he looked inside, Toyo-tama-hime had transformed into an eight-meter sea monster and was wriggling on the ground. When the birth was finished, Toyo-tama-hime told Yama-sachi-hiko, "You have shamed me, and I cannot bear to be together with you any longer." She returned to the sea and closed off the passage connecting the world of the sea to the Central Reed Plain Land. She left her younger sister Tama-yori-hime to look after the child, who she named Hiko-nagisa-take-u-gaya-fuki-aezu, meaning "valiant lord of the beach of cormorant feather thatching that is not connected." He is usually called Fuki-aezu. Toyo-tama-hime gave him this name because the cormorant feathers that Yama-sachi-hiko used to thatch the birthing hut did not completely cover the roof.

After a long time, Yama-sachi-hiko died. He is buried on Mt. Takaya in Himuka, present-day Kirishima City, Kagoshima Prefecture.

Fuki-aezu later married his aunt, Tama-yori-hime, and she gave birth to four sons. The oldest was Itsu-se, who later died in combat. Next was Ina-hi, who returned to the sea. Next was Mike-iri-no, who went to the Land of Tokoyo. Last was Kamu-yamato-iware-hiko, usually known as Jinmu. Jinmu was the first and founding emperor of Japan.

After a long time, Fuki-aezu died. He is buried on Mt. Aira in Himuka, present-day Kanoya City, Kagoshima Prefecture.

## Jinmu

When Jinmu grew up, he married Ahira-tsu-hime from the village of Ata in Himuka Province, and she gave birth to a son, Ta-gishi-mimi.

According to *Chronicles*, in 667 BCE, when Jinmu was forty-five years old, he told his older brothers and his son,

"In ancient times, the heavenly kami Taka-mi-musuhi and Amaterasu bestowed the Central Reed Plain Land on their grandson, my heavenly ancestor and great-grandfather, Ninigi. Ninigi descended from heaven and ruled this land from here in Kyushu. His son, my grandfather, succeeded him, and then my father, Fuki-aezu, took the throne. However, the lands far away from here still do not enjoy the civilizing influence of our kingly rule. Every town has its ruler, every village has its chief, and they all compete and fight with each other Also, I heard from old man Shio-tsu-chi that far to the east, there is a beautiful land surrounded by mountains. A long time ago, someone from heaven flew down to that land riding a stone boat. I think the person who came down is Nigi-hayahi, and I think that that land would be the perfect place to build my capital."

Jinmu's brothers all agreed with him, and they began preparations to depart.

Jinmu, his brothers, and his son formed an armada and sailed eastwards to found their new state. The first place they arrived was a port called Hayasui, where they met a fisherman riding a turtle. Jinmu asked the fisherman, "Who are you?" The fisherman replied that he was an earthly kami called Uzu-hiko. Jinmu asked the fisherman if he could guide the armada, and the fisherman said that he could. They gave him a long wooden rod, and he used it to guide Jinmu's boat by stretching the rod between his boat and Jinmu's. In gratitude, Jinmu renamed the fisherman Sao-ne-tsu-hiko, meaning "Lord of the Rod."

Continuing his journey, Jinmu next arrived in Usa, present-day Usa City, Oita Prefecture. There, he was welcomed by the local kami. Jinmu then arrived at the port of Oka, present-day Fukuoka City. From there Jinmu moved on to Aki, present-day Hiroshima, where he built a palace and spent the winter.

The next spring, 666 BCE, Jinmu and the armada made for Kibi, where they built Takashima Palace. During the next three years, they prepared their forces and stored up rations for the coming attack.

In 663 BCE, the armada set forth from Kibi and arrived at Naniwa, present-day Osaka City. They traveled up the Yodo River to move

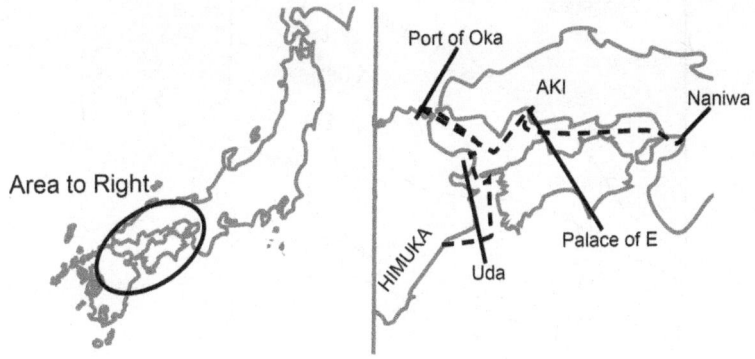

**MAP 4** Jinmu from Kyushu to Naniwa.

further inland, then disembarked to move into the Nara Basin, where Jinmu would build his new capital. At first, they tried to go south around the Ikoma mountain range that blocked their path, but because the road was very narrow, they could not pass through in formation. Jinmu decided that they should transverse the range instead, and so they backtracked to Mt. Ikoma and went due east to cross into the Nara Basin.

The chieftain who ruled the Nara area at that time, Naga-sune-hiko, was a descendant of the kami Nigi-hayahi. Naga-sune-hiko thought that Jinmu had come to steal his land, and so he blockaded Jinmu's entrance to the Nara Basin at Kusae Hill, where the two sides fought.

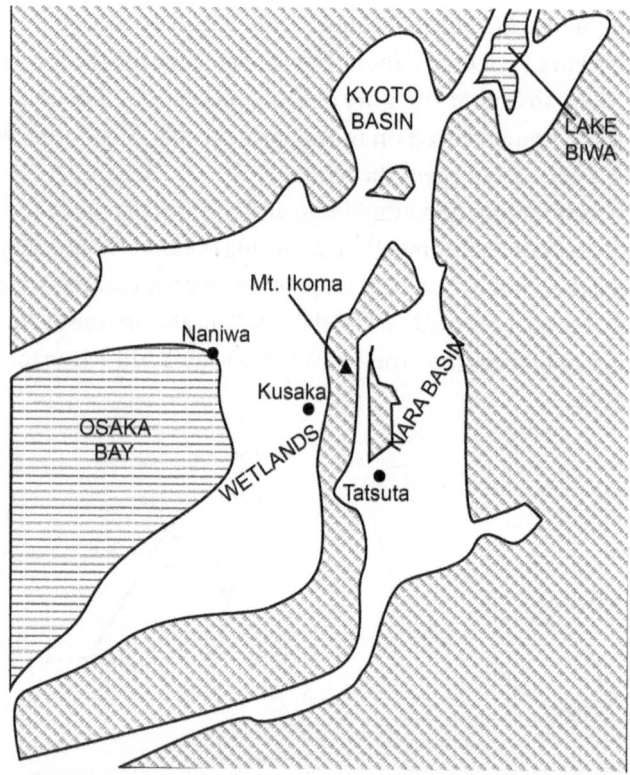

**MAP 5** Jinmu Attempts to Enter Nara from the West.

Jinmu's forces were unable to break through the blockade. Also, Jinmu's older brother Itsu-se was hit in the leg by an arrow. According to *Ancient Matters*, he was hit in the hand by an arrow. Realizing that this strategy was not going to work, Jinmu said to his forces, "This approach was a mistake. I am a descendant of the sun kami, and yet I attacked from west to east, going against the natural movement of my ancestor. For now, let us feign a retreat, then we will worship the kami of heaven and earth, find a way to put the sun at our backs, and overrun our enemies as if we were walking on our shadows."

Jinmu and his forces retreated to their boats and set back to sea. Then, port by port, they made their way around the Kii Peninsula. Itsu-se died on the march from his wound. In Kumano, the armada met with rough waves, and Jinmu's older brother Ina-hi dove into the sea with his sword, saying. "Am I not a descendant of the sea kami on my mother's side? Why would my ancestors cause me such trouble?"

Jinmu's older brother Mike-iri-no said, "I, too, am a descendant of the sea kami." Then he stepped off the boat and walked on the waves, crossing the sea to the Land of Tokoyo.

Jinmu's brothers were all gone. Jinmu and his son, Ta-gishi-mimi, landed the army in Kumano, where they met an evil spirit that spewed poisonous gas. The entire army was sickened and could no longer advance.

There was a man in Kumano named Taka-kura-ji, and he had a dream in which Amaterasu told Take-mikazuchi, "I thought that you had pacified the Central Reed Plain Land! I still hear the clamor of fighting. Go back and finish what you started."

Take-mikazuchi replied, "I will send my sword, and it will finish conquering the land." Then he said to Taka-kura-ji, "I dropped my sword in the back of your storehouse. Retrieve it and present it to Jinmu." Taka-kura-ji did as he was instructed. At that time, the emperor had fallen into a deep sleep, but when he was presented with the sword, he snapped awake along with all of his soldiers.

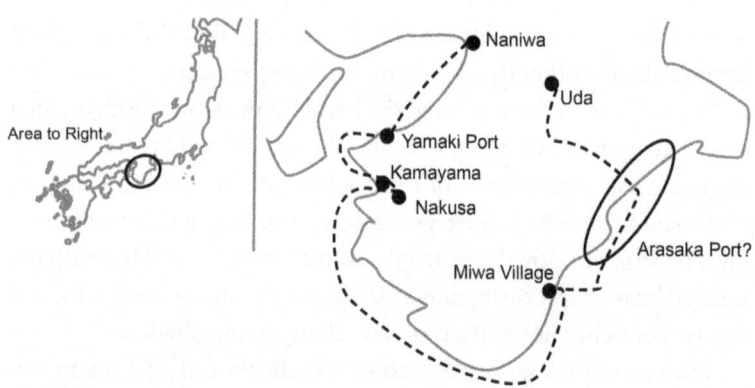

**MAP 6** Jinmu from Naniwa to Uda.

At this point, Jinmu was ready to lead his army into the Nara Basin, now from the east. However, the mountains blocking his path were steep and dense, and there was no route going through them. Amaterasu spoke to Jinmu in a dream, saying, "I will send the three-legged crow Ya-ta-garasu, who will guide you through the mountains." According to *Ancient Matters*, it was Taka-mi-musuhi who sent Ya-ta-garasu to Jinmu. Jinmu's servant Michi-no-omi, meaning "master of the way," followed the crow and led Jinmu's army through the mountains. At last, they arrived in Uda, near the southeastern edge of the Nara basin.

When Jinmu arrived in Uda, he promptly summoned the two chieftains of that region, a pair of brothers named E-ukashi and Oto-ukashi. The older brother, E-ukashi, did not answer Jinmu's summons, but the younger brother came right away. He told Jinmu, "My older brother is planning to resist your forces. At first, he raised troops and was going to attack, but when he saw your army, he knew that he would be no match and so he put all of his troops into hiding and built a new palace. He plans to invite you to this new palace for a feast, but inside, he's rigged a booby trap that he will use to kill you."

Jinmu sent Michi-no-omi to investigate this palace, and Michi-no-omi confirmed that Oto-ukashi was telling the truth. Michi-no-omi confronted the older brother, and when they came to blows, Michi-no-omi chased him inside the palace, where he stepped into his own trap and died. Michi-no-omi retrieved the body and decapitated it.

When Michi-no-omi got back to camp, Oto-ukashi threw a feast for the army. Jinmu composed a song that went,

> At the high hunting ground in Uda,
> I wait upon the sandpiper, whose trap I strung.
> I caught no sandpiper; I caught a whale!
> If your first wife asks for trimmings,
> carve a side with no meat to it,
> like a beechnut.
> If your second wife asks for trimmings,
> carve a side abundant and meaty,
> like an acorn.

This is called a "Kume Song," named after the Kume clan of warriors who were part of Jinmu's army. The whale stands for the older brother, and the second wife, which Jinmu prefers, stands for the younger brother. This song is still performed at court.

Having conquered the chieftains of Uda, Jinmu climbed to the peak of Mt. Takakura to survey his approach into the Nara Basin. A narrow river valley led into the southeast corner of the basin, but from where Jinmu stood, he could see that enemies had fortified four hills along the pass as well as set up an encampment in Iware Village. All of the roads were blocked, and there was no way to get through.

Jinmu prayed to the kami of heaven, and they spoke to him in a dream, saying, "Collect clay from Mt. Kagu and use it to make eighty plates and eighty jars. Then use those vessels to present offerings to the kami of heaven, curse your enemies, and those who oppose you will be vanquished." When Jinmu awoke, Oto-ukashi told him, "There are many enemies in this land planning to resist you. If you can collect clay from Mt. Kagu and make plates and jars for offerings to the heavenly kami, you will be able to sweep your enemies before you."

Jinmu was overjoyed that the portent he had seen in his own dream was confirmed. He made the fisherman who had guided his boat back in Hayasui, Sao-ne-tsu-hiko, put on ragged clothes and a straw raincoat, disguising him as an old man. Oto-ukashi put a grain sifter on his head like a hat, disguising him as an old woman. Jinmu told the two to go in secret to Mt. Kagu and collect the clay that he needed to make the plates and jars.

Sao-ne-tsu-hiko and Oto-ukashi set out for Mt. Kagu, but enemy troops filled the roads, and there was no way for them to get past. Then Sao-ne-tsu-hiko said, "If Jinmu is truly destined to found a new state, then somehow or another, we will be able to get past our enemies." The two went forward.

A group of enemies stopped them in the road, but then said, "Look how disgusting this old man and old woman are!" The enemies got out of the road so that the two could pass by. They made it to Mt. Kagu, retrieved the clay, and returned to Jinmu.

Jinmu used the clay to make the plates and jars, then went to the headwaters of the Yoshino River, and venerated the kami of heaven and earth. After that, he went to the Uda River and cursed his enemies. Then he performed two tests. First, he said, "I'm going to use the eighty plates that I made to make sweets. If I can make these sweets without using any water, then I will be able to conquer my enemies as a matter of course." The sweets formed all on their own. Second, he said, "I'm going to submerge the jars that I made in the river. If the fish become intoxicated and float along with the current, then my enemies will also be swept away before me." When he threw the jars in the river, the fish floated to the surface and were carried away by the current.

Jinmu set out to attack the four hills that his enemies had fortified, starting with Kunimi Hill. Jinmu's army broke through the enemy forces and executed their general. Carried by his victory, Jinmu composed a song. It went,

> Like snails that crawl about
> on the great boulders of Ise,
> (where the divine winds blow),
> like snails, my troops,
> my troops, like snails,
> that crawl about,
> strike now and end them,
> strike now and end them!

Then Jinmu made a plan to trick the remnants of his foes. He told Michi-no-omi to take a detachment of the Kume warrior clan and build a great feast hall, then to hold a banquet for the enemy. Michi-no-omi built the hall and mixed his bravest soldiers among the enemy at the feast. He told them that after he had a few rounds, he would stand up and sing. When they heard his singing, they were to immediately draw their swords and strike down their enemies. Once the enemy soldiers were drunk, Michi-no-omi got to his feet and sang,

> In the great building in Osaka,
> no matter how many people are inside,
> no matter how many people come inside,
> fiercely, fiercely the young Kume
> hold their pommeled swords,
> their pommeled swords,
> strike now and end them!

The Kume drew their swords and killed the enemy so not one remained. After this, Jinmu's forces routed the enemy at their other fortifications, and Jinmu's army prepared to move into the Nara Basin and confront Naga-sune-hiko again.

When Jinmu and Naga-sune-hiko's forces met on the field, neither was able to gain any ground against the other. Then all of a sudden, the sky went dark, and it began to hail. A golden kite flew down to the tip of Jinmu's bow, and shone so brilliantly in the darkness that all Naga-sune-hiko's soldiers were blinded and lost their way.

His troops in disarray, Naga-sune-hiko sent a message to Jinmu that said, "A long time ago, the heavenly kami Nigi-hayahi came to this land riding a heavenly rock boat. He married my younger sister and I serve him as my liege lord. You say that you are the descendant of the heavenly kami and therefore are the legitimate ruler of this land, but how can there be two heavenly kami?"

Jinmu sent a message in reply that said, "The children of the heavenly kami are many. If this Nigi-hayahi is truly a descendant of the heavenly gods, then he will have some kind object indicating his divinity. Show me this object and prove his descent to me." Naga-sune-hiko showed Nigi-hayahi's heavenly bow and arrows to Jinmu, and Jinmu said, "These are authentic." In exchange, he showed Naga-sune-hiko one of his own heavenly arrows. When Naga-sune-hiko saw that Jinmu was truly a descendant of the heavenly kami, he changed his opinion of Jinmu, but his war preparations were already in place and so he felt that he could not alter the course of events. But Nigi-hayahi knew that Jinmu was the descendant of Ninigi, chosen of the heavenly gods, and so he killed Naga-sune-hiko and surrendered to Jinmu himself.

In 662 BCE, six years after Jinmu originally set out from Kyushu, he ordered that a capital be built at Kashihara, at the base of Mt. Unebi. The next year, Jinmu wished to establish an empress, and searched far and wide among the aristocracy. He took as his wife the daughter of the kami Ō-mono-nushi, named Hime-tatara-i-suzu-hime. According to *Ancient Matters*, the reason that she is child of the kami is that her mother was very beautiful. One day when Hime-tatara-i-suzu-hime's mother was using the bathroom, Ō-mono-nushi, who is enshrined in Mt. Miwa, transformed himself into a red arrow, passed upwards through the sewage line, and penetrated her as she sat on the toilet. She hopped up in surprise and ran out of the toilet with the arrow in her hand and then placed it by her bed, where it transformed into a handsome young man.

According to *Chronicles*, the kami Koto-shiro-nushi was the father of Hime-tatara-i-suzu-hime.

**FIGURE 10**  Tomb of Jinmu. Kashihara City, Nara Prefecture Wikipedia Commons.

In 660 BCE, Jinmu took the throne for the first time at Kashihara Palace. Hime-tatara-i-suzu-hime was named empress, and they had two sons, Kamu-ya-i and Kamu-nu-na-kawa. Jinmu rewarded all of his faithful followers, especially Michi-no-omi, the Kume warriors, Oto-shiki, and the crow Ya-ta-garasu.

In the thirty-first year of his reign, 630 BCE, Jinmu went on a tour of his realm. He climbed atop a high hill and, looking at the slender and curved Nara Basin, proclaimed, "This land resembles two dragonflies mating." The land was then called Akitsu-shima, meaning "dragonfly island."

In 585 BCE, at 127 years of age, Jinmu died at Kashihara Palace. He is buried in Ushitora Tomb on the slopes of Mt. Unebi.

## Sujin

Jinmu was succeeded by his son Kamu-nu-na-kawa, known as Suizei, after killing his stepbrother Ta-gishi-mimi, who had attempted to steal the throne. The emperors from Suizei to Kaika are often called the missing eight emperors because almost no details are provided about their lives or reigns, and like Jinmu, they are clearly mythical figures.

After Kaika, the official imperial genealogy records a number of legendary emperors, some of whom appear to be founders in their own right. Both *Ancient Matters* and *Chronicles* link these founders into a single uninterrupted lineage, but it is more likely that this is a fusion of multiple distinct legendary dynasties and rulers, which explains why there appear to be multiple founding emperors, including Sujin, Ōjin, and Keitai.

Sujin was the son of Kaika, a mythical emperor who ruled from 158 to 98 BCE. Sujin's mother was affiliated with the Mononobe clan, which claimed descent from the kami Nigi-hayahi. When Kaika died, Sujin took the throne and ruled from 97 to 30 BCE.

In earlier reigns, Amaterasu was worshipped in the imperial palace. However, Sujin was anxious about sharing the same residence with this powerful kami. He assigned one of his daughters to worship this kami and built a shrine in Kasanui Village, Yamato Province, present-day Nara Prefecture. Worship of another kami venerated in the palace, Yamato-ō-kuni-tama, was charged to a woman named Nuna-ki-iri-bime, but she was unable to perform it due to poor health. In the reign of Sujin's son Suinin, the shrine to Amaterasu was moved again, this time to Ise, where it is now known as the Ise Grand Shrine.

Early in Sujin's reign, an epidemic ravaged the land and most of the people living there died. Sujin performed divination using turtle shells, upon which a kami possessed Sujin's aunt, Yamato-toto-hi-momo-so-bime. This kami spoke to Sujin through her, saying, "Why are you worried about the unrest in your land? If you worship me, then all will be at peace."

Sujin asked, "What kami are you?"

The kami replied, "I am called Ō-mono-nushi, and I live in Yamato Province at Mt. Miwa."

Sujin performed the ritual worship as he had been instructed, but there was no improvement in the plague. And so Sujin prayed, "Why is my worship not working? Please instruct me in a dream what I am to do."

That night, Sujin had a dream in which a nobleman came and identified himself as Ō-mono-nushi. He said, "Emperor, do not worry. I am the reason for this plague, and I will make it go away if you make my child, Ō-tata-neko, serve as the head priest for my worship."

The next morning, Sujin issued an order to have the land searched for Ō-tata-neko. When they found him, they made him the head priest at the Miwa Shrine, and the plague abated.

Ō-tata-neko was asked how it came to be that he was the son of Ō-mono-nushi. He explained that his mother, Iku-tama-yori-bime, was very beautiful. One night, a handsome man finer than any she had ever seen came to visit her. The two spent the night together and soon enough she was pregnant. Her parents were suspicious and asked her, "How is it that you've become pregnant without a husband?"

She replied, "There is a handsome man who comes to visit me every night, though I do not know his name or title."

The parents wanted to find out the man's identity and so they told their daughter, "Spread red clay around your bed so that we'll be able to track him by his socks when he steps on it. Also, sew a thread from a long spool through the hem of his robe."

The next morning, they saw that the thread had passed through the keyhole to her room. They followed the thread, and it led them to Mt. Miwa, stopping at the shrine for Ō-mono-nushi.

With the cooperation of the kami of Miwa, the central lands were finally at peace. However, people in distant lands still did not accept Sujin's imperial rule. Sujin chose four of his bravest servants, named them shogun, and sent one in each direction, north, south, east, and west, each with an army and orders to conquer any who opposed them.

The general who went north soon encountered a young girl sitting on top of a hill. The girl sang to the general,

> Alas, Sujin!
> While you dally with the ladies,
> you know not that secretly
> someone means to cut short
> the thread of your life.

The general asked her what she meant with her song, but she replied, "It doesn't mean anything. I'm just singing." She sang the song again and disappeared.

The general immediately went back and reported this to Sujin. Sujin's aunt, Yamato-toto-hi-momo-so-bime, understood what the song meant and told Sujin, "This is a warning that Take-hani-yasu-biko is planning a rebellion. I heard that he sent his wife, Ata-hime, to Mt. Kagu to collect soil. If you do not act quickly, it will be too late."

Sujin recalled his generals and conferred with them. Shortly thereafter, Take-hani-yasu-biko and Ata-hime each took charge of an army and attacked. The husband came from the north, the wife from the west. But because Sujin had recalled his generals, he had all of his troops available and was able to stymie the rebellion. He first sent his forces east and they killed Ata-hime and all of her soldiers. Then they marched north and routed Take-hani-yasu-biko.

Having seen to the rebellion, Sujin again dispatched his four generals in the four directions to bring order to the distant lands. The next year, the generals reported back that they had completed their missions. Shortly thereafter, Sujin issued a census of all the people in his realm, then made assignments for taxes and forced labor. The kami of heaven and earth were appeased, and the realm was at peace. Sujin then assumed the title, "First Emperor to Rule the State."

Yamato-toto-hi-momo-so-bime became the wife of the kami Ō-mono-nushi. However, the kami only visited her at night. Not once did she see him during the day. One night, she told him,

"You never come during the day and so I've never seen your face clearly. Tomorrow morning, I beg you to stay a little bit so that I can see your radiant countenance."

Ō-mono-nushi said, "Indeed. Tomorrow morning, I will go into your comb box. My one request is that you not be surprised when you see me."

The next morning, Yamato-toto-hi-momo-so-bime opened her comb box and looked inside, where she saw a small, iridescent snake. It was as tiny as a piece of thread. She was shocked and screamed.

Ō-mono-nushi was embarrassed and said, "You have shamed me, now be shamed yourself!" Then he vanished into the sky, going back to Mt. Miwa. Yamato-toto-hi-momo-so-bime looked up in the sky in regret and then plopped down on her seat, and a chopstick stabbed her in the vagina, killing her. People called the tomb Hashihaka, meaning "chopsticks tomb." It stands in present-day Sakurai City, Nara Prefecture.

In the sixtieth year of his reign, Sujin told his government officials, "I hear that the sacred treasures brought from heaven by Ame-no-hohi are in the Izumo Grand Shrine. I wish to see them." He sent someone to Izumo to retrieve the treasures.

At that time, the head priest of the Izumo shrine was away and had left his younger brother in charge. The younger brother handed the heavenly treasures over to the messenger who came from the imperial court. When the older brother returned, he blamed his younger brother for surrendering the sacred treasures of Izumo to the emperor. Because of his resentment, he hatched a plan to murder his younger brother. He had a wooden sword made that was an exact replica of the sword he usually carried. He told his brother, "Right now, the water lilies at Yamuya are quite beautiful. Let's go and see them together." When they got to the edge of the pool, the older brother invited his younger brother to go for a swim. Both took off their swords and swam out into the water. The older brother got out first and picked up the younger brother's sword. The younger brother realized something was amiss and took his older brother's sword, but because it was made out of wood, he was not able to pull it out of the sheath. Then the older brother killed his younger brother. People at the time sang,

> The scabbard of the sword worn
> by the brave man of Izumo
> is adorned with much arrowroot,
> but there is no blade inside. How sad!

When word of this deed reached the emperor, Sujin sent two of his retainers to put the older brother to death.

## Mythological Perspectives

### Comparative Axes: Relation / Cause (Thompson and Schrempp)

In *The Truth of Myth*, Thompson and Schrempp suggest that relationships between entities, such as connection, attraction, repulsion, motivation, and resistance, can characterize myths and help understand mythical traditions comparatively. These include, for example, Native American myths in which humans intermarry with other species, allowing for mutual and reciprocal relationships. In the Japanese mythical tradition, intermarriage of different groups associated with different natural features is central to the narrative. Ninigi, a heavenly deity, descends to earth, where he meets and marries an earthly deity descended from a mountain kami. His son, Luck of the Mountain, has power over the land as demonstrated by his hunting talents. Through his marriage to Toyo-tama-hime, he incorporates the power of a sea goddess into the imperial line. Their son Fuki-aezu also marries a sea goddess, Tama-yori-hime, such that the first Japanese emperor is born with control and power over both heaven and earth, mountain and sea. Notably, in the Japanese case, this does not prove beneficial for the earthly kami or the sea kami; the relationship is not reciprocal. Instead, the myths present the vision of an emperor with relationships to all the kami of heaven and earth through marriage. In a similar vein, Jinmu's second wife and empress, Hime-tatara-i-suzu-hime, is descended from a powerful kami in the Yamato region, though the identity of her father differs between *Ancient Matters*, *Chronicles*, and *Chronicles* variants. Her marriage to Jinmu reflects his new capital in Yamato and his dominion over his new realm. That relationship is further developed through the marriages of the emperors between Jinmu and Sujin, not included here, but which are primarily with women from clans from the Yamato area.

The Sujin narrative further clarifies the relationship that the emperor is expected to maintain with the kami that populate the realm and the powers they can exercise. Sujin set up the shrines for Amaterasu and Yamato-ō-kuni-tama, effectively demonstrating imperial patronage of shrines associated with deities that ruled the land (Yamato-ō-kuni-tama means "great soul of the land of Yamato"). Recall that Yamato can refer both to the province in central Japan, the present-day Nara Basin, as well as the Japanese state as a whole. The relationship between Amaterasu and the Japanese state persists in contemporary Japan. Indeed, the Japanese emperor and empress visited the Ise Shrine, which Sujin supposedly built for Amaterasu, as recently as 2019. In Sujin, we also see the emperor perform ritual worship in order to placate a raging kami, Ō-mono-nushi. The emperor was chief priest and chief ritualist for the realm, and it was his (or her; there are several female emperors in the ancient period) responsibility to ensure that all kami in the realm were placated. Finally, we see that the emperor must also maintain relationships with the children descended from kami. In this myth, Ō-mono-nushi insists that his descendant be installed as head priest in his shrine at Mt. Miwa. A similar case applies to Izumo. In the myths from the reign of Sujin, the emperor demonstrates his authority over the Izumo area by requesting divine objects, and this authority is rooted in cooperation with the descendants of Ō-kuni-nushi and the head priests of the Izumo Grand Shrine. The relationship between the emperor and the various head priests reflected the organization of the early Japanese state, in which the central authority in Yamato recognized the local rule and local deities of clans in the provinces in return for taxes and offerings paid to the Yamato court.

## South Seas Influences (Müller, Matsumoto)

One of the oldest comparative mythological theories about Japanese myths linked the lost fishhook story to Indonesia. The connection was proposed by Friedrich W. K. Müller (1863–1930). Müller was at heart a linguist involved in translation and transcription. However, his broad knowledge of Central, Southeast, and East Asian languages enabled him to readily identify parallel elements from field reports of the folklore from the many areas of the world he studied. In a brief 1893 article, Müller addressed a Dutch article from the same year by Sanskrit scholar J. H. C. Kern (1833–1917). Kern's interests had expanded to Indonesia, much of which was a Dutch colony at the time. Kern asserted that two seemingly related myths, one from the Kai Islands and another from the Minahasa Peninsula, were derived from a common source. That hypothesis suggested that the story dated from a time when the ancestors of the people in the two locations were part of a single tribe. Müller, however, was not so certain, because the same legend could be found in both *Ancient Matters* and *Chronicles*, which were written down in the eighth century. Müller then provided summaries of all three myths.

The Kai Islands story tells of three brothers—Hian, Tongil, and Parpara—and two sisters—Bikeel and Meslaang—who live in heaven. One day, Parpara went fishing in the sea of clouds with his oldest brother's fishing hook and lost it. When he returned home without a fish or the hook, his oldest brother demanded that the original hook be returned to him. Parpara piloted his boat out and dove into the clouds, where he met a fish that asked him what he was doing there. When he explained what had happened, the fish offered to help him search, and they eventually found another fish who had a sore throat and was coughing. The first fish removed the hook and returned it to Parpara.

The Minahasa story is about a man named Kawulusan, who wanted to go fishing but had no fishing tackle and so borrowed it from his friend. He set out to sea in a boat, but when he tried to pull it, the line broke and he also lost the hook. When he returned home and told his friend what had happened, the friend demanded the original hook back, telling Kawulusan that even if he gave him ten new hooks, he would only accept the original. Kawulusan went back to the sea to search, and dove in where he had lost the hook. At the bottom of the sea, he found a paved road that led him to a village. At the village, he heard a clamor from one of the houses, and when he went in, he saw that a pig was being sacrificed for a girl who had gotten a bone stuck in her throat. Kawulusan saw that the fishing hook was stuck in her throat and told the girl's parents that he could help her. He had everyone leave the room, then removed the fishing hook and hid it in his clothing. As a reward, he received gifts from the parents, and then he went back to the surface. However, when he arrived, he found that his boat was gone. Then a large fish came along, and he promised to name the fish if the fish carried him back to shore. The fish agreed, so Kawulusan rode on its back and returned home.

Müller continued with a paraphrased version of the Japanese myth largely drawn from Chamberlain's translation of *Ancient Matters*. Müller's retelling notes the exchange and loss of the hook, the older brother's refusal to accept replacements, the sea god recovering the hook from the seabream, and Yama-sachi-hiko's return on the back of a crocodile (early translations of *Ancient Matters* and *Chronicles* often use a crocodile instead of a shark). Müller noted that all the stories also involve embarrassing and punishing the lender of the hook. In the Kai Islands story, Parpara demands spilled palm wine from the older brother, and in the Minahasa story, Kawulusan demands a banana leaf that the friend had torn from

Kawulusan's tree and used for shelter from the rain. Finally, Müller added a Hawaiian story in which the fishing lines from a village were all broken because they fished in the vicinity of an underwater city. Müller was reluctant to add this fourth myth to the collection, though he notes that a flood is later sent as punishment, similar to the Japanese myth. While Müller did not go into further detail, the striking similarity in the myths led to a long-standing belief that the Yama-sachi-hiko myth demonstrated the influence of South Seas myths on Japanese myths. Future mythologists would note that the Hayato, the people group that the older brother Umi-sachi-hiko is said to have been the ancestor of, originated in southern Kyushu. The location fits the idea of people moving northwards to the Japanese archipelago from Okinawa.

As noted in Chapter 1, mythologist Matsumoto Nobuhiro used Japanese myths to propose that the Japanese people were linked to migration from the South Seas. The Yama-sachi-hiko myth was one of the clearest examples of "southern elements" in Japanese myths. Matsumoto addressed these similarities in some of his earliest work, written during World War II. Other mythologists advanced the comparative study of the Yama-sachi-hiko myth in the years that followed, notably Matsumura Takeo.

Postwar mythology tended to divide the Yama-sachi-hiko myth into three components: the return of the lost fishhook to its original owner, a repayment of kindness from the injured fish and sea god, and the taboo-breaking conduct of the husband when his wife comes to give birth. Matsumura, for example, associated the first part of the myth with the Indonesian lost fishhook stories and identified it with the South Seas. The key links were the lending of fishing gear, revenge, and the sea. Matsumura associated the repayment of kindness motif with folklore in which a wolf or lion gives a blessing to a hunter who removes a spear from their flesh, with the key elements being a lack of revenge, medical treatment, and the earth. This second narrative was widespread throughout Eurasia and even in Africa and North America. Matsumura accordingly proposed that while the lost fishhook motif certainly reached Japan from Indonesia, the lost spear motifs are of uncertain provenance—perhaps originating in the Middle East or Greece. Finally, Matsumura claimed that the marriage with Toyo-tama-hime and the taboo-breaking were linked to Melusine folklore. In this European narrative, a woman who is part fish or part snake marries a human man on the condition that he never see her bathing or giving birth. The human man eventually breaks the taboo and the woman leaves him.

Late in his career, in 1977, Matsumoto revisited the Yama-sachi-hiko myth and the fragmented analysis of Matsumura in order to reassess how the later, Melusine motif in the story was connected to the earlier, lost fishhook and lost spear motifs. Matsumoto introduced another story found on both the islands of Palau and Yap about a mahi-mahi. In this story, a man climbs a palm tree and attaches a tap and vessel to collect sap for making wine. He realizes that his wine is being stolen every night and keeps watch on the tree by day. He eventually sees a fish come to land, place its tail to the side, change into human form, and climb the tree. The man stealthily takes the tail and hides it in the shrine next to his house. The next day, he finds a naked woman squatting under the tree, and he brings her a skirt and then marries her; her name is Mahi-mahi. One day, while looking for a rod for pounding taro, Mahi-mahi finds her tail. She leaves their daughter behind and returns to the sea.

Mahi-mahi's daughter later gets married and has a son. The son is instructed by his father one day to run an errand to his uncle's house, and he is told that he must loudly sing a song as he approaches. Thinking it strange, he goes to the house and sees a beautiful oyster that shines like a lamp, and the son realizes that in the past, his uncle had always hidden this oyster when he approached. Wanting the oyster, the son speaks to his father who arranges for the son to receive a portion of the oyster shell, which the son makes into a fishhook. He loses the hook in the sea and gets scolded by his father, then follows the advice of a village elder and dives into the sea. There, he meets a fish and is guided to a land under the sea. While resting by a well, he hears about an old woman named Mahi-mahi who is sick. When he visits the patient, Mahi-mahi realizes that the young man looks like the daughter that she had abandoned. The young man realizes that Mahi-mahi's head is injured and he asks the accompanying fish to do a silly dance. When the sick woman, his grandmother, laughs, she coughs up the hook and tells him that he may catch whatever fish he likes from their land.

Matsumoto linked the Mahi-mahi story with another from Kiribati and three from the Solomon Islands. The Kiribati story is about the creation deity Nareau. Nareau lived in Samoa for seventeen generations with his daughter Kobine, who lived underground. Then Nareau lived in Tawara for seventy-seven generations. Nareau later returned to Samoa with his three sons, introducing the people of Samoa to the canoe. The people of Samoa wished to see Kobine, and so Nareau sent his oldest son Matuakeukeu to search for her, and he returned with her. Then the Samoans organized a fishing competition with the three sons of Nareau. During the competition, Nareau's youngest son Matuarang lost his fishhook. He dove in after it and met the goddess Taranga-uea. Taranga-uea had many fishhooks, and so Matuarang requested the hook in her breast, which she gave to him on the condition that he not let anyone else use it. Later, Nareau asked Matuarang to use his hook to pull up land from the deeps.

The first of the Solomon Islands stories similarly tells of a turtle who helped a fisherman pull up Santa Ana Island from the deep with a fishhook. The second, from Choiseul, tells of six brothers who go fishing, but the youngest brother, who has no hook of his own, borrows his father's. After he loses the hook at sea, his father scolds him, and so the son sets out by canoe, eventually landing on a small island. There, a giant feeds him, then summons all the fish and finds the hook. The third Solomon Islands story, from Malaita, tells of a father who made hooks from his teeth that were lost at sea by his sons. The sons go to the goddesses who protect the skipjack tuna, for the tuna seek out those goddesses whenever a hook is stuck in their mouth.

The dispersion of these stories, and especially the final story, because it involves women and skipjack tuna, prompted Matsumoto to argue that initiation ceremonies were relevant to the Yama-sachi-hiko myth. This observation is in line with Matsumoto's anthropological approach and interest in rituals, discussed in Chapter 1. Drawing especially on a report by the anthropologist Sidney Moko Mead (1927–), Matsumoto focused on the *maraufu* ceremony, held every five or six years in villages in the Solomon Islands. At this ceremony, boys to be initiated would enter a customs house and begin a period of seclusion to free them from defilement. Fishermen take charge of the initiates and go to fish for skipjack tuna. Schools of tuna are identified by birds, which compete with the tuna for small fish, and the feeding frenzy then attracts sharks that feed on the tuna. An initiate in a canoe that catches a tuna will cradle the first tuna caught in his arms until the canoe returns to shore, which will then be prepared as ritual food for the boy's family. The boy will also drink several drops of the blood from this tuna. The fishing will continue until all the initiates have caught a tuna. The boys are also shielded from women during this time. Finally, a feast concludes the ritual and the boys are recognized as adults.

Matsumoto's interest in this ceremony had more to do with the role of sharks than of tuna. Mead suggested that humans were imagined to have a special kind of communal relationship with the skipjack tuna, which also bleed red. At one point in the ritual, initiates must also pretend to be skipjack tuna and are caught with nets. Conversely, the sharks that arrive at the site of a tuna school compete with the fishermen for the tuna. At the same time, if their canoe capsizes, the fishermen will, like the tuna, be eaten by the sharks. While skipjack tuna are the supreme fish in terms of both ritual and food, sharks are never eaten and associated rather with death and ancestor worship. Matsumoto noted several islands where the souls of the deceased are imagined to go to the sea and become sharks. A shark cult also existed in the Solomon Islands but had gone extinct; the beliefs of that cult claimed that the shark played a role in guiding the fisherman to the skipjack tuna. Ultimately, Mead suggested that the shark and the skipjack tuna existed as counterinfluences: one associated with life-giving positive force and the other with negativity and death.

Mead's argument that the role of the shark was of central importance to the position of the skipjack tuna and the initiation ritual created an opportunity for Matsumoto to connect Toyo-tama-hime and the final section of the Yama-sachi-hiko myth to a South Seas story. Matsumoto argued that the Toyo-tama-hime story, in which the princess turns into a shark after Yama-sachi-hiko violates the taboo of seeing her during childbirth, is the vestige of a clan that worshipped the shark as its totem. Matsumoto noted other examples in Japanese folklore related to sharks either having connections with women or with the dead. Matsumoto also suggested that Toyo-tama-hime coming to shore with her younger sister Tama-yori-bime recalls sororate marriage, a custom in which a husband engages in intercourse with the sister of his wife, and that Tama-yori-bime marrying her nephew Fuki-aezu recalls levirate marriage, in which the brother of a deceased man marries his widow. Both types of marriage are associated, in anthropological studies of kinship, with ancient societies, leading Matsumoto to argue that the myth echoes ancient marriage practices.

The connection between sharks and humans related to fishing and partaking of the sea was, by Matsumoto's reckoning, the original form of the story, and it was augmented in ancient times with the motif of the spear removed from a lion or wolf. The fishhook motif had a smaller sphere of circulation, but Matsumoto argued that it should not be limited to Indonesia. Finally, he suggested that the version of the story seen in Palau reflects a broader spread of the Melusine story, and its convergence with the fishing/hunting narratives must have occurred at a very ancient time.

## Founding Myths and Version Comparison (Mishina)

Mythologist Mishina Shōei devoted special attention to the Ninigi descent story as a founding myth. His interest almost certainly derived from his pre–World War II research on Korea. As noted in Chapter 1, Mishina believed that Japanese myths had been influenced by myths from Northeast Asia, including Korea.

One feature of Korean myths is a wide variety of founding myths. This is due to the existence of both Korean and Chinese source materials and the multiple kingdoms and powerful clans that emerged on the ancient peninsula. The most well-known of these myths in modern Korea is the Tangun (Dangun) myth, in which Hwanung, son of the lord of heaven, descends to earth. A tiger and a bear pray to Hwanung to become human. The bear succeeded and became a human woman who gave birth to Tangun, founder of the legendary Kojosŏn (Gojoseon) Dynasty.

During Mishina's early career, Korea was a Japanese colony, and the Tangun legend was hotly debated because it provided a Korean origin story that was independent of Japan. Mishina rejected the Tangun myth for Korean origins, no doubt informed by colonial bias, and instead focused on the founding myth for the Korean kingdom of Silla. In that myth, the first king of Silla emerged from an egg that appeared on a day filled with unusual environmental phenomena. Because the egg was shaped like a gourd, the myth is also the origin for the Korean surname "Park," the Korean word for gourd. Mishina classified Korean origin myths into categories and analyzed them based on the culture areas paradigm discussed in Chapter 1. Mishina concluded that Korean myths were a composite due to the influence of multiple neighboring culture areas.

During his post–World War II career, Mishina concluded that Japanese creation myths had also changed and acquired more distinct features based on influence from other culture areas. The multiple versions of the Ninigi story in *Ancient Matters* and *Chronicles* attest to this distinctiveness. In his later career, Mishina charted the process of this narrative development by comparing all the versions. According to Mishina, versions that had the most elements in common with each other were the oldest, and then as the myth developed, parts were changed in different versions.

He began by breaking the myth into two parts: Ninigi's descent, and Ninigi's marriage and the birth of his heirs. He then divided the first part into seven elements:

(1) the kami who orders the descent
(2) the kami who receives the order and descends
(3) the appearance of the heavenly grandchild upon their descent
(4) to where they descend
(5) the gods who accompany him
(6) the bestowal of divine objects
(7) the divine proclamation to rule the land

In Table 5, these seven parts are identified by number in the leftmost column. The other columns are labeled with the different versions of the myth in *Ancient Matters* and *Chronicles*. Mishina ordered the versions from oldest to newest, so the Main Version of *Chronicles* is on the left, then Variant 6, etc. As you read from left to right, the myths become more complex or have more features, which Mishina argued was because they were developing.

The second part of Ninigi's narrative was his marriage and the birth of his heirs. Mishina divided this story into four parts:

(1) the goddess who becomes his wife
(2) the episode with Iwa-naga-hime
(3) the use of the fire
(4) the kami who are born from the fire

Mishina concluded, via this comparison. that the oldest versions of the myth were the Main Version and Variant 6 of *Chronicles*, then Variant 4 of *Chronicles*, followed by Variant 2 of *Chronicles*, then *Ancient Matters* and Variant 1 of *Chronicles*, and finally Variant 5 of *Chronicles*. The breakdown given in the tables above forms the framework for Mishina's extensive study of the foundation myths, which is over five hundred pages in length. Each development of the

**TABLE 5** Mishina on Ninigi's Descent

| | *Chronicles* Main Version | *Chronicles* Variant 6 | *Chronicles* Variant 4 | *Chronicles* Variant 2 | *Ancient Matters* | *Chronicles* Variant 1 |
|---|---|---|---|---|---|---|
| 1 | Taka-mi-musuhi | Taka-mi-musuhi | Taka-mi-musuhi | Taka-mi-musuhi, Amaterasu | Taka-mi-musuhi, Amaterasu | Amaterasu |
| 2 | Ninigi | Ninigi | Ninigi | Oshi-ho-mimi, later Ninigi | Oshi-ho-mimi, later Ninigi | Oshi-ho-mimi, later Ninigi |
| 3 | Cloak | Cloak | Cloak | Born in mid-air during descent | Born in mid-air during descent, but nothing written about appearance | Born in mid-air during descent, but nothing written about appearance |
| 4 | Takachiho in So in Himuka | Sohori in Takachiho in So in Himuka | Kushibi in Takachiho in So in Himuka | Takachiho in Kushibi in Himuka | Kujifuru in Takachiho in Himuka | Kujifuru in Takachiho in Himuka |
| 5 | n/a | n/a | Ama-no-oshi-hi, Ame-kushitsu-no-ō-kume | Ama-no-koyane, Futo-dama, various occupational gods | Five retainers (Ama-no-koyane, Futo-dama, Ame-no-uzu-me, Ishi-kori-dome, Tama-no-oya), Omoi-kane, Ta-jikara-o, Ame-no-iwa-to-wake, Toyo-uke, Saruta-hiko, Ame-no-oshi-hi, Ama-tsu-kume | Five retainers (Ama-no-koyane, Futo-dama, Ame-no-uzu-me, Ishi-kori-dome, Tama-no-oya), Saruta-hiko |
| 6 | n/a | n/a | n/a | Divine mirror and instructions | Three regalia (mirror, jewels, sword), instructions for mirror | Three regalia |
| 7 | n/a | n/a | n/a | n/a | Order to rule the fertile land | Order to rule the fertile land |

**TABLE 6** Mishina on Ninigi's Marriage

| | *Chronicles* Main Version | *Chronicles* Variant 6 | *Chronicles* Variant 2 | *Ancient Matters* | *Chronicles* Variant 5 |
|---|---|---|---|---|---|
| 1 | Kashi-tsu-hime (Kamu-ata-tsu-hime, Ko-no-hana-saku-ya-hime) | Ko-no-hana-saku-ya-hime (Toyo-ata-tsu-hime) | Kamu-ata-kashi-tsu-hime (Ko-no-hana-saku-ya-hime) | Kamu-ata-tsu-hime (Ko-no-hana-saku-ya-hime) | Ata-kashi-tsu-hime |
| 2 | n/a | n/a | Iwa-naga-hime is upset and shortens lifespan | Iwa-naga-hime is upset and shortens lifespan | n/a |
| 3 | Pregnant in one night; use fire to prove divine descent | Pregnant in one night | Pregnant in one night; use fire to prove divine descent | Pregnant in one night; use fire to prove divine descent | Pregnant in one night; use fire to prove divine descent |
| 4 | Ho-no-susori, Hiko-ho-ho-demi, Ho-no-akari | Ho-no-suseri, Ho-no-ori (Hiko-ho-ho-demi), | Ho-no-suseri, Hi-no-akari, Hiko-ho-ho-demi (Ho-no-ori) | Ho-deri, Ho-suseri, Ho-ori (Ama-tsu-hiko-hiko-ho-ho-demi) | Ho-no-akari, Ho-no-susumi, Ho-no-ori, Hiko-ho-ho-demi |

story represents the potential influence and intersection of different cultural areas.

Mishina also applied this model of layered construction to Jinmu, envisioning the Jinmu myth to have been built up and augmented as ancient Japanese history moved forward in time. The overall process resembles the model applied to the descent myths. But since there are only two versions of the Jinmu myth, one in *Ancient Matters* and one in *Chronicles*, Mishina breaks the mythical narratives into categorical elements, akin to a structural analysis. Mishina argues that by removing the later elements, older historical circumstances are revealed, and that by assigning the layers to the proper historical strata, he can trace the larger development of the mythical narrative. Again, inspired by the American anthropology of Franz Boas and his disciples, Mishina put culture at the center of his analysis, with change occurring as different groups and cultures came into contact with each other. Like Boas, Mishina depended heavily on archaeological and material evidence for determining what constituted a culture and its characteristics.

Mishina analyzed the Jinmu narrative using three mythical elements, with the third divided into four cultural aspects. The first mythical element was a South Seas influence, the oldest culture in the Japanese archipelago. These narratives were later transmogrified due to contact with land-based cultures from Northeast Asia, who worshipped the sun and sky. Finally, those two elements were incorporated into a narrative about the conquering and unification of the Yamato area of central Japan.

The oldest aspect of the Jinmu narrative was influence from the South Seas and resonated with the Yama-sachi-hiko myth discussed in Chapter 2. Mishina broke the Yama-sachi-hiko myths down into the following elements: exchange of fishing tackle; visit to a palace under the sea; marriage to a daughter of a sea god; finding the missing fishing hook; acquiring power over water; younger brother defeating the older brother; and birth of children by the daughter of a sea god.

Then, Mishina argued that Jinmu was rooted in the same mythological figure as Yama-sachi-hiko, because these elements all had parallels in the Jinmu myth. *Chronicles* records that Jinmu had multiple names, including Kamu-yamato-iware-biko-ho-ho-demi. The final part of this name, "Ho-ho-demi," is shared with Hiko-ho-ho-demi, an alternative name for Yama-sachi-hiko. The Hayato, the tribe descended from Umi-sachi-hiko, were connected with seafaring and rice rituals, especially Hayato dances used at ceremonies for imperial accession. The Kume songs which appear in the Jinmu myth are also part of imperial accession rituals. Mishina claimed that Ninigi's wife was a Hayato shamaness associated with water, and so the birth of Yama-sachi-hiko and the birth of Jinmu, son of Tama-yori-bime, are both from women with supernatural powers connected to water and so on.

Next, Northeast Asian narratives merged with the South Seas narratives to form a composite myth. Most importantly, Northeast Asian peoples worshipped the sun and sky, and they introduced the concepts of heaven, earth, and the underworld. The fusion of these elements explained, for example, why Ninigi descended to Himuka, even though the ultimate kingdom would be founded in Yamato. Mishina argued that Ninigi's descent to Himuka created a nexus between the older, South Seas myth associated with the Hayato and the sea and the Northeast Asian myths that emphasized divine descent from heaven.

The composite structure of the two cultural areas in myth is prominently given in Jinmu's navigation around Kumano. When his armada met with rough waves, Jinmu's older brother Ina-hi remarked that he was a descendant of the sea kami and went into the ocean. Another older brother, Mike-iri-no, crossed the waves to the Land of Tokoyo. Noting that the names of both brothers refer to rice, Mishina recalled an Okinawan myth about a female shamaness bringing rice from across the waves. Okinawan beliefs associated the sea with words like *Neya*, and so what was the sea to Okinawan people in South Seas mythical narratives was incorporated as the Land of Ne under the influence of Northeast Asian mythical cosmologies that included an underworld. Going into the sea is the same as going to the Land of Ne, which was entered from Kumano. Mishina also noted that in a *Chronicles* variant, Izanami—the most famous resident of the underworld—is worshipped at Kumano. Mishina argued that Jinmu and his brothers were all the same mythical figure, and so Jinmu's own problems at Kumano are a reflection of his journey to the underworld as well. Jinmu awakes from this temporary death thanks to the sword sent from heaven. Finally, the crow, a messenger from the land of the dead, is converted to the messenger of heaven in the composite version of the myths.

The last piece of Mishina's analysis was the conquest narrative of Jinmu in Yamato. The most important aspect of this narrative was the connection between Jinmu as a mythical figure to Jinmu as a historical figure. The compilers of *Ancient Matters* and *Chronicles* meant to cement this connection in writing and so created a composite Jinmu myth. Mishina breaks that myth down into four aspects. The first and primary aspect was Jinmu as Iware-biko, ruler of a specific place (Iware) in the Yamato basin and dating from the Yayoi period (300 BCE–300 CE). Guidance from the crow, the heroic actions of the Kume, the surrender of Oto-ukashi, the heroic actions of Shihi-netsu-hiko, and the connection through marriage with the Miwa kami all derived from this oldest aspect. The secondary aspect was Jinmu as a divine figure, from the Tomb Period (300–592 CE). This included putting the Kume under the control of the Ōtomo clan, the surrender of Nigi-hayahi, and the killing of the earth spiders. The third aspect was Jinmu as the first emperor. This included the conversion of the crow into a messenger of the sun goddess, the founding of the Kashihara capital, the invention of the chronology given in *Chronicles* and the 660 BCE founding date, the rewards given to the various clans that aided in conquest, and Jinmu's burial at Mt. Unebi. Mishina dated this third aspect to the Suiko era, the early seventh century. Finally, the fourth aspect dated from the Tenmu and Jitō eras (672–697 CE), discussed in Chapter 4, and included the heavenly signs given to Jinmu such as the golden kite, Jinmu's first imperial proclamation, and the creation of the name "land of the rising sun" to refer to Japan. This final aspect made Jinmu into a founder based on the legal codes that Tenmu and Jitō drafted to govern the Yamato state in the late eighth century. The primary basis for these distinctions rested on the locations and dating of tombs found in the Yamato basin and their associations with certain tribes as well as the Tenmu and Jitō records in *Chronicles*.

Mishina's approach toward breaking myths down based on a combination of extant versions and archeological data and informed by culture areas that change due to their interactions, continues to be influential among Japanese mythologists, especially in the popular arena. The potential to use differences between the versions in *Ancient Matters* and *Chronicles* to uncover or extract the oldest strata of Japanese origins, and the broad possibilities and variations for interpreting myths encouraged by this layered approach, has resulted in many books published in Japan attempting to explain Japanese origins. Diametrically opposed to Mishina are literature scholars who assert that *Ancient Matters* and *Chronicles* must be treated as separate texts and that there is no singular ancient myth that can be reconstructed through their combination.

## Kawai Hayao and the Hollow Center

As discussed in Chapter 2, psychologist Kawai Hayao used Jungian psychology to demonstrate the unique nature of the Japanese psyche. Kawai's analysis of Susano-o was one piece of his much larger "Hollow Center" theory, which he argued was the core feature of Japanese psychology. The theory is based on three repeated groups of three kami that appear in the myths of *Ancient Matters*. These are the three kami at the beginning of *Ancient Matters*: Ame-no-mi-naka-nushi, Kamu-musuhi, and Taka-mi-musuhi; the three children born when Izanagi performs ritual ablutions after his escape from Yomi: Amaterasu, Tsuku-yomi, and Susano-o; and the three children of Ninigi: Ho-deri, Ho-suseri, and Ho-ori. Kawai noted that in each of these groups, two of the three gods represent opposites or come into conflict, while the third is "hollow," that is to say, not part of the historical narrative.

Kawai's thesis rested on a structural analysis that incorporated elements from each trinity of kami. For the first three kami that appear in *Ancient Matters*, Taka-mi-musuhi is part of the heavenly gods and has the word "high" in his name. Taka-mi-musuhi is also the grandfather of the heavenly grandson, Ninigi, and has relations with the imperial line. Kamu-musuhi appears as a kind of opposite, because he is patron for the leader of the earthly kami Ō-ana-muji, resurrecting him and instructing him how to conquer his brothers. Kawai also asserted that Taka-mi-musuhi was associated with the male principle because of the kami's connection to fighting. In the *Chronicles* myth about Ō-kuni-nushi surrendering, Taka-mi-musuhi sent kami to force Ō-kuni-nushi to surrender, and later, Taka-mi-musuhi killed Ame-waka-hiko with a returned arrow. Kamu-musuhi, in contrast, was associated with the female principle, because he relates to creation and cultivation. This role is especially pronounced when resurrecting Ō-ana-muji with his mother's milk. However, in contrast to these two, Ame-no-mi-naka-nushi is essentially a non-entity. His name contains the word "center," suggesting that the kami plays the role of an axis. Ame-no-mi-naka-nushi therefore constitutes the "hollow center" between Taka-mi-musuhi and Kamu-musuhi.

This arrangement is repeated with Amaterasu, Susano-o, and Tsuku-yomi. Amaterasu has a close relationship with Taka-mi-musuhi and, though she is a goddess, embodies the male principle. This is most pointedly demonstrated when she girds herself for war to confront Susano-o. In Kawai's interpretation, Amaterasu showed that Japanese myths always demonstrate a counterbalancing effect. In *Chronicles*, Amaterasu is also known by the name "Hiru-me," meaning "sun woman," and the leech child—born because Izanami speaks before Izanagi—is called "Hiru-ko." Since the two names in

Japanese could refer to male and female deities of the sun (Jp. *hi*), Kawai argued that Izanagi reprimanding Izanami showed the male principle dominating the female. Then, casting the male god of the sun to the seas in favor of the female goddess of the sun showed the female domination of the male. For Kawai, dominance by one side must be followed by a counter-balancing effect from the other. After the female dominance of Hiru-me over Hiru-ko, Susano-o appeared as a new embodiment of the male principle, and the two continued to shift roles. In the same vein, Amaterasu mistook Susano-o's intentions when he went to heaven to bid her farewell, but then Susano-o committed violent acts against her. Because of these shifting positions, and unlike a Judeo-Christian model of God and Satan, in the Japanese case, right and wrong are not fixed; a pendulum always restores balance. The appearance of the Miwa kami, discussed in this chapter, is similarly the counterbalance between Amaterasu's offspring Sujin and the Izumo kami that his ancestors had displaced.

Most importantly for Kawai, this counterbalancing maintained a hollow center, represented by the third kami created by Izanagi when he leaves Yomi: Tsuku-yomi. Kawai called attention to the many poems about the moon in the eighth-century *Collection of Myriad Poems*, concluding that for ancient Japanese, the moon had a larger cultural impact and generated more sentimental attachment than the sun. Kawai also noted the use of the lunar calendar, highlighting the unusual absence of moon myths in Japan, and he linked this absence with that of Ame-no-mi-naka-nushi.

The story of Yama-sachi-hiko and Umi-sachi-hiko demonstrates recurrence, a characteristic that Kawai applied to both the body of Japanese myth and the entirety of Japanese history. As in the other trinities, there are three deities. Ho-ori (Yama-sachi-hiko) is clearly associated with the land and mountains and Ho-deri (Umi-sachi-hiko) with the sea, forming a binary. The middle brother, Ho-suseri, never appears in the narrative after his birth, creating a hollow center. Other structural features are repeated or repeated in variation. For example, the three brothers were born out of fire, while Amaterasu,

Tsuku-yomi, and Susano-o were born out of water. Izanagi, a heavenly kami, experienced contact with the impurity of Yomi, and Kamu-ata-tsu-hime, an earthly deity, experienced contact with the heavenly Ninigi. The three independently born deities, Taka-mi-musuhi, Kamu-musuhi, and Ame-no-mi-naka-nushi, were not related to contact between different realms. Nevertheless, they appeared at a formative and epochal moment in the development of Japanese myth. Kawai argued that this recurrence reflected a back-and-forth in which the Japanese have tried to counteract the contradictions of the previous generation by interchanging binary values like male and female. The recurrent revolution of thesis and antithesis, as Kawai put it, created a circular form of logic revealing the hollow center.

For Kawai, the primary significance of myths like the Yama-sachi-hiko narrative was their power to explain the psychology of contemporary Japanese people, an explanation that could then be applied to the therapeutic setting. These trinities of figures in the Japanese myths reflected a different way of understanding the individual psyche, especially compared to the West, which relied on a dichotomy of self and other. Monotheistic Western religious traditions placed a single, omniscient being in the center, and a number of other binary relations such as right and wrong, sacred and profane, etc., stemmed from having a single fixed pole. But in the Japanese case, because the center was empty, the mythological structure required both ends of a binary to be in balance with each other. For this reason, Kawai argued, Japanese psychology is more oriented toward the group and the group's wishes. Rather than a single viewpoint dominating the others, the empty center allowed multiple differing perspectives to exist, influencing each other, but not dominating, and the most important factor for psychological health was to maintain equilibrium. If equilibrium was disturbed, then anxiety would result.

Kawai claimed that at a societal level, the empty center theory had the possibility to influence the course of history. For example,

Japanese fascism emerged, according to Kawai, as a response to an equilibrium that had been disturbed due to global influence, because the Japanese people sought a figure who could step into the empty center and restore balance. In similar fashion, Kawai, in the symposium hosted on Susano-o discussed in Chapter 2, expressed concern that Japanese society was becoming unbalanced in the postwar era. Perhaps due to Japan's security depending on the United States, Kawai noted that society had veered too far toward the "maternal" side symbolized by Amaterasu and needed to renew interest in Susano-o. Kawai also suggested in the debate with Yoshida and Yuasa that he himself represented the empty center, preserving the balance between the other two thinkers.

## Mircea Eliade and Hierophanies

One of the most influential scholars of religion who studied myths was Mircea Eliade (1907–1986). Eliade assumed that there was a fundamental divide between the sacred and the profane, and moments in which the sacred broke into the profane world were of particular importance. Eliade called these breakthroughs "hierophanies." Hierophanies could take various forms depending on cultural context, but always involve a manifestation of the sacred. Examples could include anything from a sacred tree or rock to a constructed object of worship such as a mirror or altar. They could also describe experiences such as a human encountering a god or divine power.

Eliade argued that myths described the origins of hierophanies and then repeated them. With regards to origins, the myth expressed the original and ideal model of the breakthrough. For example, the actions or commandments of a god or hero, given in myth, created natural or social phenomena such as rain or marriage. However, hierophany is not limited to a singular moment or occurrence. Every time a marriage ritual takes place, it recalls the ideal model of the first marriage recorded in myth, and those present for the ceremony experience the manifestation of the sacred for themselves. This return to sacred time, what Eliade called the "eternal return," connects human everyday experience to the events of the mythic age and allows the humans to repeat and participate in those events. Moreover, because the myths explain the origins of phenomena, the use of myth and ritual to return to those phenomena provides structure and meaning for the lives of the participants.

While Eliade did not address Japanese myths directly, the impact of his theory of hierophany heavily influenced the approach used by American historian of religion Joseph Kitagawa (1915–1992). Kitagawa, professor and later Dean of the University of Chicago Divinity School, was a central figure in establishing the history of religion as a field and demonstrating its viability. Kitagawa worked in close contact with Eliade, who was also faculty at the University of Chicago. Kitagawa wrote broadly on world religions, including Christianity, Buddhism, and Shinto, and he wrote several books specifically on religion in Japanese history. Eliade, speaking on religion generally, argued that objects and actions acquired value and became real because they participated in the eternal return; that is, because they connected to a transcendent sacred reality. Kitagawa, writing on Shinto, quoted Eliade and asserted that for ancient Japanese, sacred reality was kami, which Kitagawa noted could also mean "sacred nature." The early Japanese believed that they all shared in this sacred nature and did not see themselves as separated from it. Rather, they were instruments of the kami, who worked through them and gave their lives and actions meaning.

Kitagawa's understanding of the myths in *Ancient Matters* and *Chronicles* hinged on the continuities, or perhaps returns, between the sacred world and the everyday that he identified in the mythical narratives. Kitagawa likened the kami who lured Amaterasu out of the heavenly rock cave to a court and identified a religious role for each of them: Futo-dama with ablution, Ame-no-uzu-me with shamanism, and Ame-no-koyane with priesthood. The historical Yamato court had the same positions, and they were filled with the descendants of these kami. The human court figures performed their roles and reinforced the linkage between the sacred world and the everyday world. The emperor, in particular, had the special charge of maintaining the relationship with Amaterasu, which Kitagawa called his "charisma." Imperial charisma was transmitted to the emperor at his enthronement through the divine objects that had originally been given by Amaterasu to Ninigi. The enthronement ceremony was an eternal return to this mythical episode.

However, the emperor could not use his charisma on other kami, who each specified their own shamans. Shamanism was another major topic of Eliade's study and informed Kitagawa's interpretation. Kitagawa drew particular attention to the myth surrounding Sujin given in this chapter. Sujin was conscientious in serving the kami of the imperial clan, but disasters and plagues still occurred. The kami responsible for the plague possessed the emperor's aunt, demanding service from Ō-tata-neko. This turn of events led Kitagawa to argue that in ancient Japan, some shamanic diviners came from clans of hereditary shamans, but others were simply charismatic individuals without other special training or qualifications. More importantly, the myth explained the origins of the shamanic worship of the Miwa kami, who provided meaning and value to the actions of the shaman.

Despite his preeminent position in the history of religion, Eliade's theories have had little influence among Japanese mythologists working in Japan. A full interpretation of the mythical narrative between Sujin and Ō-tata-neko using Eliade could be exceptionally rich. The plague itself could be interpreted as a hierophany, since it was brought about by a kami, and for the ancient Japanese person, the myth would explain why plagues occur and give them meaning and value. Eliade might even argue that this assignment of meaning at the cyclical, recurring, meta-historical level made it easier for people to bear the suffering of the plague. The possession of Sujin's aunt, Sujin's dream, and the ultimate abatement of the plague thanks to Ō-tata-neko all constitute breakthroughs of the divine into the everyday world. Perhaps, because Eliade's ultimate goal was the use of comparative religion to understand the nature of religion generally, his theories were a bad fit for Japanese mythologists, who often set out to understand Japanese religion in isolation.

## Saigō Nobutsuna and Mythical Recurrence

Literature scholar Saigō Nobutsuna (1916–2008) theorized an idea of cyclical time similar to Eliade. Saigō is best-known for his extensive commentary on *Ancient Matters*, though this is only one part of his voluminous career and body of writing. Saigō's career began with interest in ancient Japanese poetry, was informed by Marxism through the 1940s, and then pivoted toward social anthropology in the 1950s and beyond. In practice, this meant that Saigō attempted to read *Ancient Matters* as a literary text from the perspective of someone living in eighth-century Japan, much as an anthropologist might do ethnographic fieldwork in order to understand the lived experience of other people. The anthropological approach highlighted the role and importance of ritual for Saigō, which was considered integral to myth and mythology among the first generation of British anthropologists. Saigō was probably most influenced by the work of James Frazer (1854–1941), a Scottish anthropologist whose work linked ritual and myth. *The Truth of Myth* describes Frazer as focused on the transition from magic to religion and ritual to belief, with myth serving as system for understanding and controlling the world. Frazer's magnum opus *The Golden Bough* was widely read in Japan, and Japanese scholars fixated on Frazer's description of a "sacred king." Frazer's sacred king was a conceptual figure who mediated between the divine and the people, and in Japan, this role resonated with the role of the emperor and imperial family in Japanese myths. According to Frazer, the sacred king was connected to a solar deity and a yearly ritual for fertility and harvest. The king served as a consort to a goddess during this ritual, died or was sacrificed at the winter solstice, and then was reborn again for the rituals of the following year.

In Saigō's view, the first emperor, Jinmu, was a mythical personification of the inaugural Feast of First Rice ritual, the *daijōsai*, and also a mythical recurrence of his great-grandfather Ninigi. The connection between Jinmu and rice is demonstrated by the names of his brothers. Itsu-se could be a pun for "awesome rice," the "mike" in Mike-iri-no referred to rice that would be presented to the emperor, and the "ina" of Ina-hi also means "rice." This is also the case for the previous generation of ancestors—Ho-demi, Ho-suseri, and Ho-ori—"ho" could mean both "fire" and "rice ear." Jinmu himself has many names in eighth-century sources, some of which also refer to rice. One includes "hiko-ho," prince of rice, a phrase that also appears in the name of Ninigi. Saigō reads these names referring to rice and the repetition between Ninigi, Ho-ori (Hiko-ho-ho-demi/ Yama-sachi-hiko), and Jinmu as a mythical recurrence, in which each sovereign is the recurrence of Ninigi. The inaugural Feast of First Rice ritual allowed the new sovereign to step out of linear, historic time and become Ninigi within cyclical mythical time.

Based on this recurrence, Saigō interpreted Jinmu's journey as a repetition of Ninigi's descent. Jinmu moved to the east in search of an auspicious place to build his capital, just as Ninigi went around looking for land. The Hayato, based in southern Kyushu, are given in the Yama-sachi-hiko myth as the descendants of the older brother Umi-sachi-hiko and assigned a role in court ritual. Saigō drew a parallel between the land of the Hayato, where Jinmu begins his search, as the place that is both farthest from the court spatially and closest in terms of mythical time due to these rituals. Sao-ne-tsu-hiko, who guided Jinmu, was the ancestor of the provincial ruler of Yamato Province and the attendants of the main shrine to Ō-kuni-tama. Based on the Sujin myth about Amaterasu and Ō-kuni-tama being removed from the palace, Saigō inferred that Ō-kuni-tama was an important kami in the ancient period and so Sao-ne-tsu-hiko was given a prominent role in Jinmu's narrative. The same connection explains why Jinmu sends Sao-ne-tsu-hiko to collect the dirt from Mt. Kagu in Yamato prefecture. The dirt from this mountain is a metaphor for the land of the realm, and Sao-ne-tsu-hiko is associated with one of the powerful kami who inhabited it. The attack on Jinmu's forces at Kumano is meant to recall the "empty land" that Ninigi passed through during his search. The Kume and Ōtomo clans, whose ancestors served as the vanguard for Ninigi during his descent, precede Jinmu in entering Yamato.

Saigō argued that the myths related to Jinmu's pacification of Yamato were all directly linked to the *daijōsai* ceremony. Based on evidence in other historical sources, Saigō linked the crow, Ya-ta-garasu, to the Kamo clan, which was associated with imperial processions. The Ukashi brothers, the Mononobe clan, and the other kami that participated in the conquering of Yamato also played roles in the *daijōsai* ritual. Most important of these were the Kume songs, which are still performed at imperial accession rituals. The references to food in the songs refers to food from the *daijōsai* banquet, and the references to battle recall the actions of the ideal hero, presented here as Jinmu, but reenacted and recurring when a new sovereign participates in the ceremony for themselves. Noting that thirty-two of the first forty accession ceremonies took place in the twelfth, first, or second months, but that the *daijōsai* usually occurred around the winter solstice, Saigō argued that the emphasis on imperial accession at the New Year was a result of the importation of the calendar from Korea and anachronistically applied to the early emperors. In truth, the imperial accession was tied to the death and resurrection of the sun at the winter solstice, much as Frazer's sacred king would die and be reborn as a symbol of fertility and renewal.

Finally, Saigō noted that Jinmu, as a heroic ancestor linked to mythical time, was also a later creation who appeared when ritual, myth, and legend were historicized. Sujin, though equally legendary, was the first emperor in historical, linear time. Saigō argued that the eight emperors in-between Jinmu and Sujin were not a literal eight, but simply meant "many," as is common in ancient Japanese sources. This explained why Sujin was also called "first emperor to rule the state," even though Jinmu technically preceded him. For Saigō, Sujin was the first historical emperor, while Jinmu was the first mythical one.

## The Miwa God and Gods of Curses (Masuda Katsumi)

The identity and role of the kami worshipped at Mt. Miwa has prompted many mythological theories, largely due to the convoluted and conflicting information revealed about this kami in *Ancient Matters*, *Chronicles*, and other early sources. The first mention of the Miwa kami appears in the narrative of Ō-kuni-nushi finishing creation. In *Ancient Matters*, Ō-kuni-nushi laments on the seaside that he cannot finish creating the land, then a spirit comes to him to aid him. The spirit asks to be worshipped on the mountain in the east of the Yamato Basin: Mt. Miwa. A *Chronicles* variant adds that the spirit identified itself as the spirit of fortune and spirit of discernment of Ō-kuni-nushi, that is, the spirit constituted some part of Ō-kuni-nushi himself. The spirit is not identified in this entry, but at the beginning of the episode, this *Chronicles* variant notes that Ō-mono-nushi was another name for Ō-kuni-nushi. The end of the variant notes that either this Miwa kami or Koto-shiro-nushi, the son of Ō-kuni-nushi, was the father of Hime-tatara-i-suzu-hime, later empress to Jinmu. In a later variant from *Chronicles*, after Ō-kuni-nushi surrenders to the heavenly kami, Taka-mi-musuhi makes Ō-mono-nushi marry his daughter. In the Jinmu narrative in *Ancient Matters*, when Jinmu is searching for an empress, he learns of a beautiful woman who is the child of Ō-mono-nushi of Miwa, who impregnated his wife by changing into an arrow, swimming through the sewer, and penetrating her while she used the toilet. Put shortly, it is unclear if the Miwa kami is related to Ō-kuni-nushi or Koto-shiro-nushi or is another kami entirely.

Adding to the confusion, both *Ancient Matters* and *Chronicles* discuss the Miwa kami in the narrative of Emperor Sujin, but again, the information differs substantially. In both texts, Ō-mono-nushi delivers a plague upon the land, lifted only when the kami's descendant Ō-tata-neko is installed as the head priest at the Miwa Shrine. Sujin searches the realm and finds Ō-tata-neko, ending the plague, and asks Ō-tata-neko about his lineage. In *Ancient Matters*, Ō-tata-neko explains that the woman Iku-tama-yori-bime and the Miwa kami had a child, and that that child was his great-grandfather. Iku-tama-yori-bime was descended from Sue-tsu-mimi, likely associated with the Sue style of ceramic pottery. Iku-tama-yori-bime mysteriously became pregnant, and when her parents investigated, they discovered that the Miwa kami had been sneaking into her room at night through her keyhole. The lords of Miwa and Kamo are descended from this kami. In *Chronicles*, Ō-tata-neko tells Sujin that he is the direct child of Ō-mono-nushi and Iku-tama-yori-bime, without the narrative of how Iku-tama-yori-bime became pregnant. Then later in the *Chronicles* narrative, we learn of Sujin's aunt, the shamaness Yamato-toto-hi-momo-so-bime, who was secretly visited by the Miwa kami at night. When she asked the see the kami during the daytime, she found out that he was a snake and, in her surprise, is stabbed in the vagina by a set of chopsticks and dies. Finally, in the Yūryaku volume of *Chronicles*, the emperor orders a retainer named Chiisa-ko-be no Sugaru to catch the Miwa kami for him; this story is given in Chapter 4. Sugaru catches a large snake and brings it back to show Yūryaku, but because Yūryaku had failed to purify himself before seeing the kami, the kami threatened him with fire and lightning. Yūryaku had the snake returned.

A third important source for the Miwa legend is the *norito* used by the Provincial Miyatsuko of Izumo, summarized in Chapter 2. The extant recording of these prayers dates from much later than *Ancient Matters*, the 927 *Regulations and Laws of the Engi Era*, but the rituals at which the prayers were performed certainly go back earlier. Presumably the prayers were passed down via word-of-mouth, but opinions differ on whether they predate *Ancient Matters* and *Chronicles*, are from the same era, or are later products. At one ritual, the Provincial Miyatsuko of Izumo would recite the *norito* at the Yamato court. The mythical narrative of the *norito* has several major distinctions from *Ancient Matters* and *Chronicles*, most notably that Ame-no-hohi, who in *Ancient Matters* and *Chronicles* is sent to pacify the Central Reed Plain Land but betrays his charge and changes sides with Ō-kuni-nushi, is not a traitor. Instead, Ame-no-hohi is simply the ancestor of the Provincial Miyatsuko of Izumo. The other most important difference in the *norito* is that Ō-mono-nushi is the name given to the calming spirit of Ō-kuni-nushi. Similar to *Chronicles*, Ō-mono-nushi is a component part of Ō-kuni-nushi and meant to be enshrined at Mt. Miwa.

Literature scholar Masuda Katsumi (1923–2010) claimed that myths were a reflection of historical reality and were valuable because they reveal the social and cultural context of the eras in which they were created. Masuda argued that the series of myths surrounding Mt. Miwa emerged because local legends and beliefs were being conflated with mythical narratives. Examination of the Ō-mono-nushi myths clarifies what ancient people believed about kami and how they deified curses and plagues.

Masuda oriented his approach around the understandings of kami given by Yanagita Kunio and Orikuchi Shinobu, two of the greatest ethnographers and folklore scholars of twentieth-century Japan. Yanagita hypothesized that kami were ancestral spirits and that ancestor worship was the focal point of Japanese religious practice. When individuals die, their spirits become "household kami" that protect their descendants. First, the spirits of the dead head for the mountains, where they rise higher and higher. In time, they lose their individual identities, making the household kami a combination of one's ancestors. These spirits return to visit and protect their descendants at the annual *obon* festival as well as at spring and autumn festivals connected to agricultural rituals.

Orikuchi also identified kami as the spirits of the dead, but he hypothesized that these spirits go to the Land of Tokoyo, where they lost their individual features and became part of an ancestral village kami. The household vs. village distinguishes Yanagita and Orikuchi. Orikuchi also suggested that the village kami would return as *marebito*, meaning "rare visitor," to dispense blessings and good fortune. The motif of the auspicious visitor would later appear in Japanese myths and folklore, and at Japanese festivals, masked individuals reenacted these visits. Masuda, building on these two perspectives, suggested that ancient Japanese people believed in two kinds of kami. One, the kind suggested by Yanagita and Orikuchi, would visit its benefactor, but was not always present. The suppression of otherwise naturally occurring patterns wielded by this first kind of kami produced feelings of dread for the second type of kami, the *tatari-gami* or "god of curses." This second kind of kami was always present in the world and required people to venerate and pacify them.

Furthermore, the "mono" in Ō-mono-nushi can have two meanings. "Mono" can mean "thing" in Japanese, referring to concrete objects or people, and so Ō-mono-nushi could mean "great master of things" or more broadly, "master of all things." However, "mono" can also refer to negative spiritual energies, for example in the words "mono-no-ke" (evil spirt) or "mono-imi" (confinement to avoid impurity).

A key problem in Masuda's view was the uncertain relationship between Izumo and Yamato that the conflated accounts create. Mt. Miwa is in the Yamato Basin, and it is difficult to explain why Ō-mono-nushi, enshrined at Miwa, would visit Ō-kuni-nushi in Izumo or why a constituent part of Ō-kuni-nushi of Izumo would be enshrined at Miwa. Masuda argued that the Sujin myths were meant to explain the reality of the time in which they were written. As such, the most likely scenario was that the powerful clan from Izumo developed a number of explanations that fused their patron deity Ō-kuni-nushi with Ō-mono-nushi, who was at that time considered a powerful kami from Yamato. This resulted in multiple, somewhat similar explanations in which Ō-mono-nushi was a part of Ō-kuni-nushi, and as time passed, the most believable of those, which was that Ō-mono-nushi was the calm spirit of Ō-kuni-nushi, became the accepted explanation. As such, this explanation is what appeared in the ritually performed *norito*. However, there was no actual connection between Ō-kuni-nushi and Ō-mono-nushi in ancient Japan.

The reason it made sense to the ancient Japanese from Izumo to fuse Ō-mono-nushi, a god of disease and disaster, with Ō-kuni-nushi is because Ō-kuni-nushi, in the guise of his former name

Ō-ana-muji, was actually a volcano god. Masuda referred to a series of entries in the successor text to *Chronicles*, the *Continued Chronicles of Japan*, from the years 746–778. Unlike *Chronicles*, *Continued Chronicles* is considered a relatively faithful historical account of the eighth-century court. The entries to which Masuda refers describe a volcanic eruption in Kagoshima Bay. The disruption, presumably the earthquakes and ash, caused residents to flee, and created three new islands in the bay. Later, in 778, this land-creating kami was officially recognized by the court and said to be named Ō-ana-mochi, "great hole holder." Masuda argued that this kami was unique to Japan and appeared in various locations around the archipelago at different times but was ultimately connected to the intense volcanic activity in the archipelago that caused land to be created.

Masuda interpreted the Ō-mono-nushi story as given in *Chronicles*, which has more detail than *Ancient Matters*, as shorthand for explaining the connections between humans and kami. These fall into two categories: festivals, in which kami were publicly celebrated and summoned, and dreams, in which a kami could privately reveal itself to an individual. The public component of this action was the first part of the mythical narrative. At the onset of the epidemic, the emperor attempts to worship Amaterasu and Yamato-ō-kuni-tama with greater fervor by moving them out of the palace and assigning dedicated servants to them. However, these two kami, the guardians of the imperial household and the spirit of the land of Yamato, are unable to stop the plague. The emperor then sought to have Yamato-toto-bi-momo-so possessed and spoke with Ō-mono-nushi for the first time. All of these activities required the participation of multiple individuals, including the creation of vessels for offerings and the transportation of the kami. As such, they revealed the ritual worship of the kami as a social activity. Following the possession, Sujin sought instruction in a dream, and Ō-mono-nushi appeared to him in private. Masuda stressed that other people also needed to have the same dream. Hence, the episode reveals the two modes by which humans could get in touch with the kami: ritual worship and dreams.

In Masuda's explanation of the Miwa myth to illustrate the historical events of ancient Japan, the final piece of the puzzle is Ō-tata-neko's lineage. Descending from a clan that specialized in the Sue style of pottery suggests a linkage with the Korean peninsula and immigrants. The placenames given in *Ancient Matters* and *Chronicles* for Ō-tata-neko's home are different, but both are in Kōchi Province, present-day Osaka Prefecture. In ancient Japan, Osaka was a major hub for transport between the inland Yamato Basin and the outside world. Ships could move up and down the relatively peaceful inland sea between Fukuoka and Osaka, the same course used by Jinmu and his armada. Skilled ceramics immigrants from the Korean peninsula settled in Osaka in ancient times, introducing the Sue style of pottery to the Japanese archipelago. Epidemics in Japan also traveled from west to east, introduced in Fukuoka from Korea, then going up the inland sea to Osaka and on to the interior. Citing Mishina, Masuda identified numerous legends involving a snake and a woman on the Korean peninsula and in Japan, suggesting that at least one part of the legends—the mysterious pregnancy via snake god—also had connections to Korea.

The location of Kōchi created two clear plot holes with the myth as recorded. First, if Ō-tata-neko was from Kōchi, then the string used to track down his father or ancestor Ō-mono-nushi would have to be from about Osaka to Nara, at least twenty miles long. Second, the narrative suggests that Ō-mono-nushi was first worshipped at Miwa *after* the epidemic and events in the Sujin narrative, but if that was the case, then there is no explanation for why the Miwa god impregnated Iku-tama-yori-bime in the past. In Masuda's interpretation, these plot holes revealed that Ō-mono-nushi was actually a kami from Kōchi province first. The descendants of people from Kōchi in Yamato, that is, the people who came from where plagues seemed to originate, became the people who appeased the *tatari-gami* or gods of curses that caused the epidemic. For the clan worshipping the Miwa kami, the cursing kami fused with the guardian kami to become their patron, and Ō-mono-nushi fused with the snake legend that the clan had brought with them from Korea. The clan played an important ritual function in ancient Japan, and so later, Izumo aristocrats connected Ō-mono-nushi with their own patron deity, Ō-kuni-nushi.

## Intertextual Methods (Yamada)

A popular method in literature studies and intellectual history for reading mythical texts is the use of intertextuality. In this model, the linkages between texts, including citations, quotations, or references, whether explicit or implied, are identified and explored in order to clarify the meaning of authors or texts. An intertextual study might also survey the literature written around the same time as a text to get an understanding of the historical context and dominant perspectives and styles of expression in circulation at the time. Of course, for mythical texts, this approach is often difficult. For one, mythical texts can be very old, so there may not be many sources written around the same time with which to compare. Second, mythical texts often claim some descent or connection to a pre-literate oral tradition, meaning that the date the text was written may not correspond with the age of the mythical narrative.

There are few other Japanese texts from the early-eighth century when *Ancient Matters* and *Chronicles* were written. However, texts from China, especially from the Six Dynasties Period (222–589 CE), were imported to Japan through the Korean peninsula before and around the time that *Ancient Matters* and *Chronicles* were written, creating one important intellectual and potential inter-textual linkage. *Chronicles* in particular was clearly influenced by Chinese historical texts. Sino-Japanese comparative research on *Chronicles* was pioneered by Kojima Noriyuki in the contemporary era (1913–1998), and is currently applied in Japan by scholars like Endō Keita and Yamada Jun.

Yamada focuses primarily on the quasi-mythical records in *Chronicles* for emperors such as Jinmu and Sujin. By comparing

*Chronicles* with Chinese records, Yamada uncovers more complete meanings of textual material. Because the compilers of *Chronicles* were acquainted with and referred to these Chinese records, it becomes possible—or, by Yamada's interpretation, necessary—to perform comparative work between them. For example, the Sujin record uses passages from the historical record of Emperor Cheng of Han (r. 33–7 BCE) as recorded in the *Book of Han*. Because the passages in *Chronicles* are lifted almost verbatim, the parallel between the two books was observed in Japan as early as the eighteenth century, if not earlier. Yamada, however, furthered analysis by focusing on how Cheng of Han is described in the *Book of Han*. For example, Cheng regularly worshipped the gods of heaven and earth. Yamada tabulates the data for all emperors in the *Book of Han* and notes that Cheng and another emperor, Wu of Han (r. 141–87 BCE), worshipped the gods of heaven and earth the exact same number of times. As such, Yamada suggests that Sujin, known for his reverence of the gods of heaven and earth, was described in *Chronicles* in reference to not only Cheng but also Wu.

Yamada then interprets the Sujin record in *Chronicles* based on intertextual information from both the Cheng and Wu records in *Book of Han*. The most important difference between Cheng and Wu is that while the earlier emperor Wu began ritual practices of worshipping the gods of heaven and earth outside of the capital, Cheng ended this practice and worshipped them inside the capital instead. Disasters occurred as a result of Cheng's action, but his reverence for and fear of the gods allowed him to properly interpret their wishes and placate them.

Sujin also moves the location for the kami to be worshipped, but Yamada notes that the process is different from that of Cheng. In *Book of Han*, retainers first suggest the relocation to Cheng, who considers it, agrees, and then orders them to refer to classical Chinese texts for information and risk mitigation. Conversely, in *Chronicles*, when Sujin wants to relocate the god of heaven, Amaterasu, and the god of earth, Yamato-ō-kuni-tama, instead of seeking the will of the gods in classical texts, dreams, and oracles convey their wishes to humans. Furthermore, much as the Chinese historical texts were imagined in China to contain valuable precedents for kingship and prescriptions for governance from which future rulers could learn, the treatment of the kami in the Sujin volume provides an ideal version of the relationship between kami and the ruler for the Japanese emperor to emulate. The governance of the Yamato realm was accomplished through fearful and reverential worship of the kami of heaven and earth, and the emperor played a critical role as the central figure through whom the kami could make their will manifest using dreams and divination.

## Other Major Topics

### The Ise Shrine

The myth of Saruta-hiko is the first major reference to Ise in mythical texts, which is surprising given that Ise is the location of the Grand Shrine to Amaterasu, the most holy site in Shinto. Amaterasu provides the mirror that is ostensibly held by the shrine to Ninigi on his descent from heaven, but *Chronicles* identifies the mirror being moved there in the Sujin record. Another mirror was worshipped in the imperial palace in Kyoto until it was destroyed by fire in the Heian Period. Most likely, the shrine at Ise was not built until quite late, perhaps the late seventh-century reign of Jitō. If so, the association of Saruta-hiko with Ise might refer to some kami that was connected to the Ise Shrine before it became the locus for worship of Amaterasu. In medieval Japan, the Ryōbu and Watarai traditions of Shinto developed a more complex set of beliefs around the Ise Shrine that were heavily influenced by Buddhism. These traditions also created their own sacred texts, though they were all written substantially later than *Ancient Matters* and *Chronicles*.

## Court Titles

The human beings and lineage groups identified in the myths of this chapter are associated with a complicated and multi-tiered system of ranks and titles used in ancient Japan. Kimi was given to middle-ranking families in the capital area and in the periphery. It was also used for descendants of the imperial family, though written with a different character. Muraji was used for lineage groups that were allied with the Yamato court, including Mononobe and Nakatomi, and the muraji were often associated with particular artisan groups or with military affairs. The set of hereditary titles, called *kabane* in Japanese, was revised and standardized in 684 CE by Emperor Tenmu.

## Kashihara Shrine

The Kashihara Shrine, ostensibly marking the location where Jinmu founded the Japanese Empire in 660 BCE, was actually constructed in 1890. The late nineteenth century was a period in which the modern national consciousness of Japan was first being formed, and construction projects like the Kashihara Shrine played an important role in bringing the Japanese people together as a nation. The shrine is still a major site for Japanese rituals, including the February 11 celebration of "Foundation Day," the anniversary of Jinmu's founding of the empire and national holiday. A mausoleum to Jinmu is also nearby, though clearly mythical in origin.

## Eight Absent Generations

Both *Chronicles* and *Ancient Matters* record eight emperors between Jinmu and Sujin, but neither text provides much detail on their identities or the events of their reigns. One popular theory holds that these eight emperors were inserted into the narrative in order to push the foundation date of Japan back to 660 BCE, which was considered an auspicious year according to the Chinese Classic *I Ching/Yi Jing* or *Book of Changes*. Another interpretation is that the genealogical connections between each emperor and his empress and their children reveal an increasing expansion of power through marriage alliances across the Nara Basin. By this reading, the eight emperors tell the story of the Yamato state coalescing into an ever-larger polity. In either case, the dearth of historical information about these mythical figures has led to them being called *kesshi hachidai* in Japanese, or "Eight Absent Generations."

# 4

# Mythology and the Japanese State

## Japanese State-Building Myths

### Yamato Take Conquers the Kumaso, Izumo, and Emishi Peoples

Emperor Keikō had twin sons, Ō-usu, meaning "large mortar," and O-usu, meaning "small mortar." In *Ancient Matters*, the older son was killed by his younger brother when they were teenagers, while in *Chronicles*, he is a coward and leaves the court in disgrace, and is later given rule of Mino Province, present-day southern Gifu Prefecture. The younger son, O-usu, was a brave warrior. He is usually known by the name Yamato Take, meaning "brave of Yamato." In twentieth-century mythology, he was often called Yamato Takeru, though this is probably a mistaken reading of the characters for his name. In *Ancient Matters*, Yamato Take has a difficult relationship with his father, the emperor, who he believes is trying to kill him, while in *Chronicles*, he is especially beloved by his father, who praises his valor and strength.

According to *Ancient Matters*, one day, the emperor asked his younger son, O-usu, "Why does your older brother never join us for meals? Go and kindly instruct him that he is in the wrong."

Five days passed, and the older son still did not appear at meals. The emperor asked O-usu, "Why does your older brother never join us for meals? I thought that you went to talk to him about this."

O-usu replied, "I did. I've already told him about his misdeed."

Then the emperor asked, "How did you kindly instruct him that he was in the wrong?"

O-usu said, "I set an ambush for him in the bathroom. When he came in first thing in the morning, I was waiting for him, and I crushed him with my bare hands. Then I tore off his arms and legs, wrapped his body in a mat, and threw it away."

The emperor was terrified of his son's wild behavior and told him, "At the western borders of our land dwell the Kumaso. They are led by two fierce brothers. Go and slay them." O-usu received his orders, but before departing, stopped to visit his aunt, Yamato-hime. She gave him a skirt and blouse. O-usu still had the long hair of a young boy.

When he arrived in the land of the Kumaso, he found a small force guarding a newly built pit dwelling meant to serve as a meeting hall. He also overheard people talking about an upcoming feast to celebrate the new building. After scouting the area, he decided to wait for the day of the feast.

According to *Chronicles*, O-usu's father subdued the land of Kyushu, where the Kumaso dwelt, early in his reign. Later, however, the Kumaso revolted and attacked the borderlands. In response, the emperor sent O-usu to defeat the Kumaso. At the time he was sixteen years old. O-usu received the order from his father the emperor and said, "I would like a skilled archer to accompany me on my mission. Is there anyone who is skilled at archery that can come with me?"

Someone at court told him, "Otohiko no Kimi is a skilled archer." O-usu summoned Otohiko, who came with several other brave warriors in his retinue, and the small band set out for the lands of the Kumaso.

When they arrived, O-usu surveyed the geography of the land and considered its strategic value. At that time, there was a chieftain of the Kumaso named Kawakami Takeru who was holding a massive banquet.

O-usu tied his hair up in the style of a young girl and dressed up like a woman, hiding his sword underneath his clothing. He attended the feast in the company of some other women and quickly caught the attention of the Kumaso chieftain.

According to *Ancient Matters*, he quickly caught the attention of the two Kumaso brothers, who asked him to sit between them. Once the brothers were drunk, he drew his sword and stabbed the older brother in the chest. The younger brother fled, but O-usu caught up to him as he climbed the steps leading up out of the pit dwelling and stabbed him in the buttocks.

The younger brother pleaded, "Wait, stay your blade." O-usu hesitated. Then the younger brother inquired, "Who are you?"

O-usu replied, "I am the son of the Emperor of Yamato who rules over these eight great islands. The emperor sent me to kill you because of the rebellion of the Kumaso."

The younger brother replied, "I see. In the land of the Kumaso, my brother and I were the strongest. But now we have been slain by a braver man from the land of Yamato. From now on, may you be known as Yamato Take, meaning 'Brave of Yamato.'" Then O-usu sliced the younger brother up like a ripe melon. According to *Chronicles*, the name Yamato Take was given to O-usu by Kawakami Takeru, whom O-usu had stabbed through the chest.

In *Chronicles*, Yamato Take returned to the capital by sea. On the way, he killed several evil kami. Then he reported to his father the emperor, saying, "Thanks to your divine power, I have slain the Kumaso chieftain and pacified that land. The western lands are at last at peace. On the way back, there were two evil kami that were using poison gas against people traversing the inland sea. I also put them to death." His father rewarded him for his triumphs.

In *Ancient Matters*, Yamato Take returned to the capital by passing through Izumo, where he also slew the chieftain Izumo Takeru. He accomplished this by striking up a friendship with Izumo Takeru,

**FIGURE 11** Yamato Take and Kawakami Takeru. Tsukioka Yoshitoshi, *c.*1883. From the series Yoshitoshi musha murui Wikipedia Commons

but in secret, he made a fake sword out of wood. One day, he asked Izumo Takeru to go for a swim with him. Yamato Take got out of the water first and took the sword that his friend Izumo Takeru had been wearing. He told Izumo Takeru, "Let us switch swords." Izumo Takeru took the fake, wooden sword that Yamato Take had been wearing. Yamato Take challenged him to a duel. Since Izumo Takeru was unable to draw his wooden sword, Yamato Take cut him down. Then he composed a song,

> The scabbard of the sword worn
> by the brave man of Izumo
> is adorned with much arrowroot,
> but there is no blade inside. How sad!

After this, Yamato Take returned to his father and reported his triumphs.

According to *Ancient Matters*, when Yamato Take returned, his father immediately ordered him to go east and conquer the unruly people there. Before departing, Yamato Take again went to speak with his aunt, Yamato-hime. He told her, "Why is it that my father wants me to die? First, he sent me to kill the chieftains of the Kumaso; then as soon as I returned, he sent me off again by myself to conquer the people in the east. He must be hoping that I'll get myself killed."

While Yamato Take grieved, his aunt gave him a sword and a magic bag. The sword was none other than Kusanagi, the sword that Susano-o had found in the body of the eight-headed snake and surrendered to the heavenly gods, and that Amaterasu had given to Ninigi when he departed from heaven. She told Yamato Take that if he was ever in danger, he should open the bag.

According to *Chronicles*, the Emishi people of the east rebelled. The emperor conferred with his officials, saying, "Now there is unrest in the lands to the east. Who should I send to quell this rebellion?"

The government officials had no idea. Yamato Take said, "I handled the rebellion in the west. My older brother should deal with the rebellion in the east." But his older brother, Ō-usu, was terrified and ran away.

The emperor sent a message to summon Ō-usu to court. When he came, the emperor reprimanded him, saying, "You have yet to even face the rebels! How could you already be afraid?" Then he gave him a fief in Mino Province and sent him away.

Yamato Take said, "Barely any time has passed since I conquered the Kumaso, and now the Emishi in the east are rebelling. Will we ever know peace? This is an awful task, but I will handle it."

According to *Ancient Matters*, on his way eastwards, Yamato Take stayed in the house of Miyazu-hime, who dwelt in the land of Owari, present-day Nagoya City. He wanted to marry her and decided to do so on his return.

Yamato Take continued eastward and soon reached the land of Sagami. The governor of that land tricked him, saying, "In the middle of this field is a large lake inhabited by a powerful kami." Yamato Take wanted to see this kami for himself and so he set off through the wild grasses of the field. According to *Chronicles*, the governor told him that the field was full of elk and encouraged him to go hunting. As soon as Yamato Take was out of sight, the governor set the field on fire. When he realized that he had been deceived, Yamato Take drew his sword and cut down the grass around him. This is how the sword got the name Kusanagi, meaning "grass mower." Yamato Take also looked inside the bag that his aunt had given him and found a flint. He used the flint to light a counterfire and escape the trap. Then he tracked down the governor and killed him along with his family and burned the bodies.

When he reached Kamitsufusa (what is now Tokyo Bay), Yamato Take took to sea. However, once he had put out, the wind suddenly intensified and his boat was captured by the current. His consort, named Oto-tachibana-hime, was traveling with him and realized that this was the work of the sea kami. She offered to sacrifice herself to the kami in his stead. As soon as she entered the water, the wind stopped. According to *Ancient Matters*, as she sank into the depths, she sang,

> Alas, for my lord,
> who called for me
> while standing amid the fire,
> the burning flames,
> at that tiny field in Sagami.

Seven days later, her comb washed ashore. Yamato Take took the comb and buried it as if it were her.

According to *Chronicles*, Yamato Take continued to the east and entered the land of the Emishi by sea. The Emishi leaders saw his boat from afar and knew that they were no match for him. When he arrived, they asked him, "What is your name? Are you not a kami?"

Yamato Take replied, "I am the son of a kami made manifest." When he said this, the Emishi were filled with fear and reverence. They waded out into the water and helped bring his boat in. Then they surrendered. Their leader was made a servant of Yamato Take.

Yamato Take headed back toward the capital over land. When he reached the land of Kai, present-day Yamanashi Prefecture, he asked his retainers,

> Since passing Tsukuba
> and Niibari,
> how many nights have we slept?

None of them was able to reply. Then, one old man responsible for the campfire spoke up, saying,

> Counting them up,
> nights, nine,
> and days, ten.

Yamato Take was greatly pleased and rewarded the old man.

As he returned home, from a high mountain pass, Yamato Take was overcome with feelings of longing for his consort Oto-tachibana-hime, who had died when she sacrificed herself to the god of the sea. Yamato Take looked toward the east and sighed, saying, "Azuma!" This means "Alas, for my wife." For this reason, the lands of the east are sometimes called "Azuma."

As he traveled, he became hungry, and a kami from the mountain decided to torment him. The kami transformed into a white deer and stood in front of him to taunt him. Yamato Take thought it was strange and threw a piece of garlic at the deer, hitting it in the eye and killing it. It used to be that when people went through Shinano Pass, many of them were killed by poison gas that was expelled by this kami, but after Yamato Take slew it, people were able to use the pass.

Yamato Take returned at last to Owari, where he married Miyazu-hime, to whom he had previously pledged himself. After they had joined in marriage, he heard about a rampaging kami at Mt. Ibuki. He left his sword, Kusanagi, at Miyazu-hime's house, which is now the Atsuta Shrine in Nagoya City. The sword remains there to this day.

**FIGURE 12** Atsuta Shrine (location of Kusanagi Sword). Nagoya City
Wikipedia Commons

In *Chronicles*, at Mt. Ibuki, he encountered the kami of the mountain, but did not realize it because the spirit had taken on the form of a snake. According to *Ancient Matters*, it took on the form of a white boar. Since Yamato Take did not recognize it as the kami of the mountain, he ignored it and pressed on. As he continued his climb, a hailstorm suddenly broke out and he became lost in the mountains. In the end, Yamato Take was able to force his way out, but his mind was lost and he was in a complete daze. He stopped at a natural spring to recover. There he realized that the kami of the mountain had poisoned him, and he began to struggle. Though his legs began to fail him, he pressed on, but eventually he collapsed and died. Messengers swiftly went to inform the emperor.

According to *Chronicles*, when the emperor heard that Yamato Take had died, he ordered that a great tomb be constructed. According to *Ancient Matters*, it was Yamato Take's consorts and children who built the tomb. After his corpse had been interred, it transformed into a white bird and flew out of the tomb toward the capital in Yamato. The bird stopped twice on the way to Yamato, and so tombs were built at those locations as well. Finally, the bird flew off to heaven, never to return.

## Empress Jingū Conquers Korea

Yamato Take's father Keikō was succeeded by his son Seimu. However, Keikō's intended heir was Yamato Take, and so after Seimu died, the throne passed to Yamato Take's son Chūai. Chūai's reign was very short, and his wife, Empress Jingū, ruled in his stead as regent until their son, Ōjin, took the throne upon her death.

Jingū was descended from an immigrant to Japan from the Korean kingdom of Silla named Ame-no-hi-hoko, who came during the reign of the mythical emperor Suinin. This sets Jingū's conquest of Silla up as an inheritance story within the ancient mythical narrative. Sadly, this fantastical myth of foreign conquest was repurposed by the modern Japanese empire as justification for its colonization of Korea. As such, Jingū remains a controversial figure. In *Chronicles*, she is also associated with the Wa queen Himiko or Pimiko, named in Chinese historical records as the ruler of the kingdom of Yamatai. The authors of *Chronicles* were certainly familiar with this reference when they determined the chronology for Jingū, making it seem as if the two queens could be the same individual. As with the myths from the Divine Age, there are multiple differing narratives of Jingū's conquest: three in *Chronicles* and one in *Ancient Matters*.

According to *Ancient Matters*, during the reign of Chūai, his empress, Jingū, was possessed by a kami. At the time, Chūai was preparing to attack the Kumaso. When Jingū became possessed, Chūai took up his zither, and his most trusted adviser, Takeuchi no Sukune, questioned her. The empress, while possessed, told them, "In the west is a rich land of gold and silver. I bestow this land upon you."

Chūai was suspicious of this claim, for he knew of no land west of his own. When he climbed a tall hill and looked to the west, he saw only the sea. And so he pushed aside his zither and sat in silence. The kami possessing Jingū was furious and said, "You will no longer rule this realm! Quickly depart from this life!"

Takeuchi no Sukune was concerned and asked Chūai to keep playing the zither, which the emperor did unenthusiastically. Soon the music stopped, and when they raised a lantern to see what had happened, Chūai was dead.

According to *Chronicles*, when the kami possessing Jingū promised the western land of gold and silver to Chūai, he replied, "My imperial ancestors venerated all of the kami of this land already. What kami are you, and why are you trying to trick me? There is no land west of here."

Then the kami, still possessing the empress, replied angrily, "When I look down from heaven, I see the land to the west like a shadow on the water. But since you do not believe it is there, you shall never obtain it. The empress is pregnant; this land shall go to your son."

Chūai still did not believe that there was any land west of his own, and so he attacked the Kumaso, but his forces failed to subdue them, and he retreated. Shortly afterwards, he suddenly got sick and died.

Jingū knew that her unborn son's rivals for the throne would not hesitate to strike if they knew the emperor was dead, and so she asked his closest retainers to perform a temporary burial in secret. Then she waited for an auspicious day and summoned the kami that had possessed her earlier. It came, and she asked, "What kami spoke to my husband the emperor the other day?"

The kami, possessing her, replied, "Amaterasu, Waka-hiru-me, Koto-shiro-nushi, and the three Sumiyoshi gods." The empress ordered that these kami all be venerated and sent one of her generals to attack the Kumaso, who were subdued in no time at all.

Then, Jingū made several oaths confirming that she was to go west. She used a piece of flour as a lure, saying that if she caught a fish, she should seek the country in the west. She caught a sweetfish. She cleared rice fields to supply the shrines that venerated the gods, and when a large rock blocked the irrigation ditch she was digging, she held up a sword and prayed. A lightning bolt crashed from the heavens and shattered the rock. She waded into the sea and said that if her hair parted in half when she came out of the water, she would be successful in her campaign. Her hair naturally parted into two, and she tied her two locks up on the side of her head like a warrior. Finally, feeling her delivery time draw near, she took a stone and pressed it in between her legs to delay the birth.

Once her armada was ready, she set out from Tsushima. The kami of the wind gave her a powerful tailwind, and the kami of the sea raised the sea level such that the oceans spilled into the lands of Korea. Jingū's ship was carried all the way to the gate of the palace of the King of Silla, who was amazed at the supernatural phenomena that had carried the Japanese armada to his capital at Kyŏngju, twelve miles inland. Knowing that the kami must support his invaders, the king raised the white flag and surrendered. When Jingū disembarked, the King of Silla pledged that as long as the sun rose in the east and set in the west, the rudders of the tribute ships from Silla would never go dry. Shortly thereafter, the Kings of Paekche and Koguryŏ came and

**FIGURE 13**  Empress Jingū and Takeuchi no Sukune Fishing at Chikuzen. Tsukioka Yoshitoshi, 1876 Los Angeles County Museum of Art

surrendered as well. The empress then returned from Silla and gave birth to Emperor Homuta, known as Ōjin.

When Jingū returned to Japan, she put down a coup led by two imperial princes and then ruled the state from her position as Empress Dowager, the title for a mother or widow of an emperor. Her son, Ōjin, eventually succeeded her, but Jingū ruled personally for many years in the interim. For this reason, sources treat Jingū ambiguously. For example, in *Chronicles*, a volume is dedicated to Jingū, and she is the only non-emperor to receive such treatment. Conversely, *Chronicles* does not explicitly identify her as an emperor, nor does it use the specialized language befitting the supreme ruler of the state. Histories of Japan written before the end of the nineteenth century tended to count Jingū as an official ruling emperor. When the state and monarchy were modernized at the end of the 19th century, Jingū was removed from the count of historical emperors.

## Legendary Emperor Yūryaku

Ōjin was succeeded by his son, Nintoku, who is often heralded as the greatest of Japan's legendary emperors. Nintoku's devotion to benevolence and forbearance is used in the historical narratives to create a contrast with his grandson, Yūryaku. The pattern of pairing culturally enlightened rule with military virtuosity is probably modeled on the first two emperors of the Han dynasty in ancient China.

Yūryaku succeeds one of his older brothers, Ankō, after Ankō is killed by his stepson. Yūryaku then kills two of his older brothers to take the throne and one of his cousins whom he also considers a threat. He also slays Ankō's killer.

Yūryaku is the first emperor for whom the legendary accounts in Japanese sources appear to concretely intersect with historical accounts from China and with the archaeological record. During the fourth and fifth centuries, Chinese chronicles record diplomatic exchange with the so-called Five Kings of Wa. Wa was the Chinese name for the Japanese archipelago. The fifth of these kings, Wu, was described as a competent warrior king who used force to unite the warring polities of the archipelago. A pair of swords excavated from opposite ends of the ancient Yamato realm, the Eta-Funayama Sword and the Sakitama-Inariyama Sword, date from around the same time. The swords refer to a King Wowake, which is close to the vernacular Japanese name of Yūryaku, Wakatake. Based on this positive identification, the Kings of Wa in Chinese records who precede Wu are presumed to be Yūryaku's brothers, uncles, and perhaps even his grandfather, Nintoku. However, the Japanese and Chinese records are not in complete accord, and Yūryaku is the only individual who has concrete representation across sources.

Many of the famous episodes involving Emperor Yūryaku occurred when he was out on the hunt, a favorite pastime. In one episode, recorded in both *Ancient Matters* and *Chronicles*, Yūryaku was hunting around Mt. Kazuraki in the northwestern sector of the Nara basin. He saw a tall man on the other side of a valley and realized that the man looked just like him. Yūryaku knew that this meant that the man was kami and asked, "Who are you?"

The tall kami replied, "I am a kami; tell me your name and I will tell you mine."

Yūryaku replied using his vernacular name, saying, "I am Wakatake."

The kami replied to him, "I am Hito-koto-nushi, the master of one word. This is because I have the power to bring about good or evil using only a single word."

The two of them spent the entire day together hunting deer and racing their horses. At the end of the day, the kami accompanied Yūryaku to the Kume river and saw him off, making a great impression on Yūryaku's people.

In another episode, Yūryaku was hunting at Mt. Kazuraki when a mysterious bird suddenly appeared. It was the size of a sparrow, but it had a long tail that followed behind it, dragging on the ground. The bird warned Yūryaku, "Be on your guard!"

Suddenly, a wild boar rushed out of the undergrowth and attacked Yūryaku and his hunting retinue. The hunters accompanying him were terrified and all climbed up trees to escape from the boar. Yūryaku however stood his ground, and when the boar charged him, he thrust out his bow and stopped the boar's charge. Then he lifted his leg and stomped the boar underfoot, killing it instantly. Yūryaku was incensed at the cowardice of his servants and was going to kill them all. The terrified hunters composed the following poem:

> Afraid of the growl of the wild boar
> during the hunt
> of my great lord,
> I climbed to escape,
> into the branches of the alder tree
> atop the hill.
> Oh, my tree!

When the empress heard the song, she was moved with compassion and went to speak with Yūryaku. She told him, "The people in our land all say that you love hunting and animals more than you love them. If you kill your servants on account of a boar, are you any different from a wolf?"

Yūryaku was moved by the empress' words and decided to spare the lives of his hunters.

According to *Chronicles*, In the seventh year of Yūryaku's reign, he sent one of his retainers, named Sugaru, to catch the god of Mt. Miwa. The god is given as either Ō-mono-nushi or Uda-no-kurosaka. Sugaru captured the kami, which had taken the form of a great snake.

However, when Sugaru showed the snake to the Yūryaku, thunder sounded and the snake's eyes glittered because Yūryaku had not practiced the required ritual purification and abstinence before meeting the kami. Yūryaku was afraid and sent the snake back to the mountain.

A different story involving Yūryaku, Sugaru, and a thunder kami appears in the *Record of Miraculous Events in Japan* (*Nihon Ryōiki*).

Late in Yūryaku's reign, a story about a man from Tanba province named Urashima is recorded in *Chronicles*. *Chronicles* refers the reader to another source but does not provide its name. It is likely that *Chronicles* refers to the *Gazetteer of Tango Province*. There are some minor differences to the Urashima story between these sources and another retelling in *Myriad Poems*. In modern Japan, the man is known as Urashima Tarō.

Urashima was fishing in the ocean and caught a giant turtle in his net. He set the turtle free from the net and released it back into the ocean. Several days later, Urashima was out fishing when a turtle approached him and told him that the god of the sea wanted to thank him for saving the other turtle. The turtle escorted Urashima to the bottom of the ocean and the palace of the sea god. It turned out that the turtle he had saved was the daughter of the sea god, a beautiful princess.

The princess became Urashima's wife, and they lived together in the palace of the sea god. After some time, Urashima said that he wished to go back to his village and see his family. The princess gave him a magical box and told him never to open it.

Urashima returned to his village and found out that hundreds of years had passed since he left, even though his time in the palace of the sea god had only been a few days. Forlorn, he opened the box that was given to him by the princess, and a cloud puffed out leaving nothing inside the box. Urashima instantly aged all the years that he had spent in the palace of the sea god, and suddenly found that he had white hair and a long beard. He realized that the box had contained his old age.

## Myth-Making Emperors: Tenmu and Jitō

Among the historical emperors whose exploits are recorded in *Chronicles*, perhaps the most consequential are the husband-and-wife pair of Tenmu and Jitō. The prevailing opinion among historians of early Japan is that the title of emperor and the state name of Japan were both adopted after Tenmu took the throne in 673. Tenmu's reign was preceded by that of his older brother, Tenji, but after Tenji died, there was a civil war between Tenji's son Ōtomo and Tenji's younger brother Tenmu. It appears that after his victory, Tenmu not only succeeded to the throne, but also refashioned his rule as if it were a new dynastic lineage. Before he died, Tenmu named his son with Jitō, Kusakabe, as crown prince, but Kusakabe did not take the throne immediately upon Tenmu's death. Instead, Jitō took control of the state, perhaps hoping to stabilize political matters before handing power to her son, or simply waiting for him to get a little older. Unexpectedly, Kusakabe died at around twenty-six or twenty-seven years of age, only three years after the death of his father Tenmu.

The surprising death of Kusakabe resulted in Jitō staying on the throne for eight more years until she abdicated in favor of Kusakabe's son and her grandson, Monmu. Jitō's rule provided the foundations for a new kind of Japanese state based on written legal codes adapted from Tang China. She founded the first permanent capital of Japan in Fujiwara, systematized legal codes and taxation, and formalized the power structure of the court. She adopted the same title of emperor that was used by her husband, Tenmu, and in doing so, created a succession of emperors that continues to the present. Sometime during Tenmu's reign, the mythical and legendary kings of ancient Japan were posthumously promoted to the rank of emperor and arranged in a formal and official line. This line of emperors, first attested in the *Chronicles* record of Tenmu's funeral, forms the structural basis for *Ancient Matters* and *Chronicles*, the two texts that record most of the ancient Japanese myths. *Ancient Matters* was presented in 712 to Emperor Genmei, the wife of Monmu. *Chronicles* was written by one of Tenmu's sons and presented to Monmu's older sister, Emperor Genshō. Jitō, Genmei, and Genshō were women, but they held the same Japanese title as Tenmu and other emperors, so they are either called "female emperor" or just "emperor." "Empress" refers to the non-ruling wife of a male emperor.

According to the main narrative of *Chronicles*, Tenmu was named crown prince in the first year of the reign of his older brother Tenji. Four years later, Tenji fell ill and was sure that he was going to die soon. Tenji sent for Tenmu, but before Tenmu went into the room to meet him, one of Tenji's advisors advised Tenmu, "Be careful what you say." Tenmu realized that there was a plot afoot and resolved to be careful.

When Tenmu came to Tenji's bedside, Tenji ordered him to become the next emperor. Tenmu refused and said that because his health had been poor, he would be a bad fit. He asked Tenji if he could instead enter the priesthood to pray on behalf of Tenji, and if Tenji's son Ōtomo could take the throne. Tenji approved of this plan and died shortly thereafter. Tenmu left for Yoshino, south of the court capital of Ōmi, accompanied by his loyal retainers.

About six months after Tenji died, Tenmu summoned his closest servants and told them, "I've heard that the servants of the Ōmi court are planning to attack me. You three head to Mino Province, east of Ōmi, and raise the soldiers in that province. On the way, tell the other provincial governors you meet to muster their forces and close off Fuwa Pass."

The same day, Tenmu himself left Yoshino and headed east. At first, he set out on foot, but he soon met a court official who handled horse stewardship and was able to ride. His son, Kusakabe, and his wife, Jitō, were with him.

As Tenmu headed east, he was joined by more and more soldiers from each of the provinces through which he passed. Some of the imperial princes, including Prince Takechi, also came to join him, leading their own entourages. When they reached Ise, they halted to worship Amaterasu. At that moment, one of the retainers he had sent from Yoshino came riding up and reported that they had mustered three thousand soldiers and succeeded in blocking off the Fuwa Pass. Tenmu continued and camped in a place called Kuwana.

Back at the Ōmi court, Ōtomo heard that Tenmu had escaped to the east, and there was an uproar in the palace. Ōtomo asked his advisers what to do. Some suggested immediately sending a detachment of cavalry to catch Tenmu, but Ōtomo rejected the idea. Instead, he decided to send his retainers out to round up troops from distant provinces. One messenger went east, one went to the Yamato area of central Japan, one went to Kyushu in the far west, and one went to Kibi along the Sea of Japan. Ōtomo told his servants that the rulers of Kyushu and Kibi previously served Tenmu, and to kill them on the spot if they went against his orders.

Ōtomo's servants ended up killing the ruler of Kibi in order to take command of his forces. The servants who went to Kyushu were rejected; the ruler of Kyushu said that his soldiers were there to defend Japan from outside invasion, not to be deployed in the country's interior. When the servant from the Ōmi court threatened him, the sons of the ruler of Kyushu drew their swords and stood beside their father, and so the servants of Ōmi retreated with nothing. In the east, the servants of Ōmi ran into the barricaded Fuwa Pass and were unable to proceed. Their forces were routed, although their leader escaped. The two servants sent to Yamato saw which way the wind was blowing and decided to retreat to their home. The older brother decided to stay home, but the younger brother, Fukei, wanted to make a name for himself and went to fight for Tenmu with a small number of soldiers that he had gathered.

Meanwhile, Prince Takechi sent Tenmu a message asking him to come closer to the front so that they could have better communication. Jitō stayed in Kuwana, and Tenmu advanced to the blockade at Fuwa Pass. Takechi rode out to meet Tenmu and told him about the attack on the pass that he had repelled. Despite the victory, Tenmu was disconcerted when he heard that the ministers and officials in Ōmi had indeed come together to conspire against him. Takechi reassured him, saying, "Even though you are alone you are the emperor, and I, Takechi, will put my faith in your miraculous power."

Tenmu gave Takechi a fresh horse and put the military affairs completely under his command.

On that same day, in the Nara basin to the south, Fukei told his small force about a plan to remove the enemies of Tenmu off of the roads so that he could muster a larger force from the area. He said, "I'm going to pretend to be Takechi, and I'll take a small detachment of riders to face the enemy army blocking the road north of Asuka Temple. Take the rest of the force and hide west of the temple, and when you hear my signal, ride out to join me." Then Fukei sent one of his retainers to secretly mix in with the enemy army.

After the retainer was well within the enemy forces, he screamed, "Takechi has come himself from the blockade with a large army following him!" The enemy forces scattered in disarray, and at the same time, the forces that Fukei had splintered off rejoined him from the west. They captured the armory, executed its keeper, and seized the weapons. A combination of defectors and local aristocrats who had still not committed their forces to either side joined Fukei's forces. Fukei sent a messenger to Tenmu at the blockade to report that they had taken Asuka. Tenmu promoted Fukei to general, and several brave warriors rallied to Fukei's banner in hopes of fame and glory.

Fukei fortified the old capital at Asuka and pushed north, but he was defeated at Mt. Nara and retreated to the south. Meanwhile, the army manning the blockade with Tenmu pushed westwards toward Ōmi. When they heard that Fukei had been defeated at Mt. Nara, they sent a small detachment of riders racing south to his aid. Their main force pushed west and reached the enemy encampment where Ōtomo himself awaited them. Camped to the west of a bridge, it was difficult for Tenmu's army to launch an attack on Ōtomo's camp. Furthermore, Ōtomo's soldiers had removed some of the wooden planks from the bridge and replaced them with a single board running lengthwise. They had attached ropes to the board and could pull it back if anyone stepped on it to cross.

One of Tenmu's soldiers, a brave man named Wakami, put on several sets of armor to protect himself from arrows and then sprinted across the board and cut the ropes with his sword before the enemy could pull them back. Tenmu's army stormed across the bridge and routed the defending troops. They tracked down and executed the enemy commanders, and Ōtomo, who had nowhere to run, hanged himself.

Having defeated his enemy, Tenmu had a palace built in Yamato called Asuka Kiyomihara Palace, and he moved in that winter. In the spring, he officially succeeded to the throne. Jitō was named empress.

That fall, the Korean Kingdom of Silla sent envoys to the court, some to pay respects for the deceased former Emperor Tenji, and others to congratulate Tenmu on his accession to the throne. When the messengers arrived in Japan, Tenmu asked the messengers sent to mourn the former emperor to return without coming to court, but welcomed the messengers sent to congratulate him. Tenmu was not interested in simply succeeding his older brother; he wanted to start his own dynastic lineage.

In the eighth year, fifth month of his reign, Tenmu visited Yoshino Palace along with Jitō and several of his sons and nephews. There, Tenmu told them all, "I think that you should swear an alliance right here so that after I die, the succession will not fall into dispute again." Kusakabe was the first to swear that he and his brothers and cousins would never fight against each other. The other princes followed his lead, and then Tenmu swore that he would love them all equally. Jitō, too, swore that she would love them all as her own children.

After Tenmu died, Jitō attended court and handled the affairs of state, but she did not officially take the throne. Three years later, Kusakabe died.

That same year, Jitō implemented the Asuka-Kiyomihara Code, Japan's first written legal system. Since Kusakabe had died, she also acceded to the throne officially and became emperor. Takechi was appointed chancellor. Jitō frequently visited Yoshino; perhaps she meant to remind the many imperial princes of the oath they had sworn there not to fight against each other.

**FIGURE 14** Scale model of Fujiwara Capital. Held by Fujiwara-kyo Reference Room, Kashihara City

In the fifth year, tenth month of her reign, Jitō oversaw the groundbreaking of Fujiwara-kyō, the first permanent capital of Japan (not to be confused with the powerful Fujiwara clan, whose rise to power began during the reign of Tenji). Modeled on the Chinese capital of Chang-An, Fujiwara-kyō was a planned settlement with a grid layout for the streets and broad central avenue that led to the palace gate. Fujiwara-kyō served as the capital until 710.

Jitō oversaw eleven years of prosperity, during which time she ensured that laws were being effectively enforced. She promoted the spread of Buddhism in the land and improved relations with the Korean kingdom of Silla. Finally, in the eleventh year of her reign, she abdicated, and her grandson took the throne as Emperor Monmu. Although the capital was soon moved from Fujiwara-kyō to Heijō-kyō (Nara), Jitō's legacy, a historical lineage of emperors, continues to this day.

## Mythological Perspectives

### Comparative Axes: Time (Thompson and Schrempp)

Thompson and Schrempp note that time within mythical narratives can be complex. Myths may mix or juxtapose multiple kinds of time.

For example, linear time, which moves in one direction at a constant pace, could be overlaid on a recurring cyclical time, which repeats in the manner of seasonal change. Myths may contain their own periods and epochs, often with a "culture hero" or other transformative figure who makes the world safe and habitable for humans. Susano-o and Yamato Take are sometimes referred to as culture heroes because they slew dangerous and problematic kami. The notion that time passes differently in other worlds appears frequently in East Asian myths. Urashima Tarō spends only a short time in the palace of the sea god, but when he returns to our world, hundreds of years had passed. A similar narrative appears in *The Tale of the Bamboo Cutter*, one of Japan's oldest fictional narratives. In that story, the princess Kaguya-hime is sent from the moon to spend a short amount of moon time on earth, but in earthly time, this corresponds with several decades.

Tenmu and Jitō deliberately overlaid mythical time on their own historical time to legitimate their power in the wake of Tenmu's coup. The first attested reading of the Japanese emperors, whose reigns form the basis for *Ancient Matters* and *Chronicles*, occurred at Tenmu's funeral. By making Tenmu the latest in a succession of rulers going back to the descent of Ninigi from heaven, Jitō made imperial accession, rule, and death into a cyclical occurrence grafted on to historical time. The combination became more pronounced with the 720 compilation of *Chronicles*, because unlike *Ancient Matters*, *Chronicles* provided specific dates for every entry once Jinmu founded the empire in 660 BCE Obviously these dates were created after the fact and are back-dated; Jinmu and Sujin and Jingū are mythical figures, and even Yūryaku is more legend than truth. Some dates were clearly manipulated to accommodate Chinese historical sources. For example, Empress Jingū's timeline is constructed so that her rule matches that of Himiko, a Japanese queen identified in the Chinese *Book of Wei*. Beginning the official historical calendar with Jinmu also established the "Age of the Gods," an era encompassing every earlier myth, versus the historical time of the mythical emperors. *Chronicles* even specifies that the three reigns preceding Jinmu, of Ninigi, Yama-sachi-hiko, and Fuki-aezu, lasted for 1,792,470 years!

The dating of *Chronicles* counts each year from the moment the ruling emperor takes the throne. For example, Jinmu 1 is 660 BCE, then Jinmu 2 is 659 BCE, etc. In modern Japan, the calendar era is still based on the reigning emperor. The Heisei emperor, Akihito, resigned in 2019, ending the Heisei era. His son, Naruhito, became the Reiwa emperor the same year. From May 01, 2019 is "Reiwa 1," 2020 is counted as "Reiwa 2," 2021 as "Reiwa 3," and so on. When Naruhito dies or abdicates, a new emperor will begin a new era. The practice of linking the era to the life of the emperor ended in 701, when Jitō's grandson Monmu began using auspicious events as a basis for naming new eras. That practice continued until the Meiji era began in 1868 and continued until the death of Emperor Meiji.

## Intellectual History (Isomae)

The story of Yamato Take, often called Yamato Takeru, appears in both *Ancient Matters* and *Chronicles*, but the difference between the two versions has prompted mythologists to make broader observations about the attitudes, styles, and objectives of the two respective texts. Mythologist Isomae Jun'ichi interprets Japanese myth and Japanese mythology from the perspective of a post-modern intellectual historian. Isomae specializes in performing close readings of *Ancient Matters*, *Chronicles*, and others, and distinguishes them, akin to Kōnoshi discussed in Chapter 3. Isomae also studies the premodern and early modern Japanese mythological perspectives and interpretations of later scholars and situates them within their respective historical periods and context. The post-modern component of Isomae's scholarship is that he does not suggest that there is a fixed directionality, sense of progress, or increasing development of knowledge as the study of Japanese myth proceeds. Rather, each component, the original texts and later commentaries, can be historically resituated, creating an ever-transforming narrative.

In analyzing Yamato Take, Isomae separates the ancient accounts in *Ancient Matters* and *Chronicles*, from later, Heian (794–1185) and medieval (1185–1600), versions of the story. Then, finally, he addresses Norinaga and commentators from the early modern (1600–1868) period. The most famous early modern treatment was by Motoori Norinaga (1730–1801) in his commentary on *Ancient Matters*, the *Kojiki-den*. According to Norinaga, one of the foundational motifs of Japanese literature and thought is pathos, what he calls "*mono no aware*," literally "the awareness of things." Another way to translate *mono no aware* might be sensitivity, especially a sensitivity to the ephemerality of life and an accompanying sense of melancholy.

Norinaga follows earlier scholars and identifies the *mono no aware* motif in Heian literature, especially Murasaki Shikibu's classic *The Tale of Genji* (*c.*1000 CE). However, Norinaga was ultimately searching for a pattern of thought and expression that distinguished Japaneseness, and so it was important that this pattern be identifiable in ancient materials. Norinaga was also deeply influenced by *The Tale of Genji*, to the point that his own writing often mimicked Murasaki Shikibu's style of writing from seven hundred years earlier. Norinaga seized on Yamato Take's statement in *Ancient Matters* that his father wanted to see him dead as an example of *mono no aware*.

Building on Norinaga's interpretation of *Ancient Matters*, Isomae stresses that Yamato Take is introduced not as the crown prince, but as one of three potential heirs. Yamato Take is a trickster and unable to contain his strength, which causes serious problems, for example, when he misunderstands his father and kills his older brother. Yamato Take then laments that his father seems intent on sending him to his death in military expeditions. For both the eastern and western expeditions, Yamato Take receives help from his aunt Yamato-hime. Unfortunately, he forgets to take the sword Kusanagi with him to confront the evil kami of Ibuki and ultimately loses his life. In Isomae's reading, *Ancient Matters* tells the story of a son murdered by his father.

For *Chronicles*, Isomae highlights that the story of Yamato Take is only one part of a larger chronicle of the reign of his father, Keikō. Keikō himself attacks the Kumaso in the twelfth year of his reign and makes a tour of the eastern provinces in the fifty-third year of his reign. Meanwhile, Yamato Take attacks the Kumaso in the twenty-seventh year of his father's reign, and then fights the Emishi in the fortieth. As such, Yamato Take is part of a larger historical story. Unlike *Ancient Matters*, Yamato Take is clearly identified in the text as the crown prince, and in *Chronicles*, he has a good relationship with his father. Yamato Take sets out against the Kumaso and Emishi in service to his father and the throne. Yamato-hime only aids him in his eastern expedition, and then only gives him the sword Kusanagi, not the flint and bag listed in *Ancient Matters*. Finally, in *Chronicles*, Yamato Take leaves the sword behind when he goes to fight the kami at Ibuki not because he is distracted and remorseful, but because he is overconfident in his own strength.

According to Isomae, later versions of the Yamato Take myth changed in order to highlight certain components or aspects of the story that served the interests of the creators of those later versions. In the Heian era, *Original Record* summarized the Yamato Take campaign with a focus on clarifying the imperial lineages, that is, the relationship between Keikō, Yamato Take, and Yamato Take's brother Seimu. *Gleanings* focuses on the sword Kusanagi because the author of the text was interested in the use of the sword at a court ritual with which his clan was intimately connected.

In the medieval era, Isomae notes a heightened interest in the miraculous power of the Kusanagi sword, of which the Yamato Take legend constituted one part. In one such story, the *Yamato hime no mikoto seiki*, Isomae notes that the sword was no longer wielded by Yamato Take when he escaped the fire, but rather moved of its own volition. The author of this text, Watarai Yukitada (1236–1305), was associated with the Ise Grand Shrine, and by heightening the power of the sword, he also heightened the status of Yamato-hime, the priestess at the Ise Shrine associated with the Shrine's creation, and with the Shrine itself, which was the original location of the sword. Isomae argues that these transformations occurred because in medieval Japan, the collapse of imperial power meant that both the imperial court and the religious shrines that depended on it for income needed symbols like Kusanagi that could elevate their status.

Isomae's interest in Norinaga is directly connected to his own era, the late twentieth century. Isomae notes that according to Norinaga, the *Ancient Matters* version of Yamato Take exemplifies *mono no aware*, but that the *Chronicles* version lacks literary character. Isomae also notes that this perspective remained common in late twentieth-century Japan. Because of *mono no aware*, twentieth-century readers felt a closeness to the *Ancient Matters* rendition of the tale and distant from the *Chronicles* version. However, Isomae stresses that this is not due to inherent features of the text itself, but rather how the myths have been interpreted. Norinaga grafted the idea of *mono no aware* on to the *Ancient Matters* version of the story through his textual interpretation. Moreover, Norinaga's elevation of *Ancient Matters*, at the expense of *Chronicles*, which had previously been considered the official version of the myths, reflected a movement from an ancient to a modern image of myths. Because Isomae understands the myths of *Ancient Matters* and *Chronicles* as products of interpretation, his mythology takes the form of intellectual history, the history of ideas. In successive eras, new perspectives on the nature of reality and its fundamental forces influenced, and determined, the ways in which the readers of myths interpreted them.

Isomae questions Norinaga and other mythologists who attempt to claim an original understanding of mythical content. For Isomae, the claim is not only suspect, but reveals an ideological standpoint and perspective of its own that did not characterize early readers of these texts. Isomae asks why modern readers of *Ancient Matters* and *Chronicles*, beginning with Norinaga, are so invested in resurrecting an original past. Isomae calls his insistence that mythology go beyond intellectual history and include analysis of how modern readers interpret myths in relation to themselves a "meta-intellectual history of perspectives."

## Post-modern Historicism (Ōbayashi, Hirafuji, Macé and Rocher)

A post-modern approach to Japanese mythology itself, in that it seeks to historicize Japanese mythology, appears first in the work of Ōbayashi Taryō and then in the more recent scholarship of Hirafuji Kikuko. These approaches, especially that of Hirafuji, are not dissimilar to the way mythology is presented in this book: a collection of different approaches adopted at different times and yielding different interpretations. The major distinction is that Ōbayashi and Hirafuji present their histories of Japanese mythology in chronological order. Because Ōbayashi significantly predates Hirafuji, Hirafuji's work could also be seen as an extension of Ōbayashi. Both focus primarily on Japanese mythologists, though Hirafuji notes the influence of Jung on scholars like Kawai and the unusual lack of influence of Lévi-Strauss and Eliade.

Ōbayashi divides the history of Japanese mythology into four stages. The first is from 1899 to 1921, including the work by Takayama Chogyū, Takagi Toshio, and Anesaki Masaharu discussed in Chapter 1. Ōbayashi stresses that the implementation of European theoretical methods resulted in the first modern study of Japanese myths. The same period saw the rise of folklore and folk studies and the first attempt at a cosmological explanation of Japanese myths, by Inoue Tetsujirō. Finally, Ōbayashi highlights the important work of historian Tsuda Sōkichi, whose 1913 book *Jindaishi no atarashii kenkyū* brought a logical and empirical interpretation to *Ancient Matters* and *Chronicles*. François Macé and Alain Rocher have noted an alternative beginning to this period, with Tylor's 1877 essay on Susano-o, which began the study of Japanese myths in the West. This essay was succeeded by B. H. Chamberlain's English translation of *Ancient Matters* and then W. G. Aston's translation of *Chronicles*.

Hirafuji argues that scholars in this period adopted a scientific approach to the study of myth in order to avoid suspicion or punishment from traditionalists who believed in their literal quality. Several historical cases in which scholars were criticized for doubting the historical veracity of traditional literature, including Shigeno Yasutsugu, Kume Kunitake, and Kita Sadakichi, provide strong support for Hirafuji's thesis. Shigeno and Kita found themselves in trouble for their treatments of the military epic *Chronicle of Great Peace* and its description of the Northern-Southern Courts period of Japanese history (1336–1392). Kume wrote about the Japanese creation myths and argued that Shinto was derived from and continued to be a form of nature worship. At the time, it was thought that religions developed in stages, from primitive to advanced, and Kume was essentially saying that Japanese religious beliefs were primitive in comparison to established Western religions. The central problem was not only his critique of Shinto, but the fact that he was employed as university faculty at a public institution. Kume was ultimately dismissed, though he later found work at Waseda, a private college. As Hirafuji notes, the academic environment during Ōbayashi's first period restricted the degree of critique academics could use when studying mythology, leading Takayama and others to adopt models from the social sciences that seemed scientific and objective.

Ōbayashi's second period is from 1922 to 1945. This period is notable first for the wholesale incorporation of folklore and folk studies into mythology. The discipline of folk studies, pioneered by Yanagita Kunio, Takagi Toshio, and Orikuchi Shinobu, took off in the early twentieth century, but it took some time for the discipline to define itself. The mythologists in Period 2 often fused their mythology with Yanagita's folk studies, which sought to identify the defining characteristics of the Japanese people. The other notable feature of this period is the strong influence of anthropology and ethnography. This includes Matsumoto Nobuhiro, who studied in Paris and was influenced by Mauss and Durkheim, Oka Masao, who studied in Vienna and was influenced by Wilhelm Schmidt, and

Mishina Shōei, who studied in the United States and was influenced by the disciples of Franz Boas. Each of these scholars transposed a modified anthropological model they originally learned abroad to the Japanese case, and each simultaneously engaged with the folklore and folk studies of Yanagita and others. The application of folk studies pushed these theorists toward the study of the development of the Japanese people and away from the general anthropological question of the development of humanity and human society. Ōbayashi also includes the early work of Matsumura Takeo in Period 2. Matsumura was a scholar of Greek myths who went on to study comparative mythology in Europe as an exchange student.

Hirafuji calls attention to the colonial components of Matsumoto, Oka, Mishina, and Matsumura. During Period 2, Japan was a global empire that included Korea, Taiwan, parts of China, parts of Sakhalin, and South Seas islands like Yap and Palau. Matsumoto was initially interested in comparative mythology, especially with the South Seas. Combined with his study in France, which had territories in Polynesia and Indochina, Matsumoto had the opportunity to learn about the language and culture of these regions from the colonial center. When he returned to Japan, he continued scholarship on both Japanese myths and those from the South Seas and Southeast Asia. As Japan's empire expanded, Hirafuji notes, Matsumoto's scholarship began to assert that the Japanese were better positioned to rule Southeast Asia than France, due to the shared cultural history of the region and Japan. Oka went back and forth between Japan and Vienna, but in 1940, he returned to Japan to stay and worked at the Ethnic Research Institute, a Japanese government-sponsored group charged with improving colonial administration. Mishina, whose study in America had led him to focus on Northeast Asia, wrote extensively on Korean foundation myths. These, he argued, showed that Japan and Korea had been connected since antiquity, but also that Korean culture was comparatively underdeveloped. Finally, Matsumura compared Japanese ritual practice as shown in myth with that of Egyptian and European groups to demonstrate its uniqueness. All four scholars were tied to the project of defining Japaneseness, with Matsumoto and Mishina also applying their knowledge of myths to regions that had been colonized by the Japanese Empire.

Ōbayashi's Period 3 is dominated by Matsumura, Mishina, and Tsuda Sōkichi. Matsumura's most important work, *Nihon shinwa no kenkyū* (Research on Japanese Myths) was published in four volumes from 1955 to 1958 and was the most expansive and holistic treatment of Japanese myths produced to date. Matsumura's comprehensive treatment continues to be an important resource for Japanese scholars of myths to this day. Because writing about the core myths of Shinto was no longer taboo after wartime defeat, Matsumura compiled the theories of all the major scholars who had preceded him, including Matsumoto, Mishina, Oka, Orikuchi, Yanagita, Tsuda, and Takagi. He also included much of his own research in comparative mythology, creating a kind of repository of Japanese myths and interpretations. Mishina, similarly, was able to address Japanese founding narratives as myths, not scripture, and use comparison to tease out the earliest, original version of the founding myths. Tsuda, who had been put under house arrest because of his studies of Japanese mythical emperors, enjoyed something of a resurgence, surely in part due to his reputation as a scholar willing to stand up to an authoritarian state. He edited and rereleased his earlier work, which also continues to be a major resource for scholars of Japanese myth in the present. Put shortly, the postwar period was an opportunity both to take stock and compile previous work without fear of reprisals, as seen in Matsumura, and a chance to review and renew earlier work that had come under attack, as seen with Tsuda.

Ōbayashi's Period 4 begins around the middle of the 1950s until the date that he wrote the essay that created these four periods, 1973. This period somewhat overlaps with Period 3 but is made up of scholars working entirely in the postwar period. Unlike Tsuda or Matsumura, who began their work before World War II and then continued and revised it in the new postwar climate, a new generation of scholars came of age in the 1960s and 1970s who had been educated and trained almost entirely in the postwar, or at least did most of their academic work after the war had ended.

Macé and Rocher characterize this group by disciplinary approach, divided between historian, anthropologist, philologist, and comparativist. The first of these categories discusses Ueda Masaaki, who studied the ancient Japanese state. We could add historian Ishimoda Shō to this category as well. Marxism strongly influenced Japanese historiography at this time, and analysis focused on the role of the state and the despot (emperor). The Marxist approach led historians to focus on social conditions, rather than a single work of art or author. Ōbayashi's early work is among the anthropological approaches. This work applied a comparative approach to the study of ritual and of social institutions, inspired by Austro-German anthropology and ethnology. Ōbayashi's early orientation is significant because it would shape his later applications of myth theory, described later in this chapter. The philologist approach culminated in the publication of Iwanami's *Collection of Classical Japanese Literature* ( J. Nihon koten bungaku taikei) book series. This included *Ancient Matters*, Shinto prayers, and the various gazetteers in 1958, *Myriad Poems* in four volumes from 1957 to 1962, and *Chronicles* in two volumes from 1965 to 1967. Newer editions of each text have superseded these versions, but the publication of this series made myths accessible to popular and scholarly audiences in postwar Japan. Comparativists include Matsumae Takeshi, who was influenced by both Orikuchi and Yanagita.

François Macé and Alain Rocher have proposed a fifth period, from the 1970's to the present. This period is notable first because of the many mythological studies published, suggesting a steady growth (Macé and Rocher call it a "craze" or "infatuation") of interest in the subject. Second, mythologists began to challenge the genre and theoretical norms and principles that had guided research in the previous era. This includes several theorists discussed in this book.

Macé and Rocher note that literature scholar Saigō Nobustsuna applied new paradigms for literature study, especially New Criticism, that transformed the interpretation of Japanese myths. New Criticism, pioneered in the United States in the mid-twentieth century, advocated for reading texts as self-contained works of art, not as products of a particular set of historical circumstances. Instead of reading Japanese mythology by comparing and collecting accounts from *Ancient Matters* and *Chronicles*, Saigō focused on reading *Ancient Matters* as a singular and complete literary narrative. This influence led to a perspective, in later periods, in which *Ancient Matters* and *Chronicles* are imagined as distinct accounts, especially with Kōnoshi Takamitsu. In anthropology, Ōbayashi added structural methods and adapted the theoretical approach of mythologist Georges Dumézil for the Japanese case. Kawai Hayao similarly used Jungian psychology for the study of Japanese myths and the Japanese psyche. Finally, Macé and Rocher note their own work on adapting structuralism to Japanese mythology.

## Dumézil, Revisited (Hirafuji)

As noted in Chapter 2, Dumézil's tri-functional hypothesis was as major influence on Ōbayashi Taryō, who applied it to explain the relationship between the heavenly and earthly families of kami. Recall that Dumézil divided deities into three groups: a group 1 priestly and political group, a group 2 military and war group, and a group 3 agriculture and productivity group. Based on his studies of myth in Indo-European traditions, Dumézil concluded that the alliance of the first two groups and their subjugation of the third group created and constituted the world of the gods and gave structure to the pantheon. In applying this theory to Japan, Ōbayashi focused on these divisions and societal roles to classify the heavenly kami as the priestly and military groups and the earthly kami as the agriculture group. Ō-kuni-nushi's surrender of the central reed plain land to the heavenly kami demonstrated the submission of the agriculture group kami to the other, superior kami, and the resulting union created the Japanese pantheon and world of gods. The tri-functional theory, derived from study of Indo-European pantheons, appeared to apply to Japan as well.

Hirafuji Kikuko reassessed Ōbayashi's application of Dumézil and argues for a slightly more complex understanding in which both the heavenly and earthly gods have all three functions within their respective kami groups. For Hirafuji, Ō-kuni-nushi's surrender is not complete, but rather a mutual agreement between heavenly and earthly kami to each manage the functions for which their kami are superior.

Hirafuji notes several inconsistencies that appear when comparing the heavenly kami in mythical sources with Ōbayashi's application of Dumézil. The first group of kami, who take on ritual roles related to religion and politics, includes heavenly kami like Amaterasu, Taka-mi-musuhi, Omoi-kane, and others. These kami fulfill their group 1 roles both before and after the surrender of the central reed plain land, so that event does not seem especially significant in terms of defining their alignment. The group 2 kami, notably Susano-o, do not form a natural alliance with the group 1 kami. Take-mikazuchi, who forces Ō-kuni-nushi's surrender, had been in heaven all along, but had no interaction with the group 1 kami until he was specifically asked to help. During and after the surrender, the group 2 kami seem to have taken a position of servitude with regards to the group 1 kami. Ame-no-oshi-hi and Ama-tsu-kume are ordered to aid Ninigi by Amaterasu, and later, Jimmu is aided by Take-mikazuchi, but again at the order of Amaterasu. Finally, Hirafuji notes that among the heavenly kami, there are also some group 3, agricultural kami, including Tsuku-yomi and Ame-waka-hiko. However, these kami do not use their generative power on behalf of the other heavenly kami. Tsuku-yomi has a falling out with Amaterasu after killing the goddess Uke-mochi, and Ame-waka-hiko bows to the powers of the earthly kami and betrays his own heavenly kami. Because of this, Taka-mi-musuhi kills Ame-waka-hiko. Hirafuji argues that Ame-waka-hiko's betrayal demonstrates that the agricultural group of heavenly kami did not occupy the social role imagined by Dumézil.

Hirafuji also notes that there are inconsistencies for grouping the earthly kami. Ōbayashi argued that the earthly kami were all agricultural kami, but Hirafuji points out that this is clearly not the case. For example, the two sons of Ō-kuni-nushi, Koto-shiro-nushi and Take-mi-nakata, appear to be group 1 and group 2 kami, respectively, Koto-shiro-nushi is an oracle god and in the surrender episode speaks on behalf of all the earthly kami. Furthermore, this kami appears to be engaged in some kind of ritual involving fishing, and his departure from the world also takes the form of a ritual. Hence, Koto-shiro-nushi should be counted as a group 1 kami. His brother Take-mi-nakata challenges Take-mikazuchi to a battle of strength, and so is a group 2 kami. Since Take-mi-nakata did not agree to abide by Koto-shiro-nushi's agreement to surrender, the earthly group 1 kami are proved inferior to the heavenly group 1 kami since the former cannot use words to control or deploy the earthly group 2 kami.

Based on these observations, Hirafuji interprets the mythical surrender episode differently than Ōbayashi. Ōbayashi believed that Ō-kuni-nushi's surrender demonstrated the superior power of the heavenly kami and represented the subjugation of the group 3 agricultural kami by the group 1 ritualistic kami and group 2 military kami. This aligns neatly with Dumézil's tri-functional hypothesis for Indo-European myths. Hirafuji counters that the true meaning of the surrender episode lies in the agreement between the heavenly and earthly kami to combine their respective superior groups. The heavenly kami group 1 and group 2 kami proved superior to the earthly kami group 1 and group 2, and so the heavenly kami handle matters related to ritual and the military. However, the earthly group 3 kami proved superior to the heavenly group 3 kami, and so they agree to aid the heavenly group 1 and group 2 kami. For this reason, Hirafuji argues, the earthly kami that appear in the mythical narrative after Ō-kuni-nushi's surrender, like Saruta-hiko and Shio-tsu-tsu, are all group 3 kami involved with agriculture, aquaculture, or other production. The societal functions associated with deities in Japan match the groups proposed by Dumézil for Indo-European myths, as does the reconciliation of two groups of deities. However, the complimentary way in which the groups reconcile in the Japanese case does not fit Dumézil's model.

One further intervention proposed by Hirafuji identifies Jingū and the three Munakata kami created by Amaterasu and Susano-o as multi-functional water goddesses. This hypothesis is founded on several important pieces of previous scholarship by Dumézil and Yoshida Atsuhiko. First, Dumézil observed that within Indo-Iranian myth, there was often a goddess figure who combined the three societal functions of ritual, military, and agriculture. Furthermore, this goddess was usually associated with water. Yoshida applied Dumézil's thesis to Japanese myths and concluded that Amaterasu fit this role, being associated with the figure of Mithra from the Indo-Iranian mythical pantheon. In the case of Amaterasu, the Japanese myths first describe her fulfilling the military role when she defends her heavenly territory from Susano-o. Then, she engages in the production of deities with Susano-o in a ritualistic fashion, fulfilling the first and third roles of the tri-functional hypothesis. Amaterasu was also associated with water, being born from Izanaki's purification bath after his escape from Yomi. When beginning the ritual for producing kami with Susano-o, she also washes his sword in a well from heaven.

Hirafuji applies the theory of the multi-functional goddess associated with water to the three Munakata kami that are born between Amaterasu and Susano-o. These three goddesses are born from the union of Amaterasu, who embodies the first, ritualistic function of deities, and Susano-o, who embodies the second, military function. The daughters then marry Ō-kuni-nushi, who embodies the third, agriculturally productive function. When Amaterasu sends the three daughters down from heaven, they are enshrined and associated with ritual worship, connecting them to the first function. The name of one daughter, Ichi-ki-shima-hime, also appears to refer to shamanistic practice. Based on later materials, Hirafuji shows that these goddesses were worshipped at moments of military confrontation with the Korean Peninsula, suggesting a connection to the second function. Finally, the names Ta-kiri-bime and Tagitsu-hime may refer to rice paddies (Jp. *ta*), demonstrating a connection with third agricultural function. Finally, their birth following Susano-o's sword being washed in a well, their enshrinement on islands, and their instructions to guard the sea route cement their association with water.

Jingū also satisfies the conditions of the multi-functional goddess associated with water. Prior to beginning her mythical conquest of Korea, she repeatedly performs divination, clearly connecting her to the first function. She also performs as a medium for the kami. She takes on the appearance of a male warrior, and the conquest itself has the appearance of a military expedition, fulfilling the second function. Ōbayashi previously argued that Jingū fulfilled the third, productive function because when Jingū acted as a medium, the Korean Peninsula was promised to the son with whom she was pregnant, the mythical Emperor Ōjin. Later, Ōjin would trade his name with a kami related to food and provisions. Finally, the reigns of both Jingū and Ōjin have comparatively greater numbers of entries related to feasts and banquets. Hirafuji adds to Ōbayashi's point that Jingū seems to have the power to produce food, for example, when she makes sweetfish appear. Events like the mythical prevention of her son being born take place on the seaside, and Jingū's conquest is powered by the Sumiyoshi deities who are associated with the ocean. These factors connect her with the power of water.

Hirafuji's use of Dumézil to portray the three Munakata goddesses and Jingū as multi-functional goddesses associated with water satisfies a grander hypothesis made by Dumézil that links myth and ritual to actual human history. According to Dumézil, myth that is intimately tied to ritual reappears in both supernatural and realistic forms and in both the imagination of other worlds and of our own world. That reappearance includes ancient history, especially stories of heroes and legends. Hence, Hirafuji's exploration of

Jingū is an application of Dumézil's thesis. Amaterasu and the three Munakata goddesses are clearly mythical, while Jingū is a legendary figure who supposedly occupies a position in human history. Yet Dumézil proposes that Jingū is equally mythical in this regard. Hirafuji uses the linkage: Amaterasu, Munakata goddesses, and Jingū, to assert that not only are human historical events reflected in mythical narratives, but that mythical events are reflected in human narratives. Hirafuji's hypothesis and mythological interpretation explain Jingū's powers and associations.

## History (Ooms, Piggott)

Because *Chronicles* is the only written historical source for the history of the seventh century in Japan, and because both *Chronicles* and *Ancient Matters* claim to record the history of ancient Japan, historians have analyzed both texts, though they would likely not describe their work as mythology. Two of the most significant historians of ancient Japan writing in English are Joan Piggott and Herman Ooms. While working at the same time and even at universities located in the same city, their approaches are very different. Piggott focuses on specific rulers, including Yūryaku and Tenmu/Jitō, and identifies political and functional features of each reign that characterize an evolving notion of kingship. Ooms focuses on symbolic displays of power, which he argues were a critical part of Tenmu's time as sovereign. Put differently, Piggott identifies how and why sovereigns accumulated ever more power, while Ooms explores how some of those same sovereigns used symbols to demonstrate and reinforce their power. One important feature is that, as historians, both scholars are careful with the word "emperor." As the title was not used in Japan until the reign of Tenmu or Jitō, it is anachronistic to apply it to figures such as Jinmu, Sujin, or Yūryaku.

Piggott's study of Yūryaku portrays him as an epochal Great King, the title used for the sovereign at the time. A signature of Piggott's approach is the combination of sources: Chinese, archaeological, poetic, and historical material from *Chronicles*, to tease out a larger picture. The most important piece of her treatment of Yūryaku is the Chinese historical record. According to Chinese sources, the five kings of "Wa," as the Japanese archipelago was called, established diplomatic relationships with southern China during the fifth century CE. The last of these kings, called Wu, is traditionally associated with Yūryaku, and the Chinese sources make clear that there was one powerful figure in the Japanese archipelago at this time. Piggott then uses archaeological evidence to suggest that Yūryaku ruled over an area roughly corresponding to the locations of keyhole-style tombs on the archipelago, from southern Kyushu to eastern Honshu. These marked the eastern and western frontiers of Yūryaku's kingdom. Two inscribed swords excavated from sites in both locations corroborate this hypothesis, as both seem to refer to a "Great King Wakatakeru."

The literary sources used by Piggott, the *Collection of Myriad Poems* and *Chronicles*, then flesh out the nature of Yūryaku's burgeoning kingdom. The first poem in *Myriad Poems* is attributed to Yūryaku and portrays the Great King propositioning a young woman he sees while out on a ride. Piggott notes the expansive harem of Yūryaku in *Chronicles* and suggests this is meant to convey the actual use of marriage politics to build alliances and maintain control of provinces around the archipelago. At the same time, the fits of violence and raging temper seen in myths of Yūryaku reflect the demands for him to use violence to subdue chieftains that resisted him. Finally, the unusual attention to the kami in Yūryaku's reign demonstrates an increasing role for the Great King as a patron of kami all over the realm and a central figure with religious charisma. Other myths in *Chronicles* describe Yūryaku acquiring sacred objects from around the archipelago. The myth given in this chapter, in which he encounters a powerful kami that seems to be a reflection of himself, perhaps accords with Piggott's argument that Yūryaku became the center of a widespread cult network.

Ooms' interpretation of *Ancient Matters* centers on the "mythemes" proposed by Lévi-Strauss, the elements of a myth when it is reduced to its smallest narrative parts. However, rather than using these mythemes to identify universal structures, Ooms instead suggests that they demonstrate symbolic causal reversals. Historical events in memory were converted into myths, and these myths, as sacred stories, legitimized the historical events that had created them. No event is more important in this regard than Tenmu's 672 campaign, and Ooms argues that the mythemes from the myth of Jinmu are parallels with events from Tenmu's reign. For example, Jinmu himself is not mentioned in *Ancient Matters* or *Chronicles* after his reign ends until, in *Chronicles*, when Tenmu goes to worship Jinmu's grave. Amaterasu is also mostly absent, delivering aid to Jinmu, then appearing again in Tenmu's campaign. Ooms also imagines that Amaterasu is meant to be a double of Jitō, whose posthumous title called her "Princess of the High Heavenly Plain," the realm ruled by Amaterasu. In this fashion, the myth was influenced by Tenmu's actions, then functioned to reinforce the power of Tenmu and his heirs.

Several important parallels identified by Ooms include the role of the Ise Shrine, the function of grandchildren, and the structure of kingship. Ooms argues that Tenmu and Jitō were responsible for creating the Ise shrine as we know it. According to *Chronicles*, Tenmu sent one of his daughters there as priestess in 673, at the beginning of his reign, and the shrine was then first called a Grand Shrine. Jitō visited Ise in 692, seemingly marking the movement of the center of sun cult worship from Mt. Miwa to Ise. Another parallel was lineage: Jinmu was Ninigi's grandson, much as Jitō passed the throne to her own grandson, Monmu. This move was somewhat unusual; the intended heir, Tenmu and Jitō's son Kusakabe, had died unexpectedly before he could take the throne. Even more unusual was that Jitō abdicated, presumably to ensure that her grandson's power would remain unchallenged, and that no succession dispute could emerge.

Another parallel Ooms finds is the structure of kingship. In *Ancient Matters*, power from other realms is required to achieve dominance. For example, Ō-kuni-nushi uses the weapons from the underworld to conquer the central reed plain land, and Luck of the Mountain uses the jewels from the palace of the sea king to subdue his brother. Ninigi carries the regalia from the High Heavenly Plain down to earth with him. In Tenmu's era, Oom's argues, the Yamato ruler sustained their governance through interdependence with local regions ruled by their own elites who swore allegiance to the Yamato court.

While both Ooms and Piggott characterize a historical treatment of Japanese myths, their actual interpretive methods are quite different. Piggott's style of history is highly interdisciplinary, in that it brings together Chinese history, literature, history, and archeology. It is also evidentiary, in the sense that Piggott's interpretation of *Chronicles* is based not only on what the text says, but on what can be verified using other sources. The strength of this approach is that the historical narrative can be written with a high degree of certainty. The weakness is that it is difficult to evaluate mythical content that cannot be proved in an evidentiary fashion. Conversely, Ooms' approach breaks myths into mythemes, separates them from their narrative, and seeks parallels with historical events for which there is some evidence. Naturally this interpretation is highly informed by history, especially the evidence-based history written by historians like Piggott. On the other hand, the structural links between myth and history can never be more than hypothetical.

## Myth, Kingship, and Violence (Bialock, Yamaguchi)

Closely related to Ooms' use of symbols to analyze history are studies that use mythical symbols to understand deeper elements of culture or literary narratives. This approach was used by Yamaguchi Masao (1931–2013), a prominent structural anthropologist. Yamaguchi's most famous work involved analysis of tricksters and androgynous figures in myth and legends from around the world. In the case of Japan, he naturally gravitated toward Susano-o, though his writing took on a strong political element as well. For Yamaguchi, myths provided one avenue toward understanding traditional, premodern ideals and norms, and he believed that these ideals were still relevant and resonant in contemporary society. In analyzing Japanese myths, Yamaguchi argued that the ideal of a traditional Japanese village and the notion of kingship as expressed in myths constituted this deeper level of social reality.

Yamaguchi combines the miraculous visitor (*marebito*) idea from Orikuchi, the notion of inside and outside for village life from Yanigita, and the ritual sacrifice of the king described in Frazer. According to Yamaguchi, until the twentieth century, Japanese village life was defined by a sharp distinction between insiders and outsiders and a cyclical understanding of time. The outside of the village was the source of both good powers that visited in spring to encourage fertility, and of bad powers that could visit anytime, or at inappropriate times, to bring plague, pestilence, or bandits. This latter group also included itinerant merchants and priests. Villagers conducted seasonal rituals where they created an effigy of a noble hero and paraded it around the village. The hero's story was that he was banished and then died tragically, and he served as a village scapegoat to appease the rampaging kami. At the end of the ritual, the effigy was destroyed.

In a related manner, the itinerant priests who visited Japanese villages regaled the villagers with tales of the gods they served, and in those tales, the god often had a noble birth, was banished, and died a tragic death. To the villagers, the figure of the priest, who recounted the story, fused with the protagonist of the story. Like the harbinger of bad fortune, the priest came at an inappropriate or unregulated time from the outside, and like the noble hero about which they spoke, the priest was also banished to roam the countryside. In this sense, the priest was associated both with sin and redemption. Finally, Yamaguchi notes that the king performed this redemptive duty at the national level. The positive forces of the outside were manifested in the king's authority, and the negative forces of the outside were resolved using myth.

Yamaguchi identifies the parallels between Susano-o and Yamato Take as the clearest evidence that myth came to fulfill this redemptive role, and that these two figures reflect the essential character of Japanese kingship. For Susano-o, Yamaguchi divides the myth into parts, akin to a structural analysis, and notes that rather than interpreting Susano-o as a wind or storm kami, the important features are his introduction of chaos followed by his establishment of a kingdom in Izumo. Using comparative mythology from Egypt, Babylon, Greece, South America, and Chad, Yamaguchi establishes both that Susano-o fits the typology of a trickster god and of a hero who violates order, is exiled, struggles with the devil, and then reestablishes order and succeeds to the throne. The comparison with other cultures demonstrates that the hero-trickster is at its core a mythical representation of the conjunction of opposites. The hero-trickster is rude and violent, brings chaos, but then transforms himself into a hero, and his tricks are used to both introduce a known and understandable order and to introduce previously unknown artifacts to the community. Yamaguchi asserts that the mythical structure of the Susano-o narrative corresponds with the status of the visiting itinerant priests, who both bring sin into the village and are the means by which it is removed. At the national level, the king is responsible for all the calamities: incest, rebellion, epidemics, wars, contamination, and monsters, and simultaneously, is the remedy for these very problems. In Japan, this cyclical death and rebirth is demonstrated by the imperial accession ceremony, which Yamaguchi reads as the symbolic death and rebirth of the king.

The structural style of Yamaguchi's mythological analysis naturally leads him to identify parallel mythemes for the figure of the hero-trickster, and he highlights Yamato Take as a repetition of the mythical pattern of Susano-o. Like Susano-o, Yamato Take appears, in the *Ancient Matters* narrative, as a wild and rude figure at the outset. His threat to the social order maintained by his father the king is manifested in the king's fear of his son, and the king sends him to the frontier multiple times, effectively banishing him to the margins.

Yamato Take uses tricks such as cross-dressing to defeat his foes. His relationship with his aunt, which includes the exchange of clothing, an extremely intimate act in ancient Japan, suggests incest, much as Susano-o longed for his mother and then had a relationship with his sister. Yamato Take and his father were thus the epic form of Susano-o and Amaterasu from myth, and they repeated the structural model of the story. The sovereign represents order and everyday life, and the prince represents chaos and non-everyday life. In other cultures, Yamaguchi observes, this dynamic is played out by the relationship between the king and the jester, with the jester bearing those characteristics and sentiments that the king's burden of authority does not permit him to express. The analysis of myth permits the examination of the latent, hidden aspects of the political institution, a symbolic universe in which the king's order and authority makes sense to society's participants.

The goal of Yamaguchi's mythology was to identify unique features of Japanese kingship, and he locates these in political history. The hero-trickster who bears the sins of the community, the death and rebirth of the king, and the unusual relationship between the king and the clown or jester are generalizable to other societies. In the Japanese case, the unique feature was that the emperor, from the tenth century to the nineteenth, was not actually in power. Japanese kings were exiled, revolted against the military government, and were imprisoned. Put differently, the Japanese emperor became the victim of the established order and a symbol of resistance and resentment against that order. Then, after 1868, the emperor once again became the center of authority, an absolute monarch. The role of scapegoat was forced upon marginalized groups created by imperial expansion and control: communists, anarchists, Koreans, and Chinese. After 1945, the emperor was forced to declare his humanity, but Yamaguchi remains convinced that the symbolic forms of Japanese kingship continue to exert power on young people. The exiled hero idealized a spiritualized state, and people reimagined themselves as popular heroes. The suicide of Yukio Mishima, who had called for a restoration of imperial rule and tried to take over a military installation, and the student protest movements of the 1960s seem to have been especially present in Yamaguchi's mind when he analyzed Japanese myths. At the center of Japan, he claimed, remained a nostalgia for exile, and kingship myths still held power.

Literature scholar and intellectual historian David Bialock has issued an important critique of Yamaguchi while simultaneously expanding on the ambiguities surrounding kingship that Yamaguchi observed. Bialock notes that Yamaguchi's focus on identifying a persistent and unchanging ideal of Japanese kingship that displaces the king's use of violence to the mythical realm also obscures changes in the relationship of the king to violence itself. Bialock argues that differences in this relationship can be observed between *Ancient Matters* and *Chronicles* and also with texts in later eras. Ultimately, Bialock stresses historicizing the fundamental ambiguity of Japanese kingship in order to see how conceptions of royal authority changed over time.

Bialock's interpretation of Yamato Take begins with a myth in the reign of Sujin described in *Chronicles*. Sujin asks the Izumo region to present its treasures to the throne, which the younger brother of the local ruler does, his older brother being away on an errand. When the older brother returns, he blames the younger brother for surrendering the divine treasures. Still bearing the grudge years later, he kills the younger brother by tricking him with a wooden sword. Bialock stresses that prior to this event, in *Chronicles*, a succession dispute between the older and younger sons of the emperor was settled peacefully, using a divine dream. This creates a contrast between the center, where order rules, and the periphery, where might makes right. It also portrays comparatively harmonious relations within the royal family, something similarly seen in the *Chronicles* version of Yamato Take, who does not murder his brother. *Chronicles* describes Yamato Take using phrases from Chinese histories applied to ideal warriors, and the emperor's description of the Emishi also relies on Chinese phases for uncivilized peoples that associate them with bestiality and dishonesty.

The sovereign in *Chronicles* will attempt to civilize these people by virtue of their upstanding influence.

In contrast, Bialock argues that *Ancient Matters* tends toward depicting the violence of the ruler. Yamato Take in *Ancient Matters* is prone to murder and exiled from his father's court. The Izumo story from *Chronicles* about two brothers is converted in *Ancient Matters* into one in which Yamato Take kills the Izumo Brave by tricking him with a wooden sword, one of several times that Yamato Take uses a combination of trickery and brute force to overwhelm his rivals. As such, Izumo in *Ancient Matters* does not voluntarily surrender, but is made to submit. At the same time, Yamato Take himself calls out the violence of the central court, asserting that his father the emperor must want him dead. Bialock suggests that the narrative here equates the older, slain brother and the younger, who is soon to die. Both are scapegoats of collective violence. As such, the editors of *Ancient Matters* were interested in the problematic violence associated with the expansion of Yamato court rule, something that the compilers of *Chronicles*, which stressed Chinese models of kingship, were not.

## Literary and Linguistic Layers (Lurie, Duthie)

Two related mythological methods by literature scholars David Lurie and Torquil Duthie build on the text-centered approach of Kōnoshi, Bialock, and other literature scholars that treated *Ancient Matters* and *Chronicles* as discreet texts rather than part of a singular Japanese mythical corpus. Kōnoshi emphasized not only the differences between the mythical narratives of the two texts, but that each was a product of the eighth century, not a collection of ancient material. This meant understanding each text within the eighth-century historical context, a period in which the Japanese empire, as a nation centered on a written legal code, took shape for the first time. This legal code was based on the Tang Code and influenced by the legal codes used by kingdoms on the Korean peninsula. The most significant version of this code was completed in Japan in 718 CE, though

there may have been earlier versions from 701 and 689. Jitō established the first permanent capital, Fujiwara, in 694, then her
daughter-in-law Genmei (r. 707–715 CE) moved the capital to Nara
(sometimes called Heijō) in 710 CE. As *Ancient Matters* and
*Chronicles* were compiled during these changes, Lurie and Duthie
examine how the written formats (Lurie) and narrative composi-
tions (Duthie) of *Ancient Matters* and *Chronicles* evoked and imagined the new empire.

Notably, Lurie and Duthie also situate their mythological study
within Northeast Asia itself, not just the Japanese archipelago.
Historically speaking, prior to the seventh century, kingdoms on the
Korean peninsula and the Japanese archipelago sought diplomatic
recognition from Chinese states, and the Korean and Japanese states
willingly participated in an unequal diplomatic exchange that recognized Chinese superiority. Especially during periods in which China
was itself divided, this strategy was very effective, as the Korean and
Japanese kingdoms could exact a premium for their recognition of
competing Chinese states. When China unified in 581, both Korean
and Japanese kingdoms soon found themselves in conflict with
China, and by the end of the seventh century, this crucible created
the first unified kingdoms for both the peninsula and the archipelago: Silla and Japan. Japan's imagining of itself as an empire, and
equally fantastical treatment of Korea as a tributary, emerged from
this epochal seventh century for Northeast Asia. Combined with
Tenmu's 672 coup, the conditions were ripe for a new kind of
Japanese state. Lurie and Duthie argue that *Ancient Matters* and
*Chronicles* present different ideas for how this new state could and
should be imagined.

Lurie's focus is specifically on the use of writing. Writing has a
long history in Japan and is intimately associated with ruling and
kingship. Early Japanese rulers, governing small states, used writing
in their diplomatic communiqué and appear to have attached special
value to imported Chinese objects with writing on them, which they
used as burial goods. Later, domestically produced items began to

fill this same function. Literate immigrants from the Korean peninsula were integrated into the state bureaucracy as clerks, scribes, and other roles that required knowledge of letters. The grammatical difference between Japanese and Chinese (and Korean) resulted in several competing ways to write, none of which easily fit modern styles for writing Japanese or Chinese. Early writing on the Korean peninsula and the Japanese archipelago combined these competing ways of writing, such that describing these writings as being purely Chinese or Japanese is oversimplifying the reality. Confusingly, this mixed approach is also used in *Ancient Matters* and *Chronicles*. *Ancient Matters* uses characters for both meaning and sound values, and also uses both Japanese and Chinese grammar, sometimes even in the same sentence. *Chronicles* is more consistent, using Chinese grammar and the meanings of the characters for most entries, but many Japanese words are written out using the phonetic values of the characters. Both texts also include a number of Japanese poems, which are written out using the characters for their phonetic values.

Lurie argues that these two writing styles correspond to two different visions or imaginations of the Japanese empire. *Ancient Matters* is comparatively insular in focus, only rarely mentioning events outside of the Japanese archipelago, and similarly only interested in events in Japanese antiquity. The written style of *Ancient Matters* systematizes a style of writing that was widespread in ancient Japan that involved reading Chinese characters using Japanese glosses (Jp. *kundoku*). The result is a textual style of precision and attention to the Japanese vernacular, but which also does not provide direct access to speech patterns on the Japanese archipelago before the importation of writing. Lurie argues that these two elements: the insular narrative, and the written style that is attentive to the Japanese language, correspond with a text that envisions authority as distinct from Chinese models. In contrast, *Chronicles* frequently discusses historical events outside of the Japanese archipelago and frequently quotes Chinese historical texts. The structure, a historical annal and dynastic record, also mirrors Chinese models. As such,

Lurie argues that the more regular Chinese style of *Chronicles* corresponds with a text that permits the legitimacy of Chinese historiography. At the same time, *Chronicles* incorporates vernacular Japanese elements to create a second layer, an alternative mode of reading based on the use of native glosses. On the surface, *Chronicles* adheres to the established norm for historical texts, but on another level, it presents an alternative that parallels the vernacular focus used in *Ancient Matters*.

Rather than focus on language, Duthie's analysis centers on narrative. Using close reading of *Ancient Matters, Chronicles,* as well as *Myriad Poems* and other texts, Duthie identifies differences in how narrative events are described. Duthie argues that these differences demonstrate that creating an orthodox or establishment historical narrative was a complicated and contested issue. In the case of Tenmu, for example, Duthie identifies multiple narratives in *Ancient Matters* and *Chronicles.* The preface of *Ancient Matters,* which literature scholars might treat as a separate text from its mythical content, is a strong pro-Tenmu narrative. Tenmu is portrayed as an ideal sage emperor, and his order to have *Ancient Matters* created is an extension of his vision and legitimacy as a ruler. Then in *Chronicles,* we have conflicting versions of how Tenmu first fled to Yoshino, one that portrays him as an ally of his brother Tenji, and another in which Tenji is plotting against his brother in favor of his own son. In the historical record of Tenmu's own reign, there are several moments in which Tenmu acts as if he is creating a new dynasty. For example, he sends the Korean dignitaries who had come for Tenji's funeral home without entertaining them, then declares himself "first to assume the throne." Later, in Yoshino, Tenmu assembles his sons and nephews and makes them all pledge to support one son, Kusakabe, as the next ruler. At that time, he calls his nephews "sons." This need for this adoption and oath implies that the bloodline of the previous rule, Tenji, was illegitimate.

Duthie argues that one narrative, that of Tenmu's new dynasty and his rejection of the legitimacy of his older brother's bloodline, was later papered over by Jitō and her successors. They sought to create continuity between the reigns of Tenji, who was also Jitō's father, and Tenmu, her husband. For example, the opening of Jitō's chronicle portrays her as an invaluable confidant and co-ruler of the realm with Tenmu. She flees to Yoshino with Tenmu, addresses his troops, and shares in the planning for his military expedition. In this sense, Jitō's reign is really an extension of Tenmu's, because they started off together. The Jitō chronicle also adopts the position, in its description of their flight to Yoshino, of Tenji and Tenmu being allies. Later, when addressing envoys from Silla, Jitō refers to precedents from her father's reign. Put differently, while Tenmu created a new dynasty, Jitō made Tenmu and herself the latest additions to a dynasty that stretched back through Tenji to Jinmu. Duthie corroborates this hypothesis with examples from *Myriad Poems* and other eighth-century texts. For both Duthie and Lurie, the fact that these mythical accounts were recorded in the early eighth century meant that they were part of a larger political environment in which both the orthodox historical account and the true shape and vision of the Japanese empire were sites of narrative contestation.

## Myth as Symbolic Form (Steineck)

In the early twentieth century, philosopher Ernst Cassirer (1874–1945) argued that myths were an important element for understanding the development of human thought. Cassirer posited some number of "symbolic forms," such as religion, science, and myth, that ordered the human experience. As opposed to instincts, which guided animals, human beings lived in a universe of symbols, systems of signs that existed between humans and the world and which determined and guided the possible human reactions to external events. Each symbolic form possessed its own internal logic and set of symbols. For Cassirer, the symbolic form of myth was especially important because it was the most basic and primitive symbolic form. The mythical symbolic form was associated with expressive meaning, that is, with the emotional effect that events in the outside world had on the individual. Because these events were understood in terms of their emotional effect, the mythic form was fundamentally unstable, in that there was no way to distinguish the external event, the appearance of reality, from reality itself. Rather, the appearance of things and the reality of things blended together into a collection of temporary events and states.

Cassirer further theorized that natural language operated on this collection of inputs to order, distinguish, and define. This operation allowed humans to distinguish the appearance of reality from reality itself. Language permitted representation, in that a word could stand in for an object and lend it stability, and furthermore, to specify the object's temporal and spatial relationship to the observer. The process of distinguishing appearances from reality ultimately led to completely abstract symbolic forms for representing reality such as mathematics. These forms were freed from specific events or objects in the outside world and could signify universal laws or truths.

While Cassirer imagined myth as the baseline, primitive category for human thought, he also asserted that it continued to be relevant in the twentieth century. The rise of Nazi Germany depended on the appeal to and exploitation of mythic symbolic forms, irrational patterns of thought present in every human. Exposing that exploitation and overcoming the primal pull of myth was a key motivating factor for Cassirer, who fled Germany in 1933.

Philosopher Raji Steineck has applied Cassirer's theory to Japanese myths from *Ancient Matters* and *Chronicles* to assess the validity of the theory and suggest alterations as needed. Steineck ultimately argues that myths are not a primitive version of thought, but rather foundational narratives about matters of interest to the community or society that formulates them. Unlike Kōnoshi, who insisted that *Ancient Matters* and *Chronicles* had different narratives and as such cannot be read together, Steineck proposes a mythical framework common to both works alongside respective differences in content, structure, and emphasis. Steineck reduces the myths to groups of mythemes, fifteen in *Ancient Matters* and *Chronicles* and three more in *Chronicles* only. For example, group 13 is comprised of five mythemes about Nintoku. These include the debate over the legitimate successor, Nintoku's waiving of taxes, his marital problems, his fight with his half-brother Hayabusa-wake, and miraculous events during his reign. Group 14, Yūryaku, has four mythemes: killing his half-brother, being bitten by a dragonfly, encountering the kami Hito-koto-nushi, and killing the wild boar. In each of these cases, Steineck identifies the features unique to *Ancient Matters* and *Chronicles*, creating a shared set of common mythemes, while simultaneously noting distinctions based on the specific textual version.

Steineck's analysis reveals that these mythemes are oriented around a thematic center related to the origins of the government and state order. All of these myths relate to foundations: the separation of heaven and earth; the origin of the Japanese archipelago; the fight between Amaterasu and Susano-o; Susano-o and his descendant's pacification of the Central Reed Plain Land; the ruling mandate given to Amaterasu's grandson; Ninigi's descent; Ninigi and Yama-sachi-hiko being married to mountain and sea princesses; Jinmu's relocation; Sujin's creation of the Ise Shrine and tax levies; Yamato Take's pacification of the Kumaso and Emishi; Jingū's campaign; Ōjin and Nintoku's adoption of Chinese ideals of rule; and Yūryaku's consolidation of imperial authority. The focus of these myths on governmental and state order is highlighted by the fact that they are not comprehensive. That is, they do not explain the origins of everything in the universe, only selective items. Hence, swords appear without an origin story for forges, and farming and weaving exist in the myths of Amaterasu's High Heavenly Plain without an explanation of how these technologies came to be. Steineck suggests that the focus on the origins of government and order reflects the priorities of the people who created *Ancient Matters* and *Chronicles*, that is, the priorities of the Japanese ruling elite during the late seventh and early eighth centuries.

One strength of Steineck's treatment is that it considers myths before, during, and after the compilations of *Ancient Matters* and *Chronicles* as part of the effort to understand the nature of myths generally. Before the compilation of these two texts, Steineck suggests that a stock of Japanese myths existed, though not in any fashion that would allow us to recover them in the present. The compilers of *Ancient Matters* and *Chronicles* and other early texts engaged with this stock, making modifications and expanding the stock in order to create an orthodox or official narrative for the emerging centralized state. These interventions resulted in different versions, with *Chronicles* ultimately becoming the orthodox narrative, though not to the exclusion of others. Furthermore, these ancient sources never specifically referred to these narratives as "myths." Instead, they appear as historical documents, in *Ancient Matters* and *Chronicles*, and elsewhere, as poems, gazetteers, prayers, and other sorts of materials.

Cassirer would suggest that myths appeared in other forms because mythical consciousness was a lower-level, fundamental mode of thinking that appeared everywhere, but based on the Japanese case, Steineck argues that the compilers of *Ancient Matters* and *Chronicles* had an interest in fusing myth and history. For this reason, they included forms such as calendar dates, which indicate factuality, into their mythological narratives. After *Ancient Matters* and *Chronicles* were written, their mythemes were taken up in a wide variety of forms because they had been established as a narrative with binding force. Centuries later, when the state that these myths had been created to legitimize weakened, some of these mythemes were told in new versions—which often included Buddhist motifs—and served to legitimate other powers and authorities.

Steineck concludes that while Cassirer's understanding of myth as an archetype or most primitive version of symbolic forms was flawed, myth still constitutes a unique kind of symbolic form. Myth cannot be the lowest level of symbolic forms because it is a narrative, and as such, reliant on language. But instead of throwing Cassirer out, Steineck proposes modifying the definition of the symbolic form of myth such that it does not require having its own set of symbols. Instead, a symbolic form could be defined by the fact that it has a systematic organization of symbolic elements. In the case of myth, this includes something that the myth is intended to confirm or establish, and a narrative action which serves as the basis for that confirmation.

Steineck asserts that due to this systematic organization, myth operates on two timelines simultaneously. One timeline is the past, when the events narrated by the myth occurred, and it serves to establish a point of reference for the explanation or justification of some part of reality. Within the timeline of the narrative, the myth will often contain accounts of extraordinary features and events. But it will mention places or events accepted as parts of present reality to create a connection that distinguishes it from mere fantasy or fiction. The other timeline is the present, in which the myth is reenacted, read, consumed, or applied, and in this timeline, the myth legitimates the orthodox order that was established in the past. For example, Yūryaku meets the kami Hito-koto-nushi, and his special relationship with the kami confirms his preeminence among humans and legitimacy as a ruler. Yūryaku's legitimacy in turn demonstrates the legitimacy of the imperial line. The myth provides a guide for how the receiver of this narrative, in a later timeline, should understand the world by corroborating the system or order established in the past. By extension, myth functions to preserve orders and systems. Given this new definition of myth's characteristics as a symbolic form, Steineck hints that myth continues to be a relevant and powerful force, even in our modern period that imagines that objective reasons guide social organization.

## Myths and Modern Japan (Antoni)

One historically informed model for interpreting myths is to assess their function in Japan today, or in the recent past. Mythologist Klaus Antoni addresses the meanings of Japanese myth in modern and contemporary Japan. To uncover these meanings, Antoni's research moves contemporary materials to the center of analysis and the eighth-century texts like *Ancient Matters* and *Chronicles* to a supplementary position. Antoni notes that the original myths are the basis of the modern Japanese ideology that insists on Japanese ethnic and cultural uniqueness. As a political ideology, this belief used the Japanese word *kokutai,* meaning "national body," in the pre–World War II era. However, research demonstrating the influence of South Seas and Northeast Asian influence on Japanese myths clearly demonstrates that Japanese homogeneity within the *kokutai* is an ideological perspective and not an empirical reality. Yet despite the work of Japanese mythologists after World War II, who for the first time could pursue their research without fear of censorship or punishment, Japan's supposed uniqueness and homogeneity, as a concept, remains steadfastly obstinate. Antoni argues that the despite the efforts of the Allied Powers to reform the Japanese state after World War II, aspects of the *kokutai* survived in contemporary Japanese thought. Three examples used by Antoni are the debate surrounding the Yasukuni Shrine in Tokyo, the death of the Shōwa Emperor (Hirohito) in 1989, and the international perspective of Japan and the Shinto religion.

Antoni argues that the issues surrounding the intersection of Shinto shrines with the Japanese state are demonstrated by the furor surrounding the Yasukuni Shrine in Tokyo. The shrine itself was built in 1869 and commemorates those who died in military service to the Japanese empire. In 1985, on the fortieth anniversary of the end of World War II, then Prime Minister Nakasone paid respects to the dead at the shrine, the first time a government official had visited in any official capacity since the end of the war. The visit, and subsequent ones since, continue to draw criticism from Japan's former World War II adversaries. However, Antoni focuses rather on the domestic debate that occurred at the time, which involved the separation of church and state. On one side, supporters of the visit argued that the shrine was not actually religious in nature, and as such, the terms used for a visit to the shrine were "pay respects" as opposed to "worship." On the other side, domestic critics of the visit argued that the shrine was clearly a religious site and the visit was a violation of the separation of church and state guaranteed by the postwar Constitution. Worse, they claimed, it was a first step toward nationalization of Yasukuni and then all shrines and a return to the State Shinto and emperor worship systems of pre–World War II Japan.

Antoni argues that the true axis of the debate is the role of the dead. In Japanese folk tradition, the souls of the dead return to their ancestral homes on regular occasions, and their descendants pay them respects and ask for their protection. The original name for Yasukuni was "Shōkonsha," meaning "shrine for summoning the spirits of the dead." Draft legislation for nationalizing the shrine that Antoni reviewed suggests that the shrine is also meant to appease the souls of the dead. Hence, even if the shrine were to be declared non-religious, as proponents of nationalization insist, at its core, it remains a religious institution. For this reason, Yasukuni cannot be a memorial so long as the popular belief in appeasing souls continues.

To demonstrate the debate about the centrality of the emperor in contemporary Japan, Antoni analyzes the official statements and popular media surrounding the 1989 death of Hirohito and the subsequent enthronement of his son, Akihito, known as the Heisei Emperor. The seriousness of Hirohito's illness was largely concealed until September of 1988, after which Japan was paralyzed as repeated blood transfusions extended Hirohito's life until January of the following year. When the emperor actually died, the first death of an emperor since the end of World War II, the Japanese government faced a dilemma as to how to perform and finance Hirohito's funeral. Performing the burial like those of earlier emperors would mean recognition that Shinto was the national religion of Japan and supported by the Japanese state. A purely secular burial with no religious elements would most clearly fulfill the terms of the Constitution but mean disregarding the modern traditions of the imperial house. Ultimately, the Imperial Household Agency, the bureau of the

Japanese government charged with handling affairs of the royal family, determined a program for the funeral that included both private religious and public secular events. As Antoni notes, this was essentially the position of State Shinto before World War II. Shinto was not a religion, but rather Japanese custom, and while the event might have been an opportunity to rethink the relationship between state and emperor, government officials decided on a format that preserved ties to funeral ceremonies of Hirohito's father and grandfather.

Finally, Antoni assesses the impact that Japanese ideas of ethnic homogeneity and uniqueness have had on international understandings of Japan. Much as Japanese myths provide a plausible (but spurious) foundation for the *kokutai*, Antoni argues that the uniqueness and homogeneity of the *kokutai* legitimizes foreign understandings of Japan as "The Lonely Superpower." Antoni draws this characterization from influential American political scientist Samuel P. Huntington (1927–2008), whose 1993 essay "The Clash of Civilizations?" and later 1996 book divided the world into nine civilizations. Of these nine, which included Western, Orthodox, Islamic, and others, Japan was the only one in which the civilization equated to one single nation-state. African civilization, for example, included South Africa, Mozambique, Zaire, etc. Shared religion or values systems, such as Confucianism, were at the core of Huntington's framework, and so Japan's identity as a unique and lonely outlier was based on the notion of Shinto as the foundation of Japanese culture. This perspective, Antoni argues, stems not only from Western ignorance and arrogance, but also Japanese self-perception. That self-perception spreads around the world and makes its way back to Japan. Furthermore, the Japanese image serves as a validation of Huntington's theory, seemingly credible because it is provided first-hand by the Japanese. Put differently, in the nineteenth century, myth was selectively interpreted in a specific manner to support the notion of a unique and homogenous Japanese ethnicity, and that notion continues to be influential in contemporary Japan and around the world.

## New Structuralism (Macé, Rocher)

Two mythologists, François Macé and Alain Rocher, have expanded and revised the structural readings of Japanese myths performed by Lévi-Strauss and Dumézil. As discussed in Chapter 1, Lévi-Strauss advocated for breaking a myth into its smallest parts, mythemes, and using those mythemes to identify patterns at a structural level, that is, outside of the general plot and narrative of the myth. For Lévi-Strauss, this effort was directed at identifying broader structures of myth that were consistent across cultures, perhaps dating from before early humans used a land bridge from Asia to cross into the Americas. Lévi-Strauss' idea of mythical structure influenced Dumézil, who used it to identify his tri-functional hypothesis for Indo-European myths. Mythologists such as Yamaguchi and Ooms adapted structuralist approaches to link myths with kingship and power; Bialock, with kingship, power, and textual production; and Steineck, with myth as a symbolic form. Macé and Rocher revise structuralism to determine the construction and function of *Ancient Matters* and *Chronicles* as narrative texts and the relationship of myth to political ideology. In classic structuralism, myth was imagined as being a fundamental form of thought that was antithetical to the logical and rational processes that characterize ideology and political thought. But both Macé and Rocher argue that myth is ideological and characterized by its own form of logic and narrative style that is deeply self-referential.

Macé breaks *Ancient Matters* into six successions or series: Izanagi's marriage, killing of the fire kami, and escape from Yomi; Susano-o's oath with Amaterasu and descent to Izumo; Ō-kuni-nushi's rescue of the rabbit, death and rebirth, descent to Ne, and completion of creation; Ninigi's descent; emperors Sujin, Suinin, and Keikō, including Yamato Take; and emperors Seimu, Chūai, and Ōjin, including Jingū. Based on a structural analysis, Macé then breaks each of these successions into five parts: a preface, then four related elements that link together to give cohesiveness to the succession. The elements themselves are further broken down into sections, and Macé argues that between sections we can identify themes and motifs of opposition, symmetry, or inversion. The central mythical succession for this analysis is Ninigi's descent succession, which begins with a "preface" of the surrender of the land by Ō-kuni-nushi, then Ninigi's descent as section 1, Ninigi's relationship with Ko-no-hana-saku-ya-bime as section 2, Yama-sachi-hiko as section 3, and Jinmu's conquest as section 4. Macé argues that these sections constitute a single succession centered on the problem of establishing the Japanese empire.

Macé breaks the first sections of Ninigi's descent, the preface, into four more parts: Ame-no-hohi, Ame-waka-hiko, Take-mikazuchi, and the actual surrender of the land. Each of these is symmetrical or inverted to the four parts of the Ninigi's descent mythical succession that contains them, For example, Ame-no-hohi receives the order of the heavenly gods, descends to earth, and marries an earthly kami. Ninigi does the same thing during his descent. Then, Ame-waka-hiko descends to darkest Izumo and attempts to usurp control of the land, but has no children after eight years. Meanwhile, Ninigi descends to Himuka, meaning "sun facing," and has three children after only one night. In part three of the preface, Take-mikazuchi drives Koto-shiro-nushi into hiding in the ocean and confronts Take-mi-nakata. In section 3, Yama-sachi-hiko drives his wife into hiding in the ocean and confronts his brother, Umi-sachi hiko. Finally, Ō-kuni-nushi surrenders and has a palace built on his behalf, while later Jinmu will build a palace for his first capital at Kashihara. The preface of the surrender myths also forms an inverted structure with the Jinmu myths. The surrender myths begin with an oath, then a heavenly deity (Ame-no-hohi), an escapade with an arrow and bird (Ame-waka-hiko), and a sword (Take-mikazuchi's pacification). The Jinmu myth begins with a sword (Take-mikazuchi's aid), then an escapade with an arrow and a bird (the fight with E-ukashi), then a heavenly deity (Nigi-hayahi), and finally an oath. The myths that bookend the Ninigi descent myth succession are inversions of each other.

After examining each succession: six successions and the surrender episode, and breaking each down into its constituent sections, Macé circles back and recombines everything in order to identify the greater structure of the myths in *Ancient Matters*. Macé argues that there are two myth groups that contain the six successions. The first includes the creation of heaven and earth, as its preface, then the Izanagi, Susano-o, and Ō-kuni-nushi successions. The second contains the surrender episode, as its preface, and the Ninigi, Sujin, and Seimu successions. The two prefaces are symmetrical, and the second and third successions of each group are inversions of each other. The fourth succession, which ties the group together, inverts the second and third successions. Keeping track of each constituent part, especially given the brevity of the explanation here, is less critical than realizing Macé's visions for myth. The symmetries and inversions work together to create the mythical force of *Ancient Matters* as a whole. Furthermore, following Dumézil, Macé insists that myth must follow an ideology, and beyond, that myth is a form of philosophy. Beyond the simple political motivations of *Ancient Matters*, structural analysis reveals the overall framework, the logical construction of the narrative, and the symmetry and inversion in the expression. These factors work in concert to express a singular philosophical perspective and mythical ideology from a bygone era.

Like Macé, mythologist Alain Rocher approaches myth interpretation from the perspective of improving the structuralism of the past. However, for Rocher, the key is to recover the superficial and surface-level narrative elements that Lévi-Strauss ignored in favor of some supposed deeper understanding. This pursuit results in Rocher proposing the existence of a mythical style, a form of foundational narrative. Rather than the mytheme, Rocher argues that the critical aspect of the mythical form is the gesture, an action taken in the narrative that joins functional elements in the story with sacred words or magical formulas that duplicate the gesture. These gestures reverberate with each other to form, on the surface level of the narrative, gestural metonymy, that is, a structure in which the mythical story continually refers to itself. This self-reference is the signature feature of mythical style and is akin to the symmetry and inversion noted by Macé. For Rocher, the distinction is that these metonyms are in and identified not only within the text of *Ancient Matters*, but across ancient mythical narratives. The self-reference of mythical style means that myths pose problems and resolve those problems by drawing upon their own narratives.

Rocher's use of gestures to break down the narrative allows the systematic categorization of story parts that is consistent with structuralism, but also insists that the narrative content and form is relevant to the analysis. For Lévi-Strauss, mythemes released the mythologist from considering narrative, but for Rocher, gestures reveal how the narrative is significant. For example, Izanagi and Izanami's creation of the world is broken into four functions and two gestures. Functions one and two are the mission, given to Izanagi and Izanami by the heavenly gods, and the presentation of the spear to the two kami. Then, the first gesture is their thrusting and stirring of the spear. The third function is the announcement of their intentions to go around the pillar of heaven, followed by the second gesture, their union, again an act of thrusting and gyration. Finally, the fourth function is their report to the heavenly gods. The critical element, for Rocher, is that the two gestures are not spelled out in the functions that precede them. The heavenly kami tell Izanagi and Izanami to create the world, but they do not tell them what to do with the spear. Izanagi announces that they will go around the pillar, but not that they are going to consummate their marriage. These gestures were interpretative acts. Furthermore, they always link a sacred word or formula (the mission, the announcement of intention) with a magical object (the spear, the pillar) in which the object only makes sense in the context of the gesture, even though the object has presumable other uses. And of course, these two gestures are analogous to each other.

Rocher's gestures are further broken down into eight elements: the gesture itself (e1), the center of gestural activity (e2), the magic object (e3), the incantation (e4), the subjects (e5), the position (e6), the location (e7), and the element or medium (e8). The gesture in the episode of Izanagi and Izanami on the floating bridge of heaven would then resolve as follows:

| | |
|---|---|
| e1 (gesture) | penetration/gyration/withdrawal |
| e2 (center of activity) | hands |
| e3 (magic object) | spear |
| e4 (incantation) | "curdling sound" (onomatopoeia) |
| e5 (subjects) | Izanagi and Izanami |
| e6 (position) | standing |
| e7 (location) | floating bridge of heaven |
| e8 (element or medium) | ocean |

The turn around the celestial pillar would resolve as follows:

| | |
|---|---|
| e1 (gesture) | penetration/gyration/withdrawal |
| e2 (center of activity) | body |
| e3 (magic object) | heavenly pillar |
| e4 (incantation) | exclamation of the two gods |
| e5 (subjects) | Izanagi and Izanami |
| e6 (position) | standing |
| e7 (location) | Onogorojima |
| e8 (element or medium) | earth |

Rocher concludes, in breaking down these episodes, that the ritualistic interpretation of myths is misfounded because the magic object e3 is of relatively little importance for the gesture e1, and furthermore, because the usage of e3 only makes sense within the context of e1. Most importantly, these mythical gestures refer exclusively to the mythical narrative, not to ancient rituals or rites. Whatever meaning we hope to glean from the myth must come from the mythical narrative itself.

The identification of a mythical style serves, for Rocher, the added role of correcting many perceived misunderstandings about the nature of myth. These include, as noted here, its relationship with ritual, as well as language, structuralism, and politics. Analyzing myths in this fashion also permits Rocher to revise conclusions on some of the central topics of Japanese mythology, including incest, the crying baby, death, the trickster figure, and the journey to another world. Equally important for Rocher is the conclusion that mythical thought is not antithetical to political thought. *Ancient Matters* and *Chronicles* were created at the temporal end of the mythical period that they narrate, and they manage their present, the era in which they were written, through their structural and ideological organization and presentation of myths. The texts use myths to negotiate the critical issues of their era: legitimacy of rule, delegation of power, succession to the throne, and the introduction and adoption of Chinese cultural elements. Being mythical narrative, these political problems can be posed and then resolved according to the inherent logic of the narrative itself.

## Other Topics

### Horse Riders

The presence of burial artifacts related to horseback combat in Japanese tombs from around the fifth century led to a famous and controversial 1948 work by archeologist Egami Namio. Egami suggested that in the last half of the fourth century or the early fifth century, the Japanese archipelago was invaded and conquered by a group of mounted peoples. Mythologists scrambled to accept or reject this theory based on the contents of *Ancient Matters* and *Chronicles*. The Japanese vernacular name of Ōjin, Jingū's son, is unusual among Japanese rulers, and its meaning is debated. If the name were related to a Korean language, and Jingū herself had come from Korea, then the horse rider theory would seem to be borne out in myth.

## Conquering of Izumo

Yamato Take's conquest of Izumo parallels that of Sujin, given in Chapter 3. Both versions have the same poem, so it seems the compilers of *Ancient Matters* and *Chronicles* each wanted to document this conquest but disagreed on who actually did it: Yamato Take or Sujin. However, the idea that Izumo represented a distinct ethnicity, like the Kumaso and Emishi, combined with the fact that the Izumo deities are prominent in Japanese myths, has spurred a number of prehistoric conquest and assimilation theories.

# 5

# The History of Mythology in Japan

The previous chapters of this book provided retellings of the key episodes from Japanese myths as recorded in eighth-century texts along with a variety of theoretical frameworks for understanding those myths. Those frameworks are all products of the modern era, which in Japanese studies starts in the year 1868, when the Tokugawa Shogunate fell and Emperor Meiji was named head of state. Japanese mythology began several decades later at the end of the nineteenth century, with scholars like Takayama Chogyū and Takagi Toshio, or with Edmund Tylor abroad. Before the modern period, Japanese theologians, monks, poets, and historians read *Ancient Matters* and *Chronicles*, but did not call them myths. Their understanding of these texts changed over time, demonstrating that the significance of textual narratives and the fluidity of their interpretations are not restricted to the modern era.

## Premodern and Early Modern Reception

### State Ritual and New Mythical Texts

Besides Jitō's creation of a permanent capital and implementation of a written Civil and Penal Code, several of the most prominent and longest-lasting innovations of her reign involved the creation of ritual. Jitō employed pageantry and performance to symbolically reinforce her grasp of power. Through ritual, she showed the imperial court and regional elites that Tenmu's reign was legitimate and part of a grand tradition of imperial rule. She papered over the coup that had brought Tenmu to power and legitimized her own position as his successor. More importantly, she confirmed the position of Kusakabe, her son with Tenmu. Kusakabe's premature death complicated Jitō's succession plan, but her initiatives were so successful that she seemingly had little problem ensuring that Kusakabe's son would be the next to take the throne. Three key rituals legitimized Jitō's position: Tenmu's funeral, Jitō's accession ceremony, and Jitō's frequent visits to Yoshino.

While every emperor in *Chronicles* receives a burial of some kind, Tenmu's funeral ceremony is the most lavishly described. From Tenmu's death in the ninth month of 686 to the seventh month of 689, when the last foreign dignitaries sent to attend the funeral returned to Korea, the ceremonies for Tenmu were the singular focus of the court. In truth, these few years were extremely consequential for Jitō's rule for two other reasons. In 686, she preemptively addressed a challenge to Kusakabe's succession by eliminating her stepson Prince Ōtsu, and in 689, Kusakabe died. Scholars debate whether the charges against Ōtsu were real or simply used as a pretext, but judging from the numerous poems by Ōtsu contained in anthologies from the era, he was a prominent figure at court. Kusakabe's death shattered Jitō's succession plans. Both incidents are barely noted in *Chronicles*, but the two years of eulogies, funeral masses, and visits from foreign dignitaries for Tenmu's funeral are recorded in detail. Jitō and the court memorialized Tenmu time and time again, using official ceremony to cement and legitimize his rule.

One entry surrounding Tenmu's funeral is especially important for the future study of *Ancient Matters* and *Chronicles*. At Tenmu's final burial in the eleventh month of 688, which followed a long temporary interment, a courtier named Tagima no Chitoko "delivered a eulogy that recited the line of succession of imperial ancestors, and appropriate rites were performed." Chitoko also recited eulogies at the funerals of Jitō and her grandson and successor Monmu. This is the first deployment of imperial genealogy in the performance of a state ritual and had the important function of making Tenmu part of a larger grand narrative of succession going all the way back to Jinmu and the immediate descendants of Amaterasu. This succession is also the basis for the organization of *Ancient Matters* and *Chronicles*.

Jitō's accession ceremony also takes a new and peculiar form. Even today, the imperial accession ceremony is shrouded in mystery and constitutes a major public event and milestone in the reign of the Japanese emperor. In *Chronicles*, several accession ceremonies are described, probably more legendary than factual. At these ceremonies, much like at Jitō's ceremony and those in the present, a set of one or more objects was conferred upon the new ruler as a sign of their assumption of office. For example, at the accession of the legendary emperor Ingyō, government officials conferred, selected Ingyō as the new ruler, and presented a signet to him. A close comparison with Jitō's accession reveals two fundamental differences. First, Jitō is not preselected by a group of court ministers who hand over a signet or seal. Instead, representatives from three key clans perform ceremonial roles, culminating in the presentation of a sword and mirror to Jitō. Second, the objects are called "divine" at Jitō's accession, but not at those of previous rulers, suggesting that Jitō created this ceremony to elevate her status to that of a living god.

Finally, Jitō makes over thirty visits to Yoshino during her eleven years on the throne. Yoshino, famous now for its cherry blossoms, was not only the location to which Tenmu fled as he plotted his campaign to seize the throne but also the place where Tenmu had forced his sons and nephews to swear allegiance to Kusakabe. Jitō almost certainly intended these displays to remind the competitors to the throne of their oaths, which was an even more urgent matter for Jitō after Kusakabe's untimely death. Her imperial processions constituted a ritual celebrating fealty and loyalty to Kusakabe and his descendants. Numerous poems by the poet Kakinomoto no Hitomaro about these excursions appear in the poetry volume

*Myriad Poems.* While outside the scope of this guide, modern scholars like Duthie have identified discrepancies between the vision of empire and imperial power in *Myriad Poems* versus *Chronicles*, which we can call an alternative imperial mythology. Jitō's use of ritual was the occasion for the creation of myth.

Among the various mythical accounts—*Ancient Matters, Chronicles, Myriad Poems*, and others—circulating in eighth-century Japan, *Chronicles* was chosen as the official narrative. This was perhaps because of its close tie to Tenmu's court, having been composed by one of Tenmu's sons. *Chronicles* was also the text that most closely resembled a Chinese dynastic history, the dominant model for government history in East Asia at the time. *Chronicles* provided a glowing account of Tenmu's 672 coup, and as Tenmu's descendants were on the throne through most of the eighth century, there was perhaps some favoritism for *Chronicles*.

The creation of an official, canonical account of Japanese myth encouraged originality for clans interested in using myth to improve their status. Promotion and court privileges in ancient Japan often depended on lineage: a clan whose ancestors had provided important service to the ancient state, especially in the mythical era, could hope for favorable treatment in the present. But rewriting the past was not without risks. Some early evidence suggests that accounts that contradicted the information in *Chronicles* were banned or destroyed. As such, clans turned, like Jitō, to state ritual to introduce new and variant myths.

The most important examples of myth creation linked to court ritual in early Japan are the books *Gleanings*, written in 812 CE, and *Original Record*, composed sometime in the ninth century. *Gleanings*, written by Inbe no Hironari, provides an abridged version of the mythical creation story and Ninigi's descent to the archipelago. One key difference is that in *Chronicles*, Sujin orders that worship of Amaterasu be moved out of the palace, but in *Gleanings*, this is altered to say that Sujin moved a divine mirror, representing Amaterasu, and the divine sword Kusanagi, taken by Susano-o from the eight-headed serpent. Furthermore, *Gleanings* claimed that Sujin ordered the Inbe clan, the same lineage group as the author of *Gleanings*, to create replicas of these two items for use at the imperial accession ritual. In *Chronicles*, the Inbe clan plays an important ceremonial role in Jitō's accession, which includes a sword and mirror, though *Chronicles* does not state to which sword and mirror it refers.

Put together, the claims result in *Gleanings* creating a new myth with several distinct features. Jitō's accession ceremony was no longer distinct; rather, the sword and mirror, given to Ninigi by Amaterasu, were regalia that were part of every imperial accession in Japanese history. The Inbe played an important role in this ceremony. Finally, even though the original divine sword and mirror were locked away at the Atsuta and Ise Shrines, because the Inbe had made copies of the items in antiquity, the fabrications were available for the ceremony. *Gleanings* concludes, transparently, with a request that the Inbe clan be raised in rank given their important ceremonial role. Hironari's request for promotion was granted.

Perhaps because of the success of *Gleanings*, several other texts tried their hands at creating new myths linked to court ritual, but none matched the later importance or outright boldness of *Original Record*. *Original Record* made use of two key plot holes in *Chronicles* to bolster the position of the Mononobe clan, who were likely involved in the creation of the unattributed *Original Record*. First, when Jinmu sets out to conquer the Nara Basin in *Chronicles*, he refers to a kami named Nigi-hayahi, who had descended from heaven in a stone boat. Then, when Jinmu arrives in Nara, Nigi-hayahi surrenders to Jinmu after killing his son-in-law Naga-sune-hiko. However, the lineage of Nigi-hayahi is never explained in *Chronicles*. Clearly, he is a heavenly kami, but that is all we know. *Original Record* claims that Nigi-hayahi was Ninigi's older brother, sent down before Ninigi. As such, the Mononobe clan, descended from Nigi-hayahi, would have a vaunted heritage and long history of service to the state. The second plot hole employed by *Original Record* is the death of Prince Shōtoku, a legendary sage from the seventh century. *Original Record* ends with Shōtoku's death, making it seem like the prince himself authored the text. Though this attribution was eventually proved false in the eighteenth century, for one millennium, *Original Record* was counted, along with *Ancient Matters* and *Chronicles*, as an authentic record of Japanese myths and fundamental text for Shinto.

## Adapting Japanese Myths for Buddhism

The initial arrival of Buddhism in Japan sometime in the sixth century seems to have had little impact on Japanese myths, but the new religion soon made its impact on geography, theology, and cosmology. In the geographical realm, Buddhism introduced India to Japan, and the Japanese worldview was eventually reshaped to consist generally of three countries: India, China, and Japan. Conversely, *Ancient Matters* barely mentions foreign states, and *Chronicles* is primarily concerned with Korea and China. The theology underpinning the kami and their role in the world was also reframed in Buddhist principles. The diverse pantheon of Mahayana Buddhism, practiced primarily in East Asia, was accommodating to the notion of foreign deities, but the identities and relationships of the kami to Buddhist deities required explanation. Ultimately, a new creation story in which Izanagi and Izanami operated in accordance with Buddhist principles began to gain popularity, appearing in a wide variety of versions throughout medieval Japan. Finally, a series of studies and commentaries on *Chronicles*, novel for their time, introduced a new framework in the sixteenth century that reversed the positions of Buddhism and Shinto and exalted the Japanese kami above foreign competitors.

The new geographical model is exemplified in maps produced in Japan during this period. Often titled "Map of the Five Regions of India" or "Map of Jambudvīpa," these maps featured the Indian subcontinent prominently in the center of the map. China was compressed into the upper right of the map, and in the waters at the upper-right edge, the Japanese archipelago, sometimes only partially visible, sat at the edge of the world. Later versions of these maps like the one pictured here, produced after contact with Africans and Europeans, might add the Middle East, Africa, and Europe in the east as floating islands, but the ultimate geography of the world was still firmly centered on India. Placenames on the map often corresponded with locations in *Journey to the West*, a Chinese account of a monk who traveled to India to procure authentic copies of Buddhist sutras. For the Japanese viewer, tracing the journey through China to India constituted a kind of metaphorical pilgrimage. However, the spread of this new geographical reality meant that the Japanese myths, which only accounted for the creation of the archipelago itself, would need to be reimagined in a way that incorporated Jambudvīpa and the Buddhist geographical vision.

As might be expected, the new creation story integrating Japanese myths with Buddhist geography appears in multiple sources with varying details. The core myth appears for the first time in the *Nakatomi no harae kunge*, a twelfth-century commentary on a Shinto prayer used for the annual Great Purification (Ōharae) court ceremony. The myth claims that at the beginning of heaven and earth, the cosmic Buddha Dainichi desired to save living beings who were unable to escape the cycle of death and rebirth. Dainichi went to Jambudvīpa, the floating continent which contains India, China, and Japan. There, Dainichi asked King Māra, ruler of the desire realm where beings with insufficient karma to escape from the cycle of suffering are born, for his seal. When Dainichi released the power of the seal, his compassion radiated in all directions and calmed the rampaging kami. Dainichi performed this great feat under the guise of his avatar, Amaterasu.

The identification of Japanese kami as avatars of Buddhist deities, that is, as manifestations that various Buddhas and Bodhisattvas adopted in order to help mankind, appears in materials from around

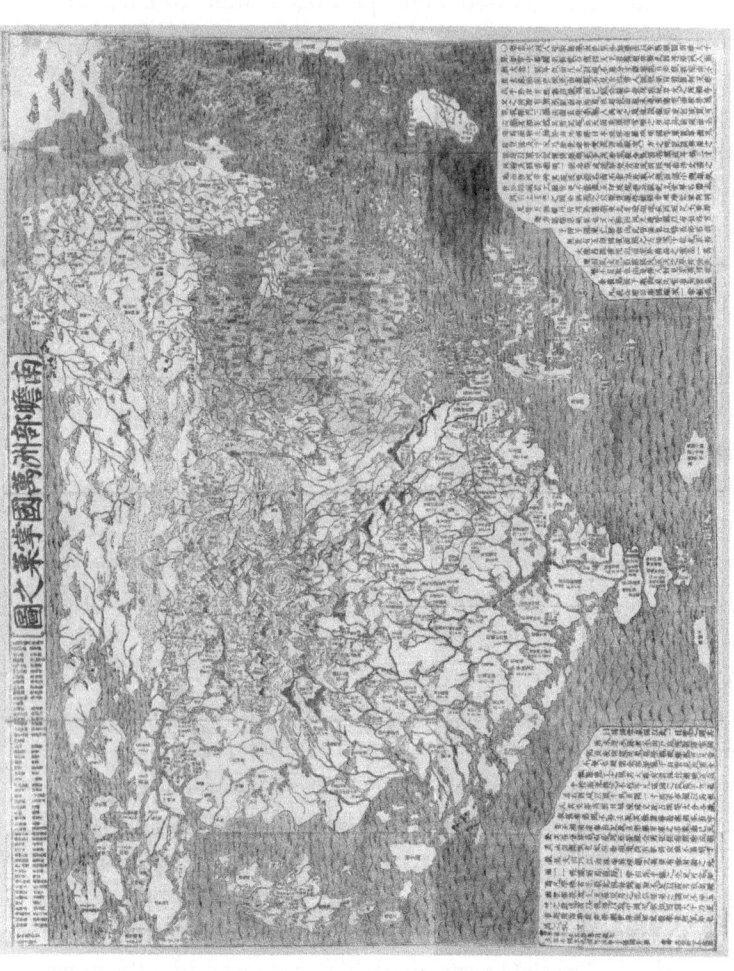

**MAP 7** Hōtan, Handy Map of the Myriad Countries of Jambudvīpa, 1710. Japan is located in the far right of the map. The Indian subcontinent dominates the center of the map, stretching from the middle to the bottom. China is colored in and compressed at center-right. Photograph courtesy of the David Rumsey Map Collection, David Rumsey Map Center, Stanford Libraries

the ninth century. Often referred to as *honji suijaku,* or "roots and traces," the theory provided a means for integrating the native Japanese kami into the Buddhist pantheon. The theory was widely applied as Buddhism spread through the archipelago and Buddhist temples developed close associations with shrines. Several of the most important kami such as Amaterasu and Ō-kuni-nushi were identified as the avatars of one or more Buddhist deities, creating a symbiotic relationship between the Japanese myths and Buddhist doctrine.

There is a time gap of several centuries between the first application of the "roots and traces" theory and the creation myth with Dainichi and Māra in *Nakatomi no harae kunge.* A few centuries later, this creation myth evolved into a much more complex narrative with deeper integration of elements from the *Ancient Matters* and *Chronicles* stories. These later narratives often begin with Izanami and Izanagi, or Amaterasu, standing on the floating bridge of heaven and looking down into the sea northeast of India. There, they see a sparkling jewel, and they thrust the spear down and stir, then pull it back up. Depending on the version of the story, the drops from the spear, or bubbles that arise from stirring, or the sparkling jewel in the deeps, results in the creation of the Japanese archipelago. This jewel, sometimes a seal, is associated with Dainichi. The literal name of Dainichi is "great sun," and Dainichi is the "root" of Amaterasu, providing "root of the sun" or "origin of the sun," i.e., the meaning of "Japan." King Māra, ruler of the desire realm, was concerned that Buddhism would flourish in this newly created group of islands, and so Dainichi, in the guise of Amaterasu, agrees to eschew Buddhism. Their agreement is confirmed using a seal, which is later conferred upon the Japanese emperor. Because of the agreement between Amaterasu and King Māra, monks are not allowed to visit Amaterasu's shrine at Ise, however, this is simply a front and Amaterasu works along with the other Japanese kami on behalf of all living things.

This new creation story is a marked departure from the narratives of *Ancient Matters* and *Chronicles*, and it appears in a wide number of sources throughout medieval Japan. Most important is that the story adapted a set of myths in a way that reshaped them to conform with prevailing understandings about the universe and Japan's place within it. The new myth also applies intellectual trends that were popular in medieval Japan such as the use of origin narratives (Jp. *setsuwa*) and associative logic. At this time in Japan, mastery of a concept was demonstrated by knowledge of how a particular phenomenon came about, and the logic frequently relied on parallels created through wordplay, numerology, or narrative similarity. The association between Dainichi and Japan, for example, hinges on wordplay, and the episode provides an origin story for the Japanese state and its name.

The suggestion that the seal used by Amaterasu and King Māra was now in the possession of the emperor fed a larger body of lore surrounding the imperial regalia that proliferated during the same period. Three objects: a seal, a sword, and a mirror, were identified as imperial regalia and expected to be passed from one emperor to the next. As noted above, *Gleanings* already claimed that the mirror and sword were needed to confirm the succession, and the same text asserted that the sword and mirror used by the imperial family were copies. However, that claim was not widely accepted in medieval Japan, and dissenting opinions argued that the mirror was destroyed in the numerous fires that ravaged the imperial palace in Kyoto. The sword had been taken from the palace by Emperor Antoku when he fled the Minamoto forces at the end of the twelfth century and was lost at sea when Antoku drowned.

## Comparative Axes: Quantity (Thompson and Schrempp)

In *The Truth of Myth*, Thompson and Schrempp note that numbers appear frequently in myths and often have pronounced significance. The most obvious of these instances is when actual numbers appear, for example, a shark claiming to be able to transport Yama-sachi-hiko to the palace of the sea god in eight days. In Japanese myths, eight is an important recurring number, including the eight great islands of the Japanese archipelago, eight mountain kami born from the body of the fire kami, eight kinds of thunder on Izanami, etc. The number appears so frequently that some scholars have suggested it might simply be an archaic way of specifying "many."

The loss of the sword Kusanagi when Antoku drowned created a new myth, again with heavy Buddhist influence, about Susano-o and the mythical sword Kusanagi and centered on the number eight. According to the new myth, Susano-o claimed the sword from the tail of the eight-headed serpent, but the serpent was in fact a manifestation of the dragon king; snakes and dragons are considered related in East Asian lore. Both are also associated with rain and bodies of water, and the greatest of the dragons resides at a palace under the sea. The Dragon King resents the loss of his sword and so reincarnates as the eighty-eighth Japanese emperor, Antoku. When Antoku reaches eight years of age, he takes the sword and plunges back into the sea, reclaiming it for himself. The incorporation of the Dragon King as a character, the use of reincarnation, and the application of an associative logic around the number "eight" illustrate how the original myths of *Ancient Matters* and *Chronicles* were adapted for the world of medieval Japan and how a mythical quantity might be used to create logical connections.

Thompson and Schrempp also discuss the power of lists, which can convey quantity in an impressionistic fashion. *Ancient Matters* and *Chronicles* contain many such lists of kami, who are born in the mythical narrative from almost every action taken by Izanagi and Izanami. Many of these have been abbreviated to simplify the retellings in this book, but in the original texts, the number of kami is so great that the narrative becomes difficult to follow. The proliferation of kami emphasizes the vastness and scope of the realm ruled by the emperor, the chief ritualist for the state. The lists also reinforce the scope of calamities, for example, when the earthly kami buzz like summer flies and the cacophony is so great that it reaches heaven.

## Chinese Writings

Chinese writings, including the mythical creation story of the giant Pangu, were also incorporated into Japanese myths using the same principles as the Buddhist-influenced stories. The Pangu story asserted that a mythical giant named Pangu was born from an egg. As Pangu grew, the heavens, which rested on his head, became further and further separated from earth. When Pangu died, his bones became mountains, his blood the waters, his fur the forests, and his eyes the sun and the moon. By and large, the myth is not easily reconcilable with the Japanese myths in *Ancient Matters* and *Chronicles*, and in a late twelfth-century lecture on *Chronicles*, an attendee asked the lecturer how the two stories could both be true. The lecturer replied that in one version of the Japanese myths, Izanagi washed his eyes after returning from Yomi, and then the sun and moon came into existence. At another point in the same lecture, the instructor recalls that when Izanagi and Izanami sent Amaterasu to heaven, Pangu had not finished growing, and so the heavens were not distantly separated from the earth at that time. The lecturer's attempt to combine these myths suggests that in this period, Chinese myth was also considered as a potential body of material that could be reconciled to understand the truth.

The differences between Indian or Buddhist, Chinese, and Japanese stories about the creation of the world was addressed directly by Kitabatake Chikafusa (1293–1394), one of the most prominent writers, theologians, and military strategists of his time. Kitabatake asserted in his history *A Chronicle of Gods and Sovereigns*, "Because they share the same world, although the beginning of the creation of the universe should be the same everywhere, the explanations of the three countries differ." Chikafusa's equation of the three countries was significant because it leveled the formerly superior position of Buddhism implied by the "roots and traces" theory. Chikafusa was likely exposed to this idea from the time he spent at Amaterasu's Ise Shrine, where a new kind of Shinto, the so-called Watarai or Ise tradition, had emerged and promised that Buddhist enlightenment could be realized through Shinto teachings.

The final chapter of medieval Japanese Shinto, realized in the work of theologian Yoshida Kanetomo (1435–1511), not only equalized India, China, and Japan but also put Japan in a superior position. Kanetomo claimed that it was Japan, not India, that constituted the roots, and that the Buddhist deities were the "traces." Building on the Watarai tradition, Kanetomo claimed that Japan was like the seed, China the stem, and India the fruit. Buddhism came to Japan like the seeded fruit falling to the ground upon maturity, returning to its original source. China connected the two via writing, by which sutras translated into Classical Chinese arrived in Japan. In terms of Japanese myths, Kanetomo's formulation meant that Buddhist and Chinese materials should be used to study Japanese myths. After all, Japan was the seed, and so concepts like Buddhist cosmology or Confucian metaphysics were ultimately products of Japan. Kanetomo's Yoshida tradition of Shinto was dominant through the early modern or Edo period, from 1600 to 1868.

## Theory versus Observation

A 1605 book by a Japanese Christian convert named Fukansai Habian assailed the Buddhist cosmological vision and the Japanese mythical creation story as delusions and fictions. The earth was a sphere, Habian claimed, and its size had been measured. Based on his calculations, the Buddhist claim that a giant mountain, Mt. Sumeru, lies at the center of the universe was wrong. Given the distance of the North Pole from Japan and the purported size of the mountain, such a mountain would be visible from Japan with the naked eye. As for the Japanese creation myths, Habian points out that the story of Amaterasu finding the seal of Dainichi at the bottom of the ocean is not in the original text of *Chronicles*. The claim by the Yoshida tradition of Shinto that the Japanese myths contained a deeper, secret meaning was equally false. For Habian, the entire matter was simply nonsense.

Habian's information about the world was probably taken from the *Compendum Catholicae Veritatis* (1593), translated into Japanese in 1594, and Matteo Richi's the *Complete Map of Myriad Countries* (Ch. Kunyu Wanguo Quantu, J. Konyo bankokuzenzu). The former was a textbook used for Jesuit education in Japan until it was banned in 1614. The latter was map of the globe produced for the Chinese Court, of which numerous manuscript copies were created. More important than the new information at Habian's disposal was his approach toward knowledge itself. Habian gave priority to measurable and verifiable data obtained through human experience: the size of the earth, the visibility of a mountain, the movements of the sun and the moon, etc., over ancient Japanese and Buddhist ways of knowing. And although Habian's ideas did not catch on in Japan for another century, they demonstrate that the seventeenth century was an inflection point. Ultimately, Habian's style of empirical reasoning would become mainstream, and Japanese myths would have to be adapted to fit.

One reason that Habian's ideas did not enjoy immediate popularity was that in seventeenth-century Japan, ideas associated with Christianity fell out of favor, and those connected to Chinese traditions rose in prominence. Of particular importance were Confucian theories that had been revised and reinterpreted during the Song Dynasty. The new version of Confucianism, sometimes called Neo-Confucianism, had a more advanced metaphysical aspect than its predecessor, and the identification of cosmic laws and principles in Neo-Confucian thought provided an alternative method of knowledge to Habian's empiricism. The principles of Neo-Confucianism espoused eternal truths, and Japanese myths could be understood by applying these known principles to them, a mode of knowledge known as rationalism.

The contrast between rationalism and empiricism in Japan is well-attested in an argument between Hayashi Razan, a famous Neo-Confucian scholar, and Habian, that purportedly happened in 1606. Only Razan's side of the story is extant, and it is certainly possible that he fabricated the story of the meeting in order to assail Christianity and empiricism more generally, but the debate is useful for seeing how knowledge claims worked in seventeenth-century Japan. As the story goes, Razan and his brother visited Habian in Kyoto through the introduction of a mutual acquaintance. At Habian's residence, Razan asked Habian about a picture of Christ and what he called a "round map." No answer is recorded about the picture of Christ, but the map prompted a serious argument. Habian attempted to explain the map to Razan, saying, "The center of the earth is down. Above the earth is heaven, and below the earth is heaven. Our country was reached by boats that crossed the ocean. The easternmost point is west, and the westernmost point is east. Based on this, we know that the earth is round."

Razan replied,

> This reasoning is impossible. How could heaven be below earth? When you look, everything in the world has a top and a bottom. This claim that there is nothing below the ground is a result of not knowing reason. And at sea, there are wind and waves. The boat goes west, then north, then south, then east. The people on the boat don't know which direction is what. They think they are going west. Saying 'this is the westernmost point, this is east,' is impossible. If the boat goes to the east, then it also goes north, or goes south, and then certainly west. Saying 'this is the easternmost point, this is west,' is impossible. Also, you don't know the reasoning by which all things have a top and a bottom. You're making the center of the earth into down, and the shape of the earth into a circle. How sad this delusion is! (Hayashi Razan, *Haiyaso*, 414)

The rationale for the two thinkers is quite different. Habian, based on the experiences of sailors who had circumnavigated the globe, knew that the earth was round. If you went far enough to the east, you would eventually reach the westernmost point on a flat map. Moreover, from any point on the surface of the globe, downwards went to the center of the earth, and the sky was above. Razan, however, knew that the earth was flat because Neo-Confucian law demanded that everything have a top and a bottom. If one somehow came to think that this were not the case, they were simply deluded. Sailors who claimed to have reached the east by going west were confused and lost. Perhaps most importantly for Razan, the suggestion that up and down were relative to where one was standing meant that other distinctions between upper and lower might also be relativized. For Confucian thought, built on a set of fundamental human relationships like lord and vassal, and which stressed the ideal of the cultivated individual as a superior form of existence, erasing top and bottom through relativizing constituted a social danger.

Some years after the alleged meeting between Habian and Razan, Razan formed his own impression of how to understand Japanese myths that was deeply informed by Confucian ideology. In principle, Confucian thought viewed supernatural deities with skepticism, but state history was of paramount importance. In this vein, Razan took up the task of writing a history of Japan, but he simply began with Emperor Jinmu and omitted the Age of the Gods. Unfortunately, this manuscript was lost in a fire, but elsewhere, Razan wrote more pointedly about Emperor Jinmu. In that writing, he also noted that one's affairs were divided into public and private. State history was public, and as such, it should be written in the public interest. For this reason, Confucius himself used historical materials in his *Spring and Autumn Annals* that he had doubts about, but he could not let his private concerns compromise public history. Razan's son Gahō later finished his father's state historical project and even added a section on the Age of the Gods, but this addition is merely a compendium of the deities that appear with no major commentarial apparatus. Gahō included the Age of the Gods because it was a public record, but it was not worth extensive effort, and privately, both he and his father had doubts about its truthfulness.

Razan's discussion of public and private was also important because he had a private theory about Emperor Jinmu that he deemed inappropriate for public history. Several Chinese sources describe legendary court figures who set sail for the far East, and one, named Wu Taibo, allegedly fled to the land of the barbarians and dwelt with a dragon. Most medieval sources like Chikafusa had dismissed this claim because it did not accord with the triad of states: Japan, China, and India, that they imagined comprised the world. Razan, however, argued that Wu Taibo in fact came to Japan, a land of barbarians, and that the story of Yama-sachi-hiko and Toyo-tama-hime in which she transforms into a sea monster while giving birth was a Japanese version of the same story. Ninigi's descent to Kyushu was, in the same way, actually a description of Wu Taibo's arrival in Japan from China. The kami who resisted Ninigi and Jinmu were local chieftains who fought and lost to Taibo's superior forces. Perhaps most important for Razan, Taibo was descended from the Kings of the Zhou Dynasty, and so if Taibo was Jinmu, it meant that the dynasty most highly regarded by Confucians still existed.

Razan's precise interpretation of Jinmu, a euhemerism that cast the gods as ancient humans, was not widely shared, but other Confucian scholars applied the same manner of interpretation. Ogyū Sorai wrote, "the age of the gods, because it was when humans who had passed away were revered as gods, should more properly be called an age when humans were worshipped as gods." Arai Hakuseki put it in similar terms, writing, "the gods are human" and taking the events of the *Chronicles*, *Ancient Matters*, and *Original Record* as metaphors for human activity. Hakuseki's analysis is of particular interest because his historical research was influential with modern historians in the Meiji Period as a model for writing the history of Japan. Hakuseki took the euhemerism that Razan had applied to Ninigi and Jinmu and formulated it into a more complete thesis that took all of the kami in *Ancient Matters* and *Chronicles* to be ancient human persons. The word "kami" itself, he contended, was derived from the Japanese word for "up," which is also "kami." The word kami was simply a title of respect or reverence used for important religious and political figures.

Within in the private sphere, Razan wrote about topics in the Age of the Gods, but Hakuseki took a more disciplined approach and wrote a well-structured twenty-five point commentary on the Age of the Gods volumes of *Ancient Matters* and *Chronicles*. Most of Hakuseki's arguments rely on the same kind of linguistic analysis that he used with "kami"; High Heavenly Plain (Takma-ga-hara) for example is rendered "Atop the Sea of Taka" with "hara" having the homophonic meaning of "atop" and "ama" of "sea." He also used narrative similarities: the spear thrust down by Izanagi and Izanami was perhaps the pole of a boater, depicting the passage of human beings to the Japanese archipelago. Despite the humanity that Hakuseki attributed to the kami, he still respected their contributions to the development of society. Moreover, while Razan's form of rationalism tended to be overdetermined, with Neo-Confucian theory rigorously providing the paradigm for understanding Japanese myths, Hakuseki introduced more interpretive freedom. An overarching confidence in the mandate of heaven, a Confucian concept of legitimacy, guided all of Hakuseki's interpretations, but beyond that, linguistic and narrative association had a major role in his interpretation of Japanese myths.

Confucian interpretations of Japanese myths dominated the intellectual landscape for the seventeenth and into the eighteenth century, but an alternative approach founded on empirical analysis gradually grew in prominence, especially through the eighteenth century. While practitioners were hardly unified in their interpretations, the general name "kokugaku," often translated as "National Learning" or "Nativism," has been applied to this group of scholars. In general, these scholars were interested in the foundational texts of Japan, including *Myriad Poems*, *Ancient Matters*, and *Chronicles*. Kokugaku readings diverged from Confucian approaches because kokugaku emphasized reading and understanding the words as they were written, rather than superimposing a top-down theoretical framework. Nativist scholars also rejected the associative logic that characterized not only Buddhist readings but the Yoshida tradition of Shinto and one of its prominent offshoots, the Suika tradition of Shinto. Yoshida and Suika suggested that there were deeper, profound meanings contained within the myths of *Ancient Matters* and *Chronicles*, but kokugaku insisted that the text meant only what it said.

In the study of Japanese myth, whether ancient or modern, the kokugaku scholar Motoori Norinaga is the preeminent figure. Norinaga's life work, called *Kojiki-den* or *Commentary on the Ancient Matters*, is a forty-four-volume commentary on *Ancient Matters*, the first full treatment on that text ever written. Not only did Norinaga provide a line-by-line commentary on the entire text, but he also reproduced the original text and added vernacular Japanese glosses. These glosses are still influential in scholarship on *Ancient Matters* today, and serious research on a topic in *Ancient Matters* often begins with a look at Norinaga. To produce the glosses, Norinaga relied primarily on *Chronicles*, which had a vernacular reading tradition dating from the ninth century, as well as *Myriad Poems* and other Japanese classics. Of course, these vernacular glosses are ultimately a best guess at the reading for much of *Ancient Matters*, but the quality and depth of Norinaga's scholarship is staggering. Despite its length, *Kojiki-den* makes up only a portion of Norinaga's output; the most recent reprinting of Norinaga's complete works is twenty volumes in total.

Norinaga's approach is best described as philological, that is, steeped in a thorough research of words and their historical usages. In order to identify the vernacular Japanese reading, and by extension, the intended meaning, of a word, Norinaga searched for attested examples in other texts from the same period. He also made use of the content in *Chronicles* that resembles material in *Ancient Matters*; the long history of study on *Chronicles* and its more orthodox written language made it easy to understand and an ideal resource for making sense of *Ancient Matters*. Norinaga also thoroughly documented his work, making it possible to follow his logic as he moved between source materials. His effort to annotate the entirety of *Ancient Matters* demonstrated a fundamental assumption at the heart of his research: Norinaga believed that *Ancient Matters* was originally an oral record in the Japanese language. Norinaga's creation of vernacular glosses was an act of recovery, because the original language had only been partially encoded. *Chronicles*, unfortunately, was too heavily influenced by Chinese styles of writing to be used for linguistic recovery, though it did record the events of antiquity with accuracy. But *Ancient Matters* offered the promise of properly understanding Japanese myths.

Norinaga's pursuit of the true words in *Ancient Matters* betrayed another important feature of his scholarly work: Norinaga believed that the myths in *Ancient Matters* were true. His dedication to literal meaning, even in the face of seeming absurdity, was extreme even among his fellow kokugaku practitioners. In a famous exchange with the author Ueda Akinari, Akinari accused Norinaga of being over-literal in interpreting the myths, to the point that Norinaga believed that Amaterasu was the actual sun. How could the sun go into a cave, Akinari argued? Norinaga's belief in the veracity of Japanese myths helps explain his *Kojiki-den* project, which was dedicated not only to resurrecting the original vernacular Japanese language of the text, but also to identifying the right and true interpretation of what the myths in *Ancient Matters* and *Chronicles* said. Norinaga believed that the truth of antiquity could be identified through rigorous textual research.

Norinaga also inferred a grander theological conception from Japanese myths. In truth, he was first and foremost a philologist, specializing in identifying the meanings of ancient Japanese words and phrases through contextual clues, linguistic similarity, and references in other sources. His theological theory, reproduced most clearly in a work called *Naobi no mitama*, was written around twenty years before he started his *Kojiki-den* commentary, and this later work is a more informed perspective on how Norinaga interpreted Japanese myths. Nevertheless, *Naobi no mitama* was extremely influential, and this short text was frequently republished through the end of World War II. Norinaga's theological interpretation hinged on the gods that were produced when Izanagi bathed himself after escaping from Yomi. Two of the kami are associated with disasters, and two of the kami are associated with repair and correction. In Norinaga's vision, evil befell the human world due to the actions of the two kami of disaster, especially Ō-maga-tsu-hi, and reprieve from the suffering of life was provided by Ō-nao-bi, from which the text *Naobi no mitama*, or "soul of Nao-hi," draws its name. This interpretation also accorded with the longstanding focus on cleanliness and purity in kami worship practices.

One of Norinaga's greatest challenges was adapting Japanese myths for the new reality of eighteenth-century Japan, in which the empirical forms of knowledge first advocated by Habian in the early 1600s at last began to seriously challenge the orthodoxy of Neo-Confucian rationalism. In the realm of cosmology, one excellent example of Norinaga's thought is recorded in a 1790 text called *Shamon Monnō ga kusen hakkai gechōron no ben* (Statement on the Explanation for Those Who Ridicule the Nine Mountains and Eight Seas by Monnō). The long title is a reference to two 1754 works by the Buddhist monk Monnō, who attempted to explain Buddhist cosmology in light of new geographical information entering Japan. Monnō held that the world was flat and located on the continent of Jambudvīpa, but his new rendering identified lands such as Australia that had not appeared in the India-centered Buddhist maps of earlier eras. He also charted empirically verified information such as the passage of the sun and moon; these he imagined orbiting the flat plane of the earth. Though Monnō had passed away by the time of Norinaga's critique, Norinaga argued forcefully that sailors had circumnavigated the globe, proving that it was round. Norinaga prioritized human experience over a theoretical framework. In a series of other writings and charts from around the same time, Norinaga sketched the passage of the sun and moon around the earth, along with the seasons, times of day, and tides.

Norinaga's interest in making astronomical observations accord with Japanese myths appeared in a pamphlet by one of his disciples, Hattori Nakatsune (1757–1824), called *Sandai kō* (Thoughts on the Three Great Celestial Bodies). This pamphlet focused on the formation of the earth, the sun, and the moon, from the perspective of *Ancient Matters*, and Norinaga included Nakatsune's pamphlet in Volume 17 of *Kojiki-den*. According to Nakatsune, the sun, moon, and earth formed as the heavens separated. Japan, which was produced by Izanami, received privileged status as the location connected to heaven by the heavenly floating bridge, though the bridge eventually separated as the three bodies moved apart from one another. The other countries of the world appeared "due to the coagu-

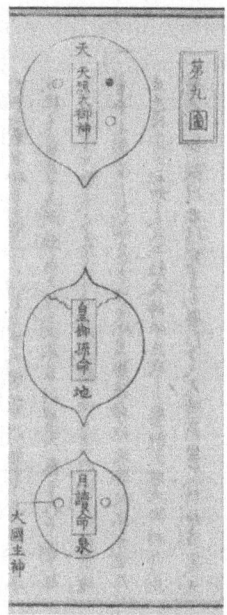

**FIGURE 15** *Sandaikō*, Figure 9. Hattori Nakatsune, 1791 National Diet Library

lation of the salt water," a line from *Ancient Matters* meant to explain
the origin of the small islands of the Japanese archipelago, but that was
expanded by Norinaga to refer to the continents of the world.
Norinaga, Nakatsune, and Norinaga's other disciples debated the location of Yomi, which Nakatsune identified with the moon. Earlier drafts
suggested that Yomi was within the earth, an underground location.

After Norinaga's death in 1801, his disciples split into pro- and
anti-*Sandai kō* factions. Hattori stood by his work in *Sandai kō*, while
other students attacked him for being overly ambitious about how
much could be known about the creation of the world. After all,
*Ancient Matters* does not describe the creation of the world itself,
and the High Heavenly Plain is already in existence when the narrative begins. In one sense, the anti-*Sandai kō* faction is even more
empirical than Norinaga himself, as these students insisted that the
only true knowledge of things that could not be observed, such as
the creation of the universe, was found in *Ancient Matters*, and if
*Ancient Matters* did not speak on these matters, then they were simply unknowable. The main defense of *Sandai kō* came from Hirata
Atsutane (1776–1843), only loosely associated with Norinaga's
school, and Atsutane himself went far beyond Nakatsune's formula-
tions. Atsutane focused on a metaphysical and theological component to Japanese myths that included statements on the nature of the
soul and an emphasis that all Japanese people were descendants of
the kami. The strong nationalist sentiment of Atsutane's writing, and
his active appeal to commoners, propelled him to fame as a Shinto
theologian and religious leader.

## Modern Reception

### Modernity, State Shinto, and Japanese Myths at War

While Atsutane's followers were instrumental in ousting the
Tokugawa shogun and reinstalling the Japanese emperor as head of
state in 1868, the new government was more immediately interested

in modernizing than in pursuing Japanese myths. The main victory for theologians was the re-establishment of the Bureau of Divinities, an ancient government body charged with managing kami affairs. However, the Bureau was soon absorbed by the Ministry of Education and did not have any major impact on state policy. From around the 1880s, state investment in universities gradually brought scholars of Japanese myths and ancient texts back into prominence. Most important were the programs in the Japanese Classics at the University of Tokyo and the Department of National Literature at Tokyo Imperial University, which replaced the University of Tokyo. The lead scholar for Japanese myth at these institutions was Konakamura Kiyonori, a student of Norinaga's adopted grandson. Kiyonori brought Norinaga's empirical and philological methods to an ever-growing body of students. Also of note in this period were the new institutions of Kokugakuin and Kōgakkan Universities, which trained Shinto priests. The English scholar and translator Basil Hall Chamberlain also worked at Tokyo Imperial University; Chamberlain produced the first full English translation of *Ancient Matters* in 1882. William George Aston, building on Chamberlain's work, translated *Chronicles* to English in 1896.

Chamberlain and Aston were insulated from the pressures on Japanese researchers of myths during the same period. Being well-informed of Chinese history, both knew that the 660 BCE founding date for the Japanese empire in *Chronicles* was fictitious. Neither believed in the existence of Japanese deities. Japanese researchers, some of whom shared Chamberlain's and Aston's position, were subject to more scrutiny. Some portion of the Japanese public believed in the literal truth of *Ancient Matters* and *Chronicles*, and others regarded Jinmu's foundation narrative as a matter of state. The most intense controversy surrounded a historian working at the Historiographical Office, Kume Kunitake, on publication of an 1892 article "Shinto is an Outmoded Form of Sun Worship." When the article was reprinted by influential historian Taguchi Ukichi, the negative attention it attracted ultimately forced Kume to resign.

The first Japanese mythologists like Takayama Chogyū and Takagi Toshio adopted a scientific approach to the study of myth to escape the kind of destructive attention that had seen Kume ousted.

Literal readings of Japanese myths also had a chilling effect on scholars of Chinese writings. In Japan, even now, major universities have a prominent department of Chinese writings, where scholars study both classics of Chinese origin such as the *Analects* of Confucius and Japanese books written in Literary Sinitic such as *Chronicles*. One such scholar, Naka Michiyo, pointed out that the year 660 BCE was of philosophical significance in a particular sect of Chinese ideology, and that it had probably been selected for the founding year of Japan based on its supposed revolutionary potential. Naka also noted that the entries in *Chronicles* take advantage of the fact that the Chinese sexagenary cycle repeats every sixty years, and so the dates 60, 120, 180, etc. are all recorded using the same year. Entries related to Empress Jingū in *Chronicles* referenced Chinese and Korean sources, but the references had a gap of 120 years. Naka concluded that the compilers of *Chronicles* had artificially inflated the reigns and lifespans of early emperors and deliberately manipulated the chronology. Adding 120 years to the chronology in certain places produced a more realistic timeline that better fit contemporaneous records from China and Korea. Naka's article was reprinted, again by Taguchi Ukichi, along with a solicitation for opinions, which poured in over the next year. Favorable readings by Kume and Aston were pitted against harsh rebukes by Shinto hardliners. The most intense of these, resulting in a long exchange with Naka, came from Konakamura Yoshikata, adopted son of Konakamura Kiyonori. In the end, there was no agreement, with literal readers of myth and those open to interpretation retreating to their respective silos.

One especially important aspect of Japanese myth at the end of the nineteenth century and beginning of the twentieth was its incorporation into imperialistic ideas. As Hirafuji has noted, during the 1930s, this effort took shape with scholars incorporating all the people of the Japanese empire, from Manchuria to Okhotsk to Palau, into the mythical narrative. This project was preceded by a similar one during the 1890s and 1900s. Based on the conquest narratives of Yamato Take, the Kumaso in southern Kyushu, the people of Izumo, and the Emishi of northeastern Honshu were all imagined as foreign races that were unified in antiquity by the imperial clan. A passage in a variant of *Chronicles* in which Susano-o lands first in Korea before crossing over to Izumo, not to mention Jingū's conquest of the peninsula, were used to argue that Korea and Japan were originally a single state, also under imperial dominion. The Kumaso were of South Seas origin and the Emishi were the ancestors of the Ainu, all of whom went on to join and intermix to create the Japanese race. This mixed-race narrative of Japanese origins was laid out most forcefully by Tokyo Imperial University Professor Inoue Tetsujirō, and at a regular national meeting for school instructors, Inoue told the teachers of the nation what became the orthodox explanation of Japanese race. As Japanese imperial ambitions widened, the myths of *Ancient Matters* and *Chronicles* were deployed to justify expansion and the further conquest and integration of new lands and peoples.

During the 1920s, scholars published several important studies of Japanese myths that used comparative or historical methodologies and did not regard the myths as truth. However, in the late 1930s and early 1940s, the more literal-minded scholars, often in departments of religion or Japanese literature, proved ascendant and ultimately dominating. Tsuda Sōkichi, whose historical readings of myths were discussed in Chapter 2, was put on trial in 1940 for claims he had made in two books published twenty years earlier. While he was acquitted for denying the veracity of the kami and the Japanese creation narrative, he was convicted of denying the historical truth of the early Japanese emperors and sentenced to house arrest, along with his publisher. Tsuda's work was banned. During the most intense years of Japanese imperialism, alternative interpretations of Japanese myths were not permitted, and scholars had to be on their guard even more so than in the days of Kume.

On the other end of the spectrum, numerous scholars of Japanese myth provided interpretations that went hand-in-glove with state propaganda. Some such work was simply guided, and enabled, by prevailing views at the time. The linguist Kanazawa Shōsaburō, for example, developed a theory linking the Japanese and Korean languages that again cited Susano-o's descent to Silla in *Chronicles* as its historical basis. For the Japanese state, the goal was not to understand Japanese linguistics but rather to weaken Korean independence and unique identity, and Kanazawa's work suited this purpose. More damning was work by scholars like Hisamatsu Sen'ichi, professor at Tokyo Imperial University, who actively produced propaganda using his knowledge of eighth-century Japanese materials. Hisamatsu chaired a committee charged with writing the document *Kokutai no hongi* or *Cardinal Principles of the National Entity of Japan*. This work used Japanese myths as a basis to argue not only for Japanese uniqueness, but also racial superiority. The work circulated in the millions of copies throughout the Japanese empire, especially in the school system, instructing citizens to put the nation before the self and ignore social unrest to achieve the inevitable future of Japan. Hisamatsu and his fellow professors used the myths of *Ancient Matters* and *Chronicles* to define the essential truths of the Japanese state, including the divine status of the emperor and the national destiny to rule over the whole world.

The use of Japanese myths for fascist propaganda at the academic level was mirrored by adaptations at the popular level. The phrase "uchite shi yaman," which translates to "strike now and end [them]" or "strike now to end [the war]," became a popular rallying cry and was featured on banners and signs across the empire. The slogan originally derives from vernacular songs in *Ancient Matters* and *Chronicles* during Jinmu's campaign to conquer the Nara Basin. Other pieces of classical Japanese literature were similarly appropriated. The national anthem, *Kimi ga yo*, had been written in 1870, but it was not until the height of World War II that the song became required for school children to sing every day. The song was taken from a tenth-century poetry anthology, the *Collection of Poems Old and New* or *Kokin wakashū*. Even more popular than *Kimi ga yo* was the song *Umi yukaba*, "If I go to the sea," taken from a poem in *Myriad Poems*. The poem expresses the wishes of the poet to die fighting alongside the emperor. Though Hirohito was not rushing into any battles, when *Umi yukaba* was set to music, it was taken to mean that citizens should willingly die in service to the empire.

## Myths in Post-World War II Japan

From 1945 to 1952, Japan was occupied by the Allied forces, and a new regime of censorship replaced the old regime of censorship. Propaganda like *Kokutai no hongi* was banned, and most importantly, the emperor renounced his divine status in a 1946 New Year's announcement. On the one hand, the epochal changes of Japan's wartime defeat and the uprooting of the imperial system cast a dark shadow on Japanese myths that had been used to drum up support for the empire. On the other, the separation of church of state and the end of legal requirements over what individuals could say about Japanese myths gave scholars and creatives new freedom to reinterpret this material.

The most immediate project for Japanese academics after the end of World War II was to reassess Japanese myths and rehabilitate them following their deployment in service to the wartime emperor. Hisamatsu and other older scholars escaped public censure, although their reputations certainly fell in the eyes of their peers. Perhaps sensing the changing winds, Hisamatsu ardently supported "new directions in Japanese literature," but his own past kept him from being seriously involved in rehabilitating Japanese myth. That task was largely accomplished by the next generation of scholars, many of whom had socialist leanings, distrusted the Japanese state both before and after the war, and resented the occupying Americans. Saigō Nobutsuna, discussed in Chapter 3, for example, published a new history of Japanese literature that imagined myth as containing the latent national energy required to stimulate a socialist revolution. However, the plunge in fortunes of the Japanese Communist Party, the signing and re-signing of the Japan-USA Security Pact, and the surge in economic growth due to the outbreak of the Korean War left any hopes for socialist revolution in the dust. Even Saigō, once an ardent Marxist, republished his earlier history of Japanese literature with a new perspective on myth. Now, according to Saigō, myth still held the raw national energy of the Japanese nation before exposure to foreign influence, but it became a dreamlike place of escape from American-influenced postwar capitalist reality.

In academic circles, the period in which Saigō was most active, the 1950s, 1960s, and 1970s, constituted a golden age for Japanese mythological study, and many researchers referenced in the first four chapters of this book were active during this period. No single factor explains this explosion of Japanese mythology, but several factors certainly contributed. The economic expansion associated with the so-called high growth era meant that Japanese universities, public and private, were growing, which meant ample budgets for faculty positions in Japanese mythology. There was also money for publishing, and multiple new editions of *Ancient Matters* and *Chronicles* were printed alongside commentaries and paperbacks targeted at a general readership. Public interest in Japanese myths also soared, as memories of wartime oppression grew distant, and theories of Japanese uniqueness grew in popularity. Japanese myths that had once demonstrated the ethnic diversity of the Japanese people, convenient for a cosmopolitan empire, were reimagined as a unique repository for a specifically Japanese past.

The de-sacralization of Japanese myths, most pointedly achieved when the emperor renounced his divinity, created the potential for adaptations and reimaginations scarcely conceivable during the repression of the early 1940s. These adaptations spread to new media as well. Osamu Tezuka, often called the godfather of Japanese manga, wrote a twelve-volume series called *Hi no tori* or "Phoenix," of which the third volume, published in 1968–1969, retells the

Yamato Take story from *Ancient Matters*. In Tezuka's treatment, Yamato Take's father, the emperor, is a despot, forcing the people to build a giant tomb for himself and employing a group of scribes to write a history of Japan that makes himself looks favorable. This, presumably, refers to *Ancient Matters*. Yamato Take travels to the land of the Kumaso and meets their princess, and also learns that the Kumaso are writing an unbiased history of Japan. Tezuka's treatment depicts both the emperor and the imperial line in an unflattering light. But perhaps more importantly, Tezuka's many alterations to the story, including the addition of the Kumaso warrior princess, a Kumaso historian, and the titular phoenix bird, demonstrated the possibilities for Japanese myth as popular entertainment in postwar Japan.

In the twenty-first century, Japanese myths have found a following outside of Japan, too. Perhaps the most well-known adaptation is the video game *Ōkami*, originally released in 2006 but with subsequent re-releases, remastered editions, and ports to new gaming systems. In the game, the player is Amaterasu, who takes the form of a white wolf. Many other characters from Japanese myths and folklore such as Susano-o and Kushi-ina-da-hime play major roles in the plot, and the player character uses special moves based on calligraphic brush strokes to vanquish *oni*, Japanese demons. Much like Tezuka's *Hi no tori*, *Ōkami* has little in common with *Ancient Matters* or *Chronicles*, but as a representation of the adaptability of Japanese myths, the game is nothing short of outstanding. And, like many media in the twenty-first century, *Ōkami* has a global following.

# GLOSSARY OF KAMI MENTIONED
# IN THIS BOOK

**AHIRA-TSU-HIME** (lady of Ahira)—first wife of Jinmu, mother of Ta-gishi-mimi

**AJI-SUKI-TAKA-HIKO-NE** (gathering plowing high lord)—earthly kami and friend of Ame-waka-hiko. Brother of Shita-teru-hime, presumed son of Ō-kuni-nushi.

**AMA-NO-KUMA-HITO** (heavenly offering presenter person)—sent by Amaterasu to investigate the body of Uke-mochi

**AMA-NO-SAGU-ME** (heavenly seeker woman)—a servant of Ame-waka-hiko who tells him to kill the pheasant

**AMA-TERASU** (heaven shining)—sun goddess and progenitor of the imperial clan, worshipped at the Ise Grand Shrine. Also called Ō-hiru-me-no-muchi.

**AMA-TSU-HIKO-HIKO-HO-NO-NI-NIGI** (heavenly lord, lord of flourishing rice ears)—son of Oshi-ho-mimi and Taku-hata-chi-ji-hime, grandson of Amaterasu and Taka-mi-musuhi, father of Yama-sachi-hiko. Usually called "Ninigi" or by his title "heavenly grandson."

**AMA-TSU-HIKO-NE** (heavenly lord)—a child of Susano-o and Amaterasu

**AMA-TSU-KUME** (heavenly Kume)—ancestor of the military Kume occupational lineage group told to aid Ninigi when he descends from heaven

**AME-NO-HATA-ORI-ME** (heavenly loom weaving woman)—a weaver goddess, perhaps a younger sister or daughter of Ama-terasu

**AME-NO-HINA-DORI** (unclear)—a son of Ame-no-hohi in the Shinto prayer of the Provincial Lord of Izumo

**AME-NO-HOHI** (heavenly rice ear spirit)—a brother of Oshi-ho-mimi sent to pacify the Central Reed Plain Land, son-in-law and head priest for worship of Ō-kuni-nushi, progenitor of the Provincial Miyatsuko of Izumo

**AME-NO-IWA-TO-WAKE** (heavenly stone door lord)—a personification of the heavenly rock cave in *Account*

**AME-NO-KOYANE** (unclear)—a god associated with ritual worship who helps lure Amaterasu out of the heavenly rock cave, progenitor of the Nakatomi lineage group

**AME-NO-MI-NAKA-NUSHI** (august center of heaven)—one of the first kami in *Account*

**AME-NO-OSHI-HI**(heavenly powerful divine spirit)—a military kami sent to descend with Ninigi, progenitor of the Ōtomo lineage group

**AME-NO-TORI-FUNE** (heavenly bird boat)—a boat god who accompanies Take-mikazuchi to pacify the Central Reed Plain Land in *Account*

**AME-NO-UZU-ME** (heavenly headdress woman)—a goddess associated with spirit possession and dance who lures Amaterasu out of the heavenly rock cave

**AME-TOKO-TACHI** (heaven always standing)—one of the first kami in *Account*

**AME-WAKA-HIKO** (young lad of heaven)—son of Ama-tsu-kuni-tama, sent to pacify the Central Reed Plain Land, son-in-law of Ō-kuni-nushi, husband of Shita-teru-hime, killed by an arrow returned from heaven

**ASHI-NA-ZU-CHI** (leg rubbing spirit)—father-in-law of Susano-o, father of Kushi-ina-da-hime

**E-UKASHI** (elder Ukashi)—the older of two brothers who ruled Uda; does not surrender to Jinmu and is killed by Michi-no-omi

**FUKI-AEZU** (thatching not connected)—son of Ho-ho-demi and Toyo-tama-hime, husband of Tama-yori-hime, father of Jinmu

**FUTO-DAMA** (opulent ritual master)—a god associated with ritual worship who helps lure Amaterasu out of the heavenly rock cave, progenitor of the Inbe lineage group

**FUTSU-NUSHI**(slicing master)—in *Chronicles*, one of the kami who successfully pacifies the Central Reed Plain Land and secures the surrender of Ō-kuni-nushi

**HANI-YAMA-HIME** (lady of clay mountains)—child of Izanagi and Izanami and kami of the earth in *Chronicles*, child born from Izanami's feces in *Account*

**HANI-YASU** (clay peace)—earth kami, child of Izanagi and Izanami, maybe the same as Hani-yama-hime

**HIKO-HO-HO-DEMI** (lord of the emerging spirit of many rice ears)—son of Ninigi and Kamu-ata-tsu-hime, husband of Toyo-tama-hime, son-in-law of the sea kami Wata-tsu-mi, father of Fuki-aezu, sometimes identified as Ho-no-ori

**HIKO-NAGISA-TAKE-U-GAYA-FUKI-AEZU** (valiant lord of the beach of cormorant feather thatching that is not connected)—full name of Fuki-aezu. Son of Yama-sachi-hiko and Toyo-tama-hime, father of Jinmu.

**HIME-TATARA-I-SUZU-HIME** (lady panic many bells lady)—empress of Jinmu, daughter Ō-mono-nushi in *Account* and Koto-shiro-nushi in *Chronicles*

**HI-NO-HAYA-HI** (fire swift spirit)—a kami born when Izanagi kills the fire kami

**HIRU-KO** (leech child)—the leech child, a crippled son of Izanagi and Izanami who is cast to the winds

**HO-DERI** (bright flame)—a son of Ninigi and Kamu-ata-tsu-hime

**HO-NO-SUSERI** (raging flame)—son of Ninigi and Kamu-ata-tsu-hime

**HO-NO-SUSUMI** (advancing flame)—a son of Ninigi and Kamu-ata-tsu-hime

**HO-ORI** (spreading flame)—a son of Ninigi and Kamu-ata-tsu-hime, husband of Toyo-tama-hime, son-in-law of the sea kami Wata-tsu-mi, father of Fuki-aezu, sometimes identified as Hiko-ho-ho-demi

**ICHI-KI-SHIMA-HIME** (lady of the island of devoted veneration)—daughter of Amaterasu and Susano-o

**IKU-KUI** (lively peg)—one of the first kami in *Account*, associated with reeds

**IKU-TSU-HIKO-NE** (lively lord)—son of Amaterasu and Susano-o and brother of Ninigi

**INA-HI** (rice ear boiled rice)—older brother of Jinmu who returns to the sea, the land of his mother

**ISHI-KORI-DOME** (stone coagulate woman)—a kami of metalwork, including mirrors, who helps lure Amaterasu out of the heavenly rock cave

**I-TAKERU** (much bravery)—a son of Susano-o and kami of trees

**ITSU-NO-OHABARI** (fierce sword swing)—a sword god, father of Take-mikazuchi

**ITSU-SE** (fierce divine rice)—oldest son of Fuki-aezu, older brother of Jinmu, is killed by Naga-sune-hiko's army

**IWA-NAGA-HIME** (lady of long rocks)—older sister of Kamu-ata-tsu-hime, rejected wife of Ninigi

**IWA-SAKU** (rock splitter)—a sword god produced when Izanagi slays the fire kami Kagu-tsu-chi

**IWA-TSUTSU-NO-ME** (rock earth woman)—a sword goddess produced when Izanagi slays the fire kami Kagu-tsu-chi

**IWA-TSUTSU-NO-O** (rock earth man)—a sword god produced when Izanagi slays the fire kami Kagu-tsu-chi

**IZANA-GI** (he who invites)—creator god of the Japanese archipelago and its kami

**IZANA-MI** (she who invites)—creator goddess of the Japanese archipelago and its kami

**IZU-NO-ME** (righteous woman)—good spirit created when Izanagi bathes himself after leaving Yomi

**JINMU** (divine warrior)—first emperor of the Japanese state, son of Fuki-aezu and Tama-yori-hime

**KA-ASHI-TSU-HIME** (lady of Kashi)—see KAMU-ATA-TSU-HIME

**KAGASE-O** (shining man)—a star god killed by Take-mikazu-chi and Futsu-nushi

**KAGU-TSU-CHI** (fire spirit)—the fire kami, kills Izanami while being born

**KAMU-ATA-TSU-HIME** (divine lady of Ata)—husband of Ninigi, daughter of Ō-yama-tsu-mi, mother of Hiko-ho-ho-demi

**KAMU-MUSUHI** (divine generative force)—one of the first kami in *Account*, father of Sukuna-bikona in *Chronicles*, benefactor of Ō-kuni-nushi in *Account*

**KAMU-NAO-BI** (divine corrective spirit)—a good kami produced during Izanagi's ablution following his escape from Yomi

**KANA-YAMA-BIKO** (lord of metal mountains)—a kami of metal born from Izanami's vomit

**KASHIKO-NE** (beautiful apprehension)—one of the first kami, wife of Omo-taru

**KASHI-TSU-HIME** (lady of Kashi)—another name for Kamu-ata-tsu-hime

**KAYA-NARU-MI** (unclear)—a son of Ō-kuni-nushi in Shinto prayer of the Provincial Lord of Izumo

**KAYA-NO-HIME** (grass field lady)—a goddess of grass, daughter of Izanagi and Izanami

**KAZURAKI-NO-HITO-KOTO-NUSHI** (one-word master of Kazuraki)—a kami that appears to Yūryaku while he is out on a hunt

**KI-MATA** (tree fork)—tree fork child of Ya-kami-hime and Susano-o

**KISA-KAI-HIME** (scrape shell lady)—A shell goddess who helps resurrect Ō-ana-muji

**KO-NO-HANA-SAKU-YA-HIME** (lady of the blooming trees and flowers)—another name for Kamu-ata-tsu-hime

**KOTO-KATSU-KUNI-KATSU-NAGA-SA** (things super land super long narrow)—an earthly kami encountered by Ninigi after he descends

**KOTO-SHIRO-NUSHI** (master of exchanged words)—an oracle kami, son of Ō-kuni-nushi

**KU-KU-NO-CHI** (spirit of trees)—a kami of trees, child of Izanagi and Izanami

**KUMANO-KUSU-HI** (miraculous spirit of Kumano)—son of Amaterasu and Susano-o, brother of Oshi-ho-mimi

**KU-NA-TO** (road fork)—a crossroads kami born from Izanagi's staff when he escapes Yomi and who guides Futsu-nushi and Take-mikazuchi during their pacification of the Central Reed Plain Land. See also **TSUKI-TATSU-FU-NA-TO**

**KUNI-NO-SA-TSUCHI** (thin strip of land)—one of the first kami in *Chronicles*

**KUNI-NUSHI-KOTO-KATSU-KUNI-KATSU-NAGASA** (land master things super land super narrow)—a personification of Cape Kasasa that gives directions to Ninigi when he descends

**KUNI-TOKO-TACHI** (land always standing)—one of the first kami in *Chronicles*

**KURA-MITSU-HA** (valley water ??)—a water kami born after the fire kami Kagu-tsu-chi is killed

**KURA-OKAMI** (valley ??)—a water kami born after the fire kami Kagu-tsu-chi is killed

**KUSHI-INA-DA-HIME** (mystical rice ear paddy lady)—daughter of Ashi-nazu-chi and Te-nazu-chi, wife of Susano-o

**MASA-KA-A-KATSU-KACHI-HAYA-HI-AME-NO-OSHI-HO-MIMI** (truly winning, I win, swiftly winning spirt, divine spirit of heavenly great rice ears). See **OSHI-HO-MIMI**.

**MICHI-NO-OMI** (road master)—a servant of Jinmu who follows the crow Ya-ta-garasu through the mountains and leads Jinmu's army

**MIKA-NO-HAYA-HI** (vigorous swift spirit)—a thunder kami created when Izanagi slays the fire kami Kagu-tsu-chi

**MIKE-IRI-NO** (august food master)—older brother of Jinmu who crosses the sea to Tokoyo

**MITSU-HA-NO-ME** (woman of waters)—a water kami born upon the death of Izanami after giving birth to the fire kami

**MIZO-KUI-HIME** (water stake lady)—daughter of Mi-shima-no-mizo-kui-mimi, wife of Ō-mono-nushi/Ō-kuni-nushi/Koto-shiro-nushi, mother of Hime-tatara-i-suzu-hime

**NAGA-SUNE-HIKO** (lord of long shanks)—a relative by marriage of Nigi-hayahi who resists Jinmu's conquest of the Nara Basin

**NAKA-TSU-TSU-NO-O** (man of the middle seaport)—produced by Izanagi during his ablution following his escape from Yomi, one of the three gods of the Sumiyoshi Grand Shrine

**NAKA-TSU-WATA-TSU-MI** (spirt of the middle sea)—produced by Izanagi during his ablution following his escape from Yomi

**NAKI-SAWA-ME** (crying swamp woman)—produced from the tears of Izanagi after the death of Izanami

**NE-SAKU** (root splitter)—a sword kami produced when Izanagi slays the fire kami Kagu-tsu-chi

**NIGI-HAYAHI** (flourishing swift spirit)—heavenly deity encountered by Jinmu, progenitor of the Mononobe, older brother of Ninigi in later sources

**NINIGI** (flourish)—son of Oshi-ho-mimi, grandson of Taka-mi-musuhi and Amaterasu, father of Hiko-ho-ho-demi, husband of Kamu-ata-tsu-hime, often referred to as the "heavenly grandson" or the "heavenly descendant"

**NUNAKAWA-HIME** (lady of Nunakawa)—third wife of Ō-kuni-nushi, who he woos with song

**Ō-ANA-MUJI** (great ?? noble)—the original name of Ō-kuni-nushi. See **Ō-KUNI-NUSHI**.

**Ō-GETSU-HIME** (great food lady)—an agriculture goddess killed by Susano-o in *Account* and, as Uke-mochi, by Tsuku-yomi in *Chronicles*

**Ō-HIRU-ME-NO-MUCHI** (noble lady of the great sun)—see **AMA-TERASU**

**Ō-KAMU-ZU-MI** (great divine spirt)—the deified name for the peaches used by Izanagi to fend off his pursuers during his escape from Yomi

**OKI-TSU-SHIMA** (lady of the deep sea island)—another name for Ta-kiri-bime

**Ō-KUNI-NUSHI** (great land master)—descendant of Susano-o, completes creation of the land in *Account* and a *Chronicles* variant, surrenders Central Reed Plain Land to the heavenly kami, worshipped at the Izumo Grand Shrine

**Ō-MAGA-TSU-HI** (spirit of great disaster)—an evil kami produced during Izanagi's ablution following his escape from Yomi

**O-MIZU-NO** (master of flood waters)—a descendant of Susano-o and ancestor of Ō-kuni-nushi in *Account*. Maybe the same as Ya-tsuka-mizu-o-mizu-no from *Records of Wind and Earth of Izumo*.

**OMOI-KANE** (layered thoughts)—son of Taka-mi-musuhi who formulates plans for luring Amaterasu out of the heavenly rock cave and for pacifying the Central Reed Plain Land

**Ō-MONO-NUSHI** (great object master)—earthly kami sometimes associated with Ō-kuni-nushi, worshipped at the Miwa shrine, causes a plague in the reign of Sujin

**OMO-TARU** (complete face)—one of the first kami, associated with having a face

**Ō-NAO-BI** (great corrective spirit)—a good kami produced during Izanagi's ablution following his escape from Yomi

**OSHI-HO-MIMI** (powerful superior mysterious power)—son of Amaterasu and Susano-o, father of Ninigi

**Ō-TOMA-BE** (great woven mat woman)—one of the first kami, associated with femininity

**Ō-TO-NO-JI** (great door pathway man)—one of the first kami, associated with masculinity

**OTO-UKASHI** (younger Ukashi)—the younger of two brothers who ruled Uda; surrenders to Jinmu

**Ō-YA-BIKO** (lord of great buildings)—a building kami from Ki Province who helps Ō-ana-muji

**Ō-YAMA-TSU-MI** (great mountain spirit)—see **YAMA-TSU-MI**

**Ō-YA-TSU-HIME** (great house lady)—daughter of Susano-o, sister of I-takeru

**SAO-NE-TSU-HIKO** (lord of the rod)—a boat kami who guides Jinmu during his conquest of the Nara Basin

**SARUTA-BIKO** (lord of Saruta)—earthly kami who comes to the crossroads of heaven to greet Ninigi, associated with Ise, later drowns in *Account*

**SA-YORI-HIME** (lady of divine possession)—another name for Ichi-ki-shima-hime

**SHI-NAGA-TSU-HIKO** (lord of long breath)—a wind kami produced by Izanagi's breath

**SHIO-TSU-CHI** (sea current spirit)—a kami of the ocean currents, helps Hiko-ho-ho-demi reach the palace of the sea kami, helps Ninigi and Jinmu in *Chronicles*

**SHITA-TERU-HIME** (red shining lady)—daughter of Ō-kuni-nushi, wife of Ame-waka-hiko

**SOKO-TSU-TSU-NO-O** (man of the deep seaport)—produced by Izanagi during his ablution following his escape from Yomi, one of the three gods of the Sumiyoshi Grand Shrine

**SOKO-TSU-WATA-TSU-MI** (spirit of the deep sea)—produced by Izanagi during his ablution following his escape from Yomi

**SU-HIJI-NI** (sandy earth)—one of the first kami, associated with mud and sand

**SUKUNA-BIKO-NA-NO-KAMI** (small lord)—son of Taka-mi-musuhi in *Chronicles* and Kamu-musuhi in *Account*, aids Ō-kuni-nushi to complete the creation of the land

**SUSA-NO-O** (man of Susa; raging man)—son of Izanagi and Izanami, brother of Amaterasu, ancestor of Ō-kuni-nushi

**SUSERI-BIME** (lady of rage)—daughter of Susano-o and second wife of Ō-ana-muji; helps Ō-ana-muji steal weapons from Susano-o and return to the Central Reed Plain Land

**TAGITSU-HIME** (lady of rushing waters)—daughter of Susano-o and Amaterasu

**TA-JIKARA-O** (hand power man)—kami who pulls Amaterasu out of the heavenly rock cave

**TAKA-KURA-JI** (high storage room man)—a man who receives the sword from Take-mikazuchi and saves Jinmu's army

**TAKA-MI-MUSUHI** (high august generative force)—one of the first kami in *Account*, grandfather of Ninigi, called the "imperial ancestor" in *Chronicles*

**TAKE-HAYA-SUSA-NO-O** (brave swift raging man)—a name for Susano-o in *Account*

**TAKE-MIKAZUCHI** (brave vigorous spirit or brave august lightning)—a thunder kami born when Izanagi slays the fire deity Kagu-tsu-chi who pacifies the Central Reed Plain Land so that Ninigi can descend

**TAKE-MI-NA-KATA** (fierce direction of the waters)—son of Ō-kuni-nushi who resists Take-mikazuchi

**TA-KIRI-BIME** (lady of mist)—daughter of Susano-o and Amaterasu

**TAKU-HATA-CHI-JI-HIME** (lady of one thousand paper mulberry flags)— daughter of Taka-mi-musuhi, wife of Oshi-ho-mimi, and mother of Ninigi

**TAMA-NO-OYA** (jewel ancestor)—kami associated with jewel-making, ancestor of the jeweler occupational lineage group

**TAMA-YORI-BIME** (spirit drawing lady)—daughter of the sea kami, sister of Toyo-tama-hime, wife of Fuki-aezu

**TE-NA-ZU-CHI** (hand rubbing spirit)—mother of Kushi-ina-da-hime, mother-in-law of Susano-o

**TOYO-KUMU-NU** (richly watered swamp)—one of the first kami in *Chronicles*

**TOYO-UKE-BIME** (rich food lady)—an agriculture kami enshrined at the Ise Shrine

**TOYO-TAMA-BIME** (rich jewel lady)—daughter of the sea kami, wife of Hiko-ho-ho-demi, mother of Fuki-aezu

**TSUKI-TATSU-FU-NA-TO** (post stand road fork)—crossroads kami created by Izanagi's belt when he flees Yomi, made to guide the heavenly kami during their pacification of the Central Reed Plain Land in *Chronicles*. See also **KU-NA-TO.**

**TSUKU-YOMI** (moon counting)—moon kami, brother of Amaterasu and Susano-o

**TSUMA-TSU-HIME** (lumber lady)—a daughter of Susano-o

**TSUNO-KUI** (horned peg)—one of the first kami in *Account,* associated with reeds

**U-HIJI-NI** (muddy earth)—one of the first kami, associated with mud and sand

**UKA-NO-MITAMA** (soul of rice storage)—a rice kami created by Izanagi

**UKE-MOCHI** (food preserver)—see **Ō-GETSU-HIME**

**UMASHI-ASHIKABI-HIKOJI** (fine reed man)—one of the first kami

**UMI-SACHI-HIKO** (luck of the sea)—see **HO-DERI**

**UMU-KAI-HIME** (mother shell lady)—a shell goddess who helps resurrect Ō-ana-muji

**UWA-TSU-TSU-NO-O** (man of the surface seaport)—produced by Izanagi during his ablution following his escape from Yomi, one of the three gods of the Sumiyoshi Grand Shrine

**UWA-TSU-WATA-TSU-MI** (spirit of the upper sea)—produced by Izanagi during his ablution following his escape from Yomi

**UZU-HIKO** (extraordinary lord; whirlpool lord, perhaps)—a kami encountered by Jinmu who guides his boat out of Kyushu

**WAKA-MUSUHI** (young generative force)—agriculture kami, child of Kagu-tsu-chi and Hani-yama-hime

**WATA-TSU-MI** (sea spirit)—kami of the sea, child of Izanagi and Izanami, father of Toyo-tama-hime and Tama-yori-hime, father-in-law of Hiko-ho-ho-demi

**WAZURAI-NO-KAMI** (illness kami; disaster kami)—see **WAZURAI-NO-USHI**

**WAZURAI-NO-USHI** (illness master; disaster master)—an evil kami born during Izanagi's ablution following his escape from Yomi

**YACHI-HOKO** (many halberds)—a name used by Ō-kuni-nushi when he woos Nunakawa-hime

**YA-KAMI-HIME** (unclear)—first wife of Ō-ana-muji, promised to him by the rabbit from Oki

**YAMA-SACHI-HIKO** (luck of the mountains)—see **HO-ORI**

**YAMATA-NO-OROCHI** (eight fork serpent)—eight-headed snake killed by Susano-o

**YAMATO-Ō-KUNI-TAMA** (great land spirit of Yamato)—kami venerated by Suinin, enshrined in Cape Nagaoka

**YAMA-TSU-MI** (mountain spirit)—a mountain kami, child of Izanagi and Izanami, father of Ka-ashi-tsu-hime in *Account*, mother of Ka-ashi-tsu-hime in *Chronicles*

**YASO-MAGA-TSU-HI** (spirit of many disasters)—an evil kami produced during Izanagi's ablution following his escape from Yomi

**YA-TA-GARASU** (eight shaftment crow)—a crow sent by Amaterasu to guide Jinmu into the Nara Basin

**YA-TSUKA-MIZU-O-MIZU-NO** (many handbreadths deep flood master)—see **O-MIZU-NO**

**YOROZU-HATA-HIME** (myriad looms lady)—daughter of Taka-mi-musuhi, wife of Oshi-ho-mimi, mother of Fuki-aezu

# REFERENCES

**TRANSLATIONS OF PRIMARY MYTH SOURCES (JAPANESE TITLE, ENGLISH TITLE, ABBREVIATION):**

*Kojiki* (An Account of Ancient Matters; Ancient Matters)

Chamberlain, Basil Hall, trans. 2025. Kojiki: Fully Revised Edition: *Records of Ancient Matters.* New York: Tuttle.

Heldt, Gustav, trans. 2014. *The Kojiki: An Account of Ancient Matters.* New York: Columbia University Press.

Philippi, Donald L., trans. 1968. *Kojiki; Translated with an Introduction and Notes by Donald L. Philippi.* Tokyo: University of Tokyo Press.

*Nihon shoki* (Chronicles of Japan; *Chronicles*)

Aston, William. G., trans. 1956. *Nihongi: Chronicles of Japan from the Earliest Times to A.D. 697.* London: Allen & Unwin.

Bentley, John R., trans. 2025. *Nihon shoki: The Chronicles of Japan.* Echo Mount Zion Publishing.

Felt, Matthieu, trans. 2026. *The Chronicles of Japan: Volume I: Age of the Gods and Legendary Sovereigns.* The Hsu-Tang Library of Classical Chinese Literature. New York: Oxford University Press.

*Kojiki* and *Nihon shoki*

Borgen, Robert, and Marian Ury. 1990. "Readable Japanese Mythology: Selections from *Nihon Shoki* and *Kojiki.*" *The Journal of the Association of Teachers of Japanese* 24 (1): 61–97.

*Sendai kuji hongi* (Original Record of Previous Reigns and Past Matters; *Original Record*)

Bentley, John R. 2006. *The Authenticity of Sendai Kuji Hongi : A New Examination of Texts, with a Translation and Commentary*. Leiden; Boston, MA: Brill.

*Kogo shūi* (*Gleanings from Ancient Stories; Gleanings*)

Genchi Katō, and Hikoshirō Hoshino, trans. 1926. *Kogo shui: Gleanings from Ancient Stories*. Tokyo: Zaidan-Hōjin-Meiji-Seitoku-Kinen-Gakkai (Meiji Japan Society).

*Norito* (Shinto Prayers)

Philippi, Donald L., trans. 1990. *Norito: A Translation of the Ancient Japanese Ritual Prayers*. Princeton, NJ: Princeton University Press.

*Engi Shiki* (Procedures of the Engi Era; Procedures)

Bock, Felicia Gressitt, trans. 1970. *Engi-Shiki; Procedures of the Engi Era*. Tokyo: Sophia University.

*Izumo no kuni fudoki* (Records of Wind and Earth; Records)

Aoki, Michiko Yamaguchi, trans. 1997. *Records of Wind and Earth: A Translation of Fudoki, with Introduction and Commentaries*. Ann Arbor, MI: Association for Asian Studies.

*Kojiki, Nihon shoki,* and *Izumo no kuni fudoki*

Felt, Matthieu. 2024. "Ancient Japanese Chronicles and Gazetteers." In *Norton Anthology of World Literature*. Fifth Edition, Volume A. New York: W.W Norton & Company, 33–44.

*Harima no kuni fudoki* (Records of Wind and Earth of Harima)

Palmer, Edwina, trans. 2016. *Harima Fudoki: A Record of Ancient Japan Reinterpreted, Translated, Annotated, and with Commentary*. Leiden: Brill.

*Man'yōshū* (Collection of Myriad Poems; Myriad Poems)

Cranston, Edwin A., trans. 1993. *A Waka Anthology Volume One: The Gem-Glistening Cup*. Stanford, CA: Stanford University Press.

Kojima, Takashi, trans. 1995. *Written on Water: Five Hundred Poems from the Manyōshū*. First edition. Rutland, VT: Tuttle.

Levy, Ian Hideo, trans. 1981. *The Ten Thousand Leaves: A Translation of the Man'yōshū, Japan's Premier Anthology of Classical Poetry*. Princeton, NJ: Princeton University Press.

Nippon, Gakujutsu Shinkōkai, ed. 1969. *The Manyoshu: The Nippon Gakujutsu Shinkokai Translation of One Thousand Poems*. New York: Columbia University Press.

Vovin, Alexander. 2009–2020. *Man'yōshū: A New English Translation Containing the Original Text, Kana Transliteration, Romanization, Glossing and Commentary*. 11 vols. Leiden: Brill.

Wright, Harold, trans. 1986. *Ten Thousand Leaves: Love Poems from the Manyōshū* Woodstock, NY: Overlook Press.

## TRANSLATIONS OF OTHER PREMODERN MATERIAL MENTIONED IN THE TEXT (800–1900)

### Shoku Nihongi

Bender, Ross, trans. 2013. *The Imperial Edicts in the Shoku Nihongi: A Translation with Text and Transliteration*. CreateSpace Independent Publishing Platform.

Bender, Ross, trans. 2016. *Nara Japan, 758–763: A Translation from Shoku Nihongi*. CreateSpace Independent Publishing Platform.

Bender, Ross, trans. 2016. *Nara Japan, 764–766: A Translation from Shoku Nihongi*. CreateSpace Independent Publishing Platform.

Bender, Ross, trans. 2016. *Nara Japan, 767–770: A Translation from Shoku Nihongi*. CreateSpace Independent Publishing Platform.

### Nakatomi no harae kunge

Teeuwen, Mark, and H. van der Veere. 1998. *Nakatomi Harae Kunge: Purification and Enlightenment in Late-Heian Japan*. München: Iudicium.

### A Chronicle of Gods and Sovereigns

Varley, H. Paul, trans. 1980. *A Chronicle of Gods and Sovereigns: Jinnō Shōtōki of Kitabatake Chikafusa*. New York: Columbia University Press.

### Chronicle of the Great Peace

McCullough, Helen Craig, trans. 1959. *The Taiheiki: A Chronicle of Medieval Japan*. New York: Columbia University Press.

### Kokutai no hongi

Gauntlett, John Owen, and Robert King Hall, trans. 1949. *Kokutai No Hongi. Cardinal Principles of the National Entity of Japan.* Cambridge, MA: Harvard University Press.

### Collection of Poems Old and New

Cranston, Edwin A. 2006. *A Waka Anthology, Volume Two: Grasses of Remembrance.* Stanford, CA: Stanford University Press.
Duthie, Torquil, trans. 2023. *The Kokinshū: Selected Poems.* New York: Columbia University Press.

### SECONDARY SOURCES ON MYTH USED IN THIS BOOK

Anesaki, Masaharu. 1899. "Susano-o no mikoto no shinwa densetsu." *Teikoku bungaku* 5 (8:1–25; 9:1–29; 11:14–35; 12:1–25).
Anesaki, Masaharu. 1900. "Gengogaku ha shinwagaku o hyō shite Takagi kun no so mikoto fūron ni oyobu." *Teikoku bungaku* 6 (1): 13–39.
Anesaki, Masaharu. 1930. *History of Japanese Religion, with Special Reference to the Social and Moral Life of the Nation.* London: K. Paul, Trench, Trubner & Co., Ltd.
Antoni, Klaus. 2016. *Kokutai: Political Shintô from Early-Modern to Contemporary Japan.* Tübingen: Eberhard Karls University.
Aston, W. G. 1905. *Shinto, the Way of the God.* London: Longmans, Green, 1905.
Bialock, David T. 2007. *Eccentric Spaces, Hidden Histories: Narrative, Ritual, and Royal Authority from the Chronicles of Japan to the Tale of the Heike.* Stanford, CA: Stanford University Press.
Buckley, Edmund. 1896. "The Shinto Pantheon." In *The New World; a Quarterly Review of Religion, Ethics and Theology (1892–1900).* Vol. 5. Boston, MA: American Periodicals Series III, 719–44.
Campbell, Joseph. 1949. *The Hero with a Thousand Faces.* New York: Pantheon Books.
Clover Studio. 2006. *Ōkami.* Capcom. PlayStation 2.
Douglas, Mary. 1966. *Purity and Danger: An Analysis of Concepts of Pollution and Taboo.* New York: Praeger.
Dumézil, Georges. 1973. *The Destiny of a King,* trans. Alf Hiltebeitel. Chicago, IL: University of Chicago Press.
Duthie, Torquil. 2014. *Man'yōshū and the Imperial Imagination in Early Japan.* Leiden: Brill.

Ebersole, Gary L. 1992. *Ritual Poetry and the Politics of Death in Early Japan.* Princeton, NJ: Princeton University Press.

Egami, Namio. 1964. "The Formation of the People and the Origin of the State in Japan." *The Memoirs of the Toyo Bunko* 23: 35–70.

Eliade, Mircea. 1961. *The Sacred and the Profane: The Nature of Religion.* New York: Harper & Row.

Hayashi Razan. 1970. *Haiyaso.* Kirishitan sho Yaso sho, ed. H. Chiisuriku, Doi Tadao, and Ōzuka Mitsunobu. NST 25. Tokyo: Iwanami shoten.

Hirafuji, Kikuko. 2004. *Shinwagaku to Nihon no kamigami.* Tōkyō: Kōbundō.

Hirafuji, Kikuko. 2013. "Colonial Empire and Mythology Studies: Research on Japanese Myth in the Early Shōwa Period." In *Kami Ways in Nationalist Territory: Shinto Studies in Prewar Japan and the West,* ed. Bernhard Scheid and Kate Wildman Nakai. Wien: Verlag der Österreichischen Akademie der Wissenschaften, 75–107.

Hoshino, Hisashi. 1890. "Honpō no jinshu gengo ni tsuite hikō o nobete yo no magokoro aikokusha ni tadasu." *Shiggakkai zasshi* 11: 17–43.

Isomae, Jun'ichi. 1999. "Myth in Metamorphosis: Ancient and Medieval Versions of the Yamatotakeru Legend." *Monumenta Nipponica* 54 (3): 361–85.

Isoame, Jun'ichi. 2000. "Reappropriating the Japanese Myths: Motoori Norinaga and the Creation Myths of the Kojiki and Nihon Shoki," trans. Sarah E. Thal. *Japanese Journal of Religious Studies* 27 (1/2): 15–39.

Kanazawa, Shōsaburō. 1910. *Nikkan ryōkokugo dōkeiron.* Tokyo: Sanseidō Shoten.

Kanazawa, Shōsaburō. 1929. *Nissen dōsoron.* Tokyo: Tōkō shoin.

Kawai, Hayao, Yuasa Yasuo, and Yoshida Atsuhiko. 1983. *Nihon shinwa no shisō: Susanoo ron.* Kyōto: Mineruva Shobō.

Kawai, Hayao. 1985. "The Japanese Mind as Reflected in Their Mythology." *Psychologia* 28 (2): 71–76.

Kawai, Hayao, and Hori Tadashi. 1986. "The Hollow Center in the Mythology of *Kojiki.*" *Review of Japanese Culture and Society* 1 (1): 72–77.

Kitagawa, Joseph Mitsuo. 1987. *On Understanding Japanese Religion.* Princeton, NJ: Princeton University.

Kōnoshi, Takamitsu. 1995. *Kojiki: tennō no sekai no monogatari.* NHK Books 746. Tokyo: Nihon hōsō shuppan kyōkai.

Kōnoshi, Takamitsu. 1999. *Kojiki to Nihon shoki: "Tennō shinwa" no rekishi.* Kōdansha gendai shinsho 1436. Tokyo: Kōdansha.

Kōnoshi, Takamitsu. 2008. *Kojiki no sekaikan.* Tokyo: Yoshikawa kōbunkan.

Kume, Kunitake. 1891. "Shintō wa saiten no kozoku." *Shigakkai zasshi* 23–25.

Lévi-Strauss, Claude. 1973. *From Honey to Ashes*, trans. John Weightman and Doreen Weightman. New York: Harper & Row.

Lurie, David Barnett. 2011. *Realms of Literacy: Early Japan and the History of Writing*. Cambridge, MA: Harvard University Asia Center.

Macé, François. 1989. *Kojiki shinwa no kōzō*. Tokyo: Chūō Kōronsha.

Masuda, Katsumi. 2006. *Kazan rettō no shisō*. In *Masuka Katsumi no shigoto* vol. 2, ed. Suzuki Hideo and Amano Kiyokio. Tokyo: Chikuma shobō, 11–298.

Matsumoto, Nobuhiro. 1928. *Essai sur la mythologie Japonaise*. Paris: P. Geuthner, 1928.

Matsumoto, Nobuhiro. 1971. *Nihon shinwa no kenkyū*. Tokyo: Heibonsha.

Matsumoto, Nobuhiro. 1977. "Nankai no tsuribari sōshitsu shō: saisetsu Toyotamahime setsuwa." In *Nihon shinwa kenkyū* 3, ed. Ōbayashi Taryō and Itō Seiji. Gakuseisha, 130–41.

Matsumura, Takeo. 1954–1958. *Nihon shinwa no kenkyū*. 4 vols. Baifūkan.

Matsumura, Takeo. 2005. *Shinwagaku genron*. 2 vols. Shinwagaku meicho senshū 16–17. Yumani shobō.

Mishina, Shōei. 1971. *Kenkoku shinwa no shomondai*. Mishina Shōei ronbunshū vol. 2. Heibonsha.

Mishina, Shōei. 1971. *Shinwa to bunkashi*. Mishina Shōei ronbunshū vol. 3. Heibonsha.

Müller, Friedrich W. K. 1893. "Eine Mythe der Kêi-Insular und Verwandtes." *Zeitschrift für Ethnologie* 25: 533–37.

Ōbayashi, Taryō. 1973. "Nihon shinwa no kenkyū shi." In *Nihon shinwa no kigen*, ed. Ōbayashi Taryō. Tokyo: Kadokawa Shoten, 272–77.

Ōbayashi, Taryō. 1975. *Nihon shinwa no kōzō*. Tokyo: Kōbundō.

Ōbayashi, Taryō. 1975. *Shinwa to shinwagaku*. Tokyo: Daiwa Shobō.

Oka, Masao. 1994. *Ijin sono ta: hoka jūni hen*. Oka Masao ronbun shū, ed. Ōbayashi Taryō. Tokyo: Iwanami Shoten.

Oka, Masao. 2012. *Kulturschichten in Alt-Japan*, ed. Josef Kreiner. 2 vols. Bonn: Bier'sche Verlagsanstalt.

Ooms, Herman. 2009. *Imperial Politics and Symbolics in Ancient Japan: The Tenmu Dynasty, 650–800*. Honolulu: University of Hawai'i Press.

Orikuchi, Shinobu. 1955. *Kokubungaku*. In Orikuchi Shinobu zenshū vol. 14, ed. Orikuchi hakase kinenkai. Chūō kōronsha.

Piggott, Joan R. 1997. *The Emergence of Japanese Kingship*. Stanford, CA: Stanford University Press.

Rocher, Alain. 1997. *Mythe et souveraineté au Japon*. Paris: Presses Universitaires de France.

Saigō, Nobutsuna. 1967. *Kojiki no sekai*. Tokyo: Iwanami Shoten.

Saigō, Nobutsuna. 1973. *Kojiki kenkyū*. Tokyo: Miraisha.

Segal, Robert Alan. 2004. *Myth: A Very Short Introduction*. New York: Oxford University Press.

Steineck, Raji C. 2017. *Kritik der Symbolischen Formen II: Zur Konfiguration aljapanischer Myhologien*. Stuttgart-Bad Cannstatt: Frommann-Holzboog.

Stockdale, Jonathan. 2013. "Origin Myths: Susano-o, Orikuchi Shinobu, and the Imagination of Exile in Early Japan." *History of Religions* 52 (3): 237–66.

Takagi, Toshio. 1899. "Takayama shi no Kojiki ron." *Teikoku bungaku* 5 (4) (anonymous): 79–84.

Takagi, Toshio. 1899. "Soshin fūjin ron 1." *Teikoku bungaku* 5 (11): 35–60.

Takayama, Chogyū. 1905. "Kojiki jindaikan no shinwa oyobi rekishi." In *Chogyū zenshū* vol. 3. Hakubunkan, 419–39.

Tezuka, Osamu. 2003. *Phoenix, Vol. 3: Yamato/Space*. San Francisco: VIZ Media LLC.

Thompson, Tok Freeland, and Gregory Allen Schrempp. 2020. *The Truth of Myth: World Mythology in Theory and Everyday Life*. New York: Oxford University Press.

Tsuda, Sōkichi. 1963. *Nihon koten no kenkyū*. Tsuda Sōkichi zenshū vol. 1. Iwanami Shoten.

Turner, Victor W. 1967. *The Forest of Symbols: Aspects of Ndembu Ritual*. Ithaca, NY: Cornell University Press.

Tylor, Edward B. 1877. "Remarks on Japanese Mythology." *Journal of the Anthropological Institute of Great Britain and Ireland* 6: 55–60.

Weiss, David. 2022. *The God Susanoo and Korea in Japan's Cultural Memory: Ancient Myths and Modern Empire*. First edition. London: Bloomsbury Academic.

Yamada, Jun. 2018. *Nihon shoki tenkyō ron*. Shintensha.

Yamaguchi, Masao. 1977. "Kingship, Theatricality, and Marginal Reality in Japan." In *Text and Context: The Social Anthropology of Tradition*, ed. Ravindra K. Jain. Philadelphia, PA: Institute for the Studies of Human Issues, 151–79.

Yanagita, Kunio. 1988. *About Our Ancestors: The Japanese Family System*, trans. Fanny Hagin Mayer, Yasuyo Ishiwara, and Nihon Yunesuko Kokunai Iinkai. New York: Greenwood Press.

Yoshida, Atsuhiko. 1974. *Nihon shinwa to In-ō shinwa: kōzōronteki bunseki no kokoromi*. Kōbundō.

Yoshida, Atsuhiko. 1977. "Japanese Mythology and the Indo-European Trifunctional System." *Diogenes* 25 (98): 93–116.

## FURTHER READING ON JAPANESE MYTHS AND EARLY JAPAN IN ENGLISH, GENERAL AUDIENCES:

Ashkenazi, Michael. 2003. *Handbook of Japanese Mythology*. Santa Barbara, CA: ABC-CLIO.

Foster, Michael Dylan. 2009. *Pandemonium and Parade: Japanese Monsters and the Culture of Yokai*. Berkeley, CA: University of California Press.

Foster, Michael Dylan. 2015. *The Book of Yokai: Mysterious Creatures of Japanese Folklore*. Berkeley, CA: University of California Press.

Frydman, Joshua. 2022. *The Japanese Myths: A Guide to Gods, Heroes and Spirits*. New York: Thames & Hudson Ltd.


## FURTHER READING ON JAPANESE MYTHS AND EARLY JAPAN IN ENGLISH, ACADEMIC AUDIENCES:

Akima, Toshio. 1982. "The Songs of the Dead: Poetry, Drama, and Ancient Death Rituals of Japan." *The Journal of Asian Studies* 41 (3): 485–509.

Akima, Toshio. 1993. "The Myth of the Goddess of the Undersea World and the Tale of Empress Jingū's Subjugation of Silla." *Japanese Journal of Religious Studies* 20 (2/3): 95–185.

Allen, Chizuko. 2003. "Empress Jingū: A Shamaness Ruler in Early Japan." *Japan Forum* 15 (1): 81–98.

Antoni, Klaus J. 2002. *Religion and National Identity in the Japanese Context*. Münster: Lit.

Aoki, Michiko Yamaguchi. 1974. *Ancient Myths and Early History of Japan: A Cultural Foundation*. New York: Exposition Press.

Barnes, Gina Lee. 2007. *State Formation in Japan: Emergence of a 4th-Century Ruling Elite*. London: Routledge. Durham East Asia Series.

Batten, Bruce Loyd. 2003. *To the Ends of Japan: Premodern Frontiers, Boundaries, and Interactions*. Honolulu: University of Hawai'i Press.

Batten, Bruce Loyd. 2006. *Gateway to Japan: Hakata in War and Peace, 500–1300*. Honolulu: University of Hawai'i Press.

Breen, John, and Mark Teeuwen. 2000. *Shinto in History: Ways of the Kami*. Honolulu: University of Hawai'i Press.

Brownlee, John S. 1999. *Japanese Historians and the National Myths, 1600–1945: The Age of the Gods and Emperor Jinmu*. Vancouver: UBC Press.

Burns, Susan L. 2003. *Before the Nation: Kokugaku and the Imagining of Community in Early Modern Japan*. Durham, NC: Duke University Press.

Carlqvist, Anders. 2010. "The Land-Pulling Myth and Some Aspects of Historic Reality." *Japanese Journal of Religious Studies* 37 (2): 185–222.

Como, Michael. 2003. *Shōtoku: Ethnicity, Ritual, and Violence in the Japanese Buddhist Tradition.* New York: Oxford University Press.

Como, Michael. 2009. *Weaving and Binding: Immigrant Gods and Female Immortals in Ancient Japan.* Honolulu: University of Hawaii Press.

De Veer, Henrietta. 1976. "Myth Sequences from the Kojiki." *Japanese Journal of Religious Studies* 3 (2): 175–214.

Edwards, Walter. 1983. "Event and Process in the Founding of Japan: The Horserider Theory in Archeological Perspective." *The Journal of Japanese Studies* 9 (2): 265–95.

Ellwood, Robert S. 1993. "A Japanese Mythic Trickster Figure: Susa-no-o." In *Mythical Trickster Figures: Contours, Contexts, and Criticisms,* ed. William J. Hynes and William G. Doty. Tuscaloosa, AL: University of Alabama Press, 141–58.

Ellwood, Robert S. 1990. "The Sujin Religious Revolution." *Japanese Journal of Religious Studies* 17 (2/3): 199–217.

Fairchild, William P. 1965. "'Mika'-Jar Deities in Japanese Mythology." *Asian Folklore Studies* 24 (1): 81–101.

Farris, William Wayne. 1985. *Population, Disease, and Land in Early Japan, 645–900.* Cambridge, MA: Council on East Asian Studies, Harvard University.

Farris, William Wayne. 1998. *Sacred Texts and Buried Treasures: Issues in the Historical Archaeology of Ancient Japan.* Honolulu: University of Hawaii Press.

Faure, Bernard. 2016. *Gods of Medieval Japan.* Honolulu: University of Hawai'i Press.

Felt, Matthieu. 2021. "Nihongi Banquet Poetry: Rewriting Japanese Myth in Verse." *Monumenta Nipponica* 76 (2): 249–90.

Felt, Matthieu. 2023. *Meanings of Antiquity: Myth Interpretation in Premodern Japan.* Cambridge, MA: Harvard University Asia Center.

Grapard, Allan G. 1991. "Visions of Excess and Excesses of Vision: Women and Transgression in Japanese Myth." *Japanese Journal of Religious Studies* 18 (1): 3–23.

Grapard, Allan G. 1992. "The Shinto of Yoshida Kanetomo." *Monumenta Nipponica* 47 (1): 27–58.

Grayson, James H. 2002. "Susa-no-o: A Culture Hero from Korea." *Japan Forum* 14 (3): 465–87.

Hardacre, Helen. 2017. *Shinto: A History.* New York: Oxford University Press.

Horton, H. Mack. 2012. *Traversing the Frontier: The Man'yōshū Account of a Japanese Mission to Silla in 736–737.* Cambridge, MA: Harvard University Asia Center.

Isomae, Jun'ichi. 2009. *Japanese Mythology: Hermeneutics on Scripture.* Kyoto: International Research Center for Japanese Studies (Nichibunken), Equinox Publishing.

Kelsey, W. Michael. 1981. "The Raging Deity in Japanese Mythology." *Asian Folklore Studies* 40 (2): 213–36.

Kidder, J. Edward. 1959. *Japan before Buddhism.* New York: Praeger.

Kidder, J. Edward. 1974. "Ancient Myths and Early History of Japan. A Cultural Foundation." *Monumenta Nipponica.* https://doi.org/10.2307/2383673.

Kōnoshi, Takamitsu. 2000. "Constructing Imperial Mythology: *Kojiki* and *Nihon Shoki.*" In *Inventing the Classics,* ed. Haruo Shirane and Tomi Suzuki. Stanford, CA: Stanford University Press, 51–68.

Kurosawa, Kōzō. 1982. "Myths and Tale Literature." *Japanese Journal of Religious Studies* 9 (2/3): 115–25.

Ledyard, Gari. 1975. "Galloping along with the Horseriders: Looking for the Founders of Japan." *The Journal of Japanese Studies* 1 (2): 217–54.

Littleton, C. Scott. 1981. "Susa-Nö-Wo Versus Ya-Mata Nö Woröti: An Indo-European Theme in Japanese Mythology." *History of Religions* 20 (3): 269–80.

Littleton, C. Scott. 1995. "Yamato-Takeru: An 'Arthurian' Hero in Japanese Tradition." *Asian Folklore Studies* 54 (2): 259–74.

Matsumae, Takeshi. 1978. "Origin and Growth of the Worship of Amaterasu." *Asian Folklore Studies* 37 (1): 1–11.

Matsumae, Takeshi. 1980. "The Heavenly Rock-Grotto Myth and the Chinkon Ceremony." *Asian Folklore Studies* 39 (2): 9–22.

Matsumae, Takeshi. 1983. "The Myth of the Descent of the Heavenly Grandson." *Asian Folklore Studies* 42 (2): 159–79.

McCallum, Donald F. 2009. *The Four Great Temples: Buddhist Archaeology, Architecture, and Icons of Seventh-Century Japan.* Honolulu: University of Hawaii Press.

McNally, Mark. 2005. *Proving the Way: Conflict and Practice in the History of Japanese Nativism.* Cambridge, MA: Harvard University Asia Center.

Metevelis, Peter. 1993. "A Reference Guide to the 'Nihonshoki' Myths." *Asian Folklore Studies* 52 (2): 383–88.

Miller, Alan L. 1984. "'Ame No Miso-Ori Me' (The Heavenly Weaving Maiden): The Cosmic Weaver in Early Shinto Myth and Ritual." *History of Religions* 24 (1): 27–48.

Miller, Richard J. 1974. *Ancient Japanese Nobility: The Kabane Ranking System.* Berkeley, CA: University of California Press.

Miller, Richard J. 1978. *Japan's First Bureaucracy: A Study of Eighth-Century Government.* Ithaca: China-Japan Program, Cornell University.

Murakami, Fuminobu. 1988. "Incest and Rebirth in Kojiki." *Monumenta Nipponica* 43 (4): 455–63.

Nakanishi, Susumu. 1985. "Spatial Structure of Japanese Myth: The Contact Point between Life and Death." In *Principles of Classical Japanese Literature*, ed. Sumie Jones, Earl Miner, and Joint Committee on Japanese Studies. Princeton, NJ: Princeton University Press, 106–29.

Naumann, Nelly. 1982. "'Sakahagi': The 'Reverse Flaying' of the Heavenly Piebald Horse." *Asian Folklore Studies* 41 (1): 7–38.

Nishimura, Sey. 1986. "Retrospective Comprehension: Japanese Foretelling Songs." *Asian Folklore Studies* 45 (1): 45–66.

Ōbayashi, Taryō. 1984. "Japanese Myths of Descent from Heaven and Their Korean Parallels." *Asian Folklore Studies* 43 (2): 171–84.

Ouwehand, Cornelius. 1958. "Some Notes on the God Susa-No-o." *Monumenta Nipponica* 14 (3/4): 384–407.

Pai, Hyung Il. 2000. *Constructing "Korean" Origins: A Critical Review of Archaeology, Historiography, and Racial Myth in Korean State-Formation Theories.* Boston, MA: Harvard University Asia Center.

Ruoff, Kenneth J. 2014. *Imperial Japan at Its Zenith: The Wartime Celebration of the Empire's 2,600th Anniversary.* Ithaca, NY: Cornell University Press.

Simpson, Emily B. 2022. "Like a Fierce God: Reenvisioning the Enemy in the Legend of Empress Jingū in the Wake of the Mongol Invasions." *Religions (Basel, Switzerland)* 13 (8): 695.

Strand, Kendra. 2017. "Jingū: Narratives of Motherhood and Imperial Rule in Early Japan." In *Motherhood in Antiquity*, ed. Dana Cooper and Claire Phelan. Cham: Palgrave Macmillan, 123–42.

Teeuwen, Mark, and Fabio Rambelli. 2003. *Buddhas and Kami in Japan: Honji Suijaku as a Combinatory Paradigm.* New York: RoutledgeCurzon.

Teeuwen, Mark, John Breen, Nobutaka Inoue, Satoshi Ito, Jun Endo, and Mizue Mori. 2003. *Shinto, a Short History.* New York: RoutledgeCurzon.

Thal, Sarah. 2002. "Redefining the Gods: Politics and Survival in the Creation of Modern Kami." *Japanese Journal of Religious Studies* 29 (3/4): 379–404.

Torrance, Richard. 2019. "Ōnamochi: The Great God Who Created All under Heaven." *Japanese Journal of Religious Studies* 46 (2): 277–318.

Wachutka, Michael. 2001. *Historical Reality or Metaphoric Expression? Culturally Formed Contrasts in Karl Florenz' and Iida Takesato's Interpretations of Japanese Mythology.* Hamburg: Lit.

Wachutka, Michael. 2013. *Kokugaku in Meiji-Period Japan: The Modern Transformation of "National Learning" and the Formation of Scholarly Societies.* Leiden: Global Oriental.

Weiss, David. 2014. "The Japanese Trickster and His Connection to Metallurgy: The Myth of Susanoo." In *Sources of Mythology: Ancient and Contemporary Myths*, ed. Klaus Antoni and David Weiss. Berlin: Lit, 337–47.

Yamaguchi, Masao. 1972. "Kingship as a System of Myth: An Essay in Synthesis." *Diogenes* 20 (77): 43–70.

Zhong, Yijiang. 2016. *The Origin of Modern Shinto in Japan: The Vanquished Gods of Izumo*. New York: Bloomsbury Academic.

# INDEX

For the benefit of digital users, indexed terms that span two pages (e.g., 52–53) may, on occasion, appear on only one of those pages.